The Kubernetes Book

Starfleet edition

Paperback edition authorised for use on lower decks

Stardate: -300109.58

Nigel Poulton   **@nigelpoulton**

About this edition

This edition was published on stardate -300109.58.

Everything in this edition is up-to-date with the latest trends and patterns in the industry. All examples and hands-on tasks are also tested against **Kubernetes 1.26**. Finally, all references to Pod Security Policies have been removed and replaced with new sections covering Pod Security Standards and Pod Security Admission.

Good luck deploying Kubernetes in Starfleet!

Nigel Poulton

Commisioned by Starfleet Command

Following successful testing of Kubernetes by Starfleet Corps of Engineers and Starfleet R&D, Starfleet Command have announced plans to rollout Kubernetes as the official infrastructure and orchestration platform for all new Starfleet builds. Starfleet have also announced an extensive technology refresh program to install Kubernetes on all existing fleet assets, including:

- Starships
- Starbases
- Shipyards
- Other ground, orbital, and deep space assets

Trials consisted of Kubernetes 1.26 installations at the Utopia Planitia Fleet Yard, Starbase 74, as well as all Galaxy-class starships and Oberth-class science vessels in the home fleet. K3d and MicroK8s have also been tested and authorised for use on resource-constrained assets and Starfleet edge assets such as tricorders, probes, sub-space relays, and small deep space objects in Federation territory.

To aid with this rollout, Starfleet has commissioned this edition of **The Kubernetes Book** and made it required reading for all engineering cadets at Starfleet Academy. A hardback copy is mandatory on the engineering deck of all Starships and space stations. Paperback editions may be kept on lower decks.

About the authors

I'd like to thank Pushkar for his contributions to the security chapters. Pushkar approached me at a KubeCon and asked if he could contribute content on real-world security. Collaborating on content wasn't something I'd done previously and I tried to tell him "no thanks" (I'm quite disorganized and can be hard to work with). However, he was keen, so we made it happen. To be clear, the technical content for the security chapters is Pushkar's. I just tweaked the writing style so that the book has a consistent feel.

Author: Nigel Poulton (@nigelpouton)

Nigel is a technology geek who spends his life creating books, training videos, and online hands-on training. He's the author of best-selling books on Docker and Kubernetes, as well as the most popular online training videos on the same topics. Nigel is a Docker Captain and always playing with new technology -- his latest interest is cloud native WebAssembly (Wasm). In the past, Nigel has held various senior infrastructure roles at large enterprises.

When he's not playing with technology, he's dreaming about it. When he's not dreaming about it, he's reading and watching sci-fi. He wishes he lived in the future so he could explore space-time, the universe, and other mind-blowing stuff. He likes cars, football (soccer), and learning. He lives in England with his fabulous wife and three children.

Contributing author: Pushkar Joglekar

Pushkar contributed the technical content for chapters 15 and 16.

He currently works as a Cloud Native Security Engineer at a FinTech company in the San Francisco Bay Area. In the last few years, he's built multiple "secure by design" production container deployments for a Fortune 500 company and worked as a Security Engineer at VMware Tanzu. He is currently a Tech Lead for the CNCF Security Technical Advisory Group (STAG) and leads the Kubernetes Security Tooling sub-project with a goal to "Make Kubernetes Secure for All".

When he's not securing containers, he spends his time exploring neighborhood bike trails, capturing beautiful sunsets through his camera, and sipping home-made masala ginger chai. He lives with his wonderful wife, who happens to be the real engineer among them.

Contents

0: Preface

Kubernetes is developing fast. With this in mind, I'm fully committed to updating this book every year. And when I say "update", I mean real updates – every word and every concept will be reviewed, and every example will be tested and updated against the latest versions of Kubernetes. I'm 100% committed to making this the best Kubernetes book in the world.

As an author, I'd love to write a book and never touch it again for 5 years. Unfortunately, that doesn't work for Kubernetes – a two-year-old book on Kubernetes could be dangerously out of date.

Editions Paperbacks, hardbacks, eBooks, audio, and translations

The following editions of the book are available, or soon will be:

- **Paperback:** English, Simplified Chinese, Spanish, Portuguese
- **Hardback:** English
- **eBook:** English, Russian, Spanish, Portuguese

eBook copies are available on Kindle and from LeanPub.

Previous editions had a large-print paperback edition. However, Amazon does not have a useful way of listing and searching for large-print books and the book was almost impossible to find. If this changes in the future I will make a large-print edition available.

Finally, there's a couple of collector's editions:

- Klingon paperback
- Borg hardback

The Klingon edition has a special front-cover written in Klingon text. The Borg edition has a special front-cover written in Borg text. The rest of the books is exactly the same as the English language edition.

The sample app and GitHub repo

There's a GitHub repo with all the YAML and code used throughout the book.

You can clone it with the following command. You'll need `git` installed. This will create a new folder in your current working directory called `TheK8sBook` with all the files you need to follow the examples.

```
$ git clone https://github.com/nigelpoulton/TheK8sBook.git
```

Don't stress if you've never used git. The book walks you through everything you need to do.

Responsible language

The book follows guidelines issued by the *Inclusive Naming Initiative* (inclusivenaming.org) which promotes responsible language and tries to avoid harmful terms. As an example, the Kubernetes project has replaced the term "master" with "control plane node". This book does the same and attempts to follow all published guidance.

Feedback and contacting me

If you like the book, I'd consider you *family* if you leave a review and a few stars on Amazon.

You can also reach me on any of the following:

- Twitter: twitter.com/nigelpoulton
- LinkedIn: linkedin.com/in/nigelpoulton
- Mastodon: @nigelpoulton@hachyderm.io
- Web: nigelpoulton.com
- YouTube: youtube.com/nigelpoulton

If you have a content suggestion or a potential fix, drop me an email at `tkb@nigelpoulton.com`. I'll do my best to respond.

Let's get started!

1: Kubernetes primer

This chapter is split into two main sections:

- Kubernetes background – where it came from etc.
- Kubernetes as the Operating System of the cloud

Kubernetes background

Kubernetes is an *application orchestrator*. For the most part, it orchestrates containerized cloud-native microservices apps. That's a lot of buzzwords, so let's take some time to clarify some jargon.

What is an orchestrator

An *orchestrator* is a system that *deploys* and *manages* applications. It can deploy your applications and dynamically respond to changes. For example, Kubernetes can:

- Deploy your application
- Scale it up and down dynamically based on demand
- Self-heal it when things break
- Perform zero-downtime rolling updates and rollbacks
- Lots more…

And the best part about Kubernetes… it does all of this *orchestration* without you having to supervise or get involved. Obviously, you have to set things up in the first place, but once you've done that, you sit back and let Kubernetes work its magic.

What is a containerised app

A *containerized application* is an app that runs in a container.

Before we had containers, applications ran on physical servers or in virtual machines. Containers are just the next iteration of how we package and run apps. As such, they're faster, more lightweight, and more suited to modern business requirements than servers and virtual machines.

Think of it this way:

- Apps ran on physical servers in the open-systems era (1980s and 1990s)
- Apps ran in virtual machines in the virtualisation era (2000s and into the 2010s)
- Apps run in containers in the cloud-native era (now)

While Kubernetes can orchestrate other workloads, including virtual machines, serverless functions, and WebAssembly, it's most commonly used to orchestrate containerised apps.

What is a cloud-native app

A *cloud-native application* is one that's designed to meet cloud-like demands of auto-scaling, self-healing, rolling updates, rollbacks and more.

It's important to be clear that cloud-native apps are not applications that will only run in the public cloud. Yes, they absolutely can run on public clouds, but they can also run anywhere that you have Kubernetes, even your on-premises datacenters.

So, *cloud-native* is about the way applications behave and react to events.

What is a microservices app

A *microservices app* is built from lots of small, specialised, independent parts that work together to form a meaningful application. For example, you might have an e-commerce app comprising all of the following small, specialised, independent components:

- Web front-end
- Catalog service
- Shopping cart
- Authentication service
- Logging service
- Persistent store

As each of these features is developed and deployed as its own small app, or small service, we call each one a ***microservice***. Typically, each is coded and owned by a different development team. Each can have its own release cycle and can be scaled independently. For example, you can patch and scale the shopping cart *microservice* without affecting any of the others.

Building applications this way is vital for cloud-native features.

For the most part, each microservice runs as a container. Assuming this e-commerce app with the 6 microservices, there'd be one or more web front-end containers, one or more catalog containers, one or more shopping cart containers etc.

With all of this in mind, let's re-phrase that definition that was full of buzzwords…

Kubernetes deploys and manages (orchestrates) applications that are packaged and run as containers (containerized) and that are built in ways (cloud-native microservices) that allow them to scale, self-heal, and be updated in-line with modern cloud-like requirements.

We'll talk about these concepts a lot throughout the book, but for now, this should help you understand some of the main industry buzzwords.

Where did Kubernetes come from

Let's start at the beginning…

Amazon Web Services (AWS) changed the world when it brought us modern cloud computing. Since then, everyone else has been playing catch-up.

One of the companies trying to catch-up was Google. Google had its own very good cloud and needed a way to abstract the value of AWS, **and** make it easier for potential customers to get off AWS and onto their cloud.

Google also had a lot of experience working with containers at scale. For example, huge Google applications, such as Search and Gmail, have been running at extreme scale on containers for a lot of years – since way before Docker brought us easy-to-use containers. To orchestrate and manage these containerised apps, Google had a couple of in-house proprietary technologies called Borg and Omega.

Well, Google took the lessons learned from these in-house systems, and created a new platform called Kubernetes that it donated to the newly formed Cloud Native Computing Foundation (CNCF) in 2014 as an open-source project.

https://www.cncf.io

Kubernetes enables two things Google and the rest of the industry needed:

1. It abstracts underlying infrastructure such as AWS
2. It simplifies moving applications on and off clouds

Since its introduction in 2014, Kubernetes has become the most important cloud-native technology on the planet.

Kubernetes and Docker

Docker and Kubernetes have worked well together since the beginning of Kubernetes. Docker builds applications into container images and can run them as containers. Kubernetes can't do either of those. Instead, it sits at a higher level and orchestrates things.

Consider the following quick example. You have a Kubernetes cluster with 10 nodes for running your production applications. The first step is for your development teams to use Docker to package their applications as containers. Once this is done you give those containerised apps to Kubernetes to run. Kubernetes makes high-level orchestration decisions such as which nodes should run the containers, but Kubernetes itself cannot start and stop containers. In the past, each Kubernetes cluster node ran a copy of Docker that would start and stop containers. In this model, the Docker build tools are used to package applications as containers, Kubernetes makes scheduling and other orchestration decisions, and the Docker container runtime performs the low-level job of running containers.

From the outside everything looked good. However, on closer inspection, the Docker runtime was bloated and overkill for what Kubernetes needed. As a result, the Kubernetes project began work to make the container runtime layer pluggable so that users could choose the best runtime for their needs. We'll get into more detail later in the book, but in 2016 Kubernetes introduced the container runtime interface (CRI) that made this container runtime layer pluggable. Since then, lots of different container runtimes have been developed for Kubernetes.

At the time of writing, containerd (pronounced "container dee") has replaced Docker as the default container runtime in most Kubernetes clusters. However, containerd is a stripped-down version of Docker that's optimized for Kubernetes. As such, all container images created by Docker will continue to work on Kubernetes. In fact, both Docker and Kubernetes work with containers that support the Open Containers Initiative (OCI) specification.

Figure 1.2 shows a simple Kubernetes cluster with worker nodes using different container runtimes. Configurations like this are fully supported.

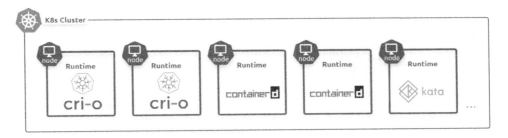

Figure 1.2

While all of this is interesting, it's low-level stuff that shouldn't impact your Kubernetes learning experience. For example, no matter which container runtime you use, the regular Kubernetes commands and patterns will work as normal.

What about Kubernetes vs Docker Swarm

In 2016 and 2017 we had the *orchestrator wars* where Docker Swarm, Mesosphere DCOS, and Kubernetes competed to become the de-facto container orchestrator. To cut a long story short, Kubernetes won.

However, Docker Swarm is still under active development and is popular with small companies that need a simple alternative to Kubernetes.

Kubernetes and Borg: Resistance is futile!

There's a good chance you'll hear people talk about how Kubernetes relates to Google's *Borg* and *Omega* systems.

As previously mentioned, Google has been running containers at scale for a long time – crunching through billions of containers a week. Orchestrating these containerised apps was the job of a couple of in-house technologies called *Borg* and *Omega*. So, it's not a huge stretch to make the connection with Kubernetes – all three are in the game of orchestrating containers at scale, and they're all related to Google.

However, it's important to understand that Kubernetes is **not** an open-source version of *Borg* or *Omega*. It's more like Kubernetes shares its DNA and family history with them.

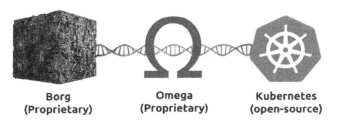

Figure 1.3 - Shared DNA

The point is, all three are separate, but all three are related. In fact, some of the people who built Borg and Omega were, and still are, involved with Kubernetes. So, although Kubernetes was built from scratch, it leverages much of what was learned at Google with Borg and Omega.

As things stand, Kubernetes is an open-source project donated to the CNCF in 2014. It's licensed under the Apache 2.0 license, version 1.0 shipped way back in July 2015, and at-the-time-of-writing, we're deep into the 1.20's and averaging three major releases per year.

Kubernetes – what's in the name

The name "Kubernetes" (koo-ber-net-eez) comes from the Greek word meaning *Helmsman* – the person who steers a ship. This theme is reflected in the logo, which is the wheel (helm control) of a ship.

Figure 1.4 - The Kubernetes logo

Some of the people involved in the creation of Kubernetes wanted to call it *Seven of Nine*. If you know Star Trek, you'll know that *Seven of Nine* is a **Borg** drone rescued by the crew of the USS Voyager under the command of Captain Kathryn Janeway. Sadly, copyright laws prevented it from being called *Seven of Nine*. So, the creators gave the logo **seven** spokes as a subtle reference to *Seven* of Nine.

One last thing about the name before moving on. You'll often see it shortened to "K8s" (pronounced "kates"). The number 8 replaces the 8 characters between the "K" and the "s".

Kubernetes as the operating system of the cloud

Kubernetes has emerged as the de facto platform for deploying and managing cloud-native applications. In many ways, it's like an operating system (OS) for the cloud. Consider this:

- You install a traditional OS (Linux or Windows) on a server, and it *abstracts* server resources and *schedules* application processes
- You install Kubernetes on a cloud, and it *abstracts* cloud resources and *schedules* application microservices

In the same way that Linux *abstracts* the hardware differences between server platforms, Kubernetes *abstracts* the differences between different private and public clouds. Net result... as long as you're running Kubernetes, it doesn't matter if the underlying infrastructure is on premises in your own datacenters, or in the public cloud.

With this in mind, Kubernetes is a major step towards a true *hybrid cloud*, allowing you to seamlessly move and balance workloads across multiple different public and private cloud infrastructures. You can also migrate *to* and *from* different clouds, meaning you can choose one cloud today and switch to a different one in the future.

Cloud scale

Generally speaking, cloud-native microservices applications make our previous scalability and complexity challenges look easy – we've just said Google goes through billions of containers every week!

That's great, but most of us are nothing like Google.

Well, as a general rule, if your legacy apps have hundreds of VMs, there's a good chance your containerized cloud-native microservices apps will have thousands of containers. With this in mind, you'll need help managing them.

Say hello to Kubernetes.

Also, we live in a business and technology world that's increasingly fragmented and constantly in a state of disruption. With this in mind, we desperately need a framework and platform that is widely accepted and hides complexity.

Again, say hello to Kubernetes.

Application scheduling

A typical computer is a collection of CPU, memory, storage, and networking. But modern operating systems have done a great job abstracting that. For example, how many developers care which CPU core or exact memory address their application uses? Not many, we let the OS take care of things like that. And it's a good thing as it makes the world of application development a far friendlier place.

Kubernetes does a similar thing with cloud and datacenter resources. At a high-level, a cloud or datacenter is a pool of compute, network, and storage resources. Kubernetes abstracts them, meaning you don't have to hard code which node or storage volume your applications run on, you don't even have to care which cloud they run on. Kubernetes takes care of all that.

So, gone are the days of naming your servers, mapping storage volumes and IP addresses in spreadsheets, and otherwise treating your infrastructure assets like *pets*. Modern cloud-native apps don't usually care. In the cloud-native world, we just say *"Hey Kubernetes, here's an app. Please deploy it and make sure it keeps running...".*

A quick analogy...

Consider the process of sending goods via a courier service.

You package the goods in the courier's standard packaging, slap on one of their labels and hand it over to the courier. The courier is responsible for everything else. This includes all the complex logistics of which planes and trucks it goes on, which highways to use, and who the drivers should be etc. They also provide services that let you do things like track your package and make delivery changes. The point is, the only thing *you* have to do is package and label the goods. The courier does everything else.

It's the same for apps on Kubernetes. You package the app as a container, give it a Kubernetes manifest, and let Kubernetes take care of deploying it and keeping it running. You also get a rich set of tools and APIs that let you introspect (observe and examine) it. It's a beautiful thing.

Chapter summary

Kubernetes was created by Google based on lessons learned running containers at scale for a lot of years. It was donated to the community as an open-source project and is now the industry standard platform for deploying and managing cloud-native applications. It runs on any cloud or on-premises datacenter and abstracts the underlying infrastructure. This allows you to build hybrid clouds, as well as migrate on, off and between different clouds. It's open-sourced under the Apache 2.0 license and lives within the Cloud Native Computing Foundation (CNCF).

Don't be afraid by all the new terminology and how fast things are moving. Embrace it, and remember, I'm here to help and I can be reached at any of the following:

- Twitter: @nigelpoulton
- LinkedIn: linkedin.com/in/nigelpoulton/
- Mastodon: @nigelpoulton@hachyderm.io
- Insta: https://www.instagram.com/nigel.poulton/
- TikTok: https://www.tiktok.com/@nigelpoulton
- Web: nigelpoulton.com

2: Kubernetes principles of operation

In this chapter, you'll learn about the major components required to build a Kubernetes cluster and deploy an app. The aim is to give you an overview of the major concepts. So don't worry if you don't understand everything straight away, we'll cover most things again as you progress through the book. Plus, the hands-on demos will help everything fall into place.

The chapter is divided as follows:

- Kubernetes from 40K feet
- Control plane nodes and worker nodes
- Packaging apps for Kubernetes
- The declarative model and desired state
- Pods
- Deployments
- Services

Some of the information in this chapter is covered in more depth the next couple of chapters. I've tried to keep this to a minimum; however, repetition is key to learning. It also caters for readers who skip this chapter and dive straight into the detail.

Kubernetes from 40K feet

At the highest level, Kubernetes is two things:

- A cluster to run applications on
- An orchestrator of cloud-native microservices apps

Kubernetes as a cluster

Kubernetes is like any other cluster – a bunch of machines to host applications. We call these machines "nodes", and they can be physical servers, virtual machines, cloud instances, Raspberry Pis, and more.

A Kubernetes cluster consists of a *control plane* and *worker nodes*. The *control plane* implements the intelligence. It exposes the API, has a scheduler for assigning work, and is responsible for keeping apps healthy. This includes self-healing, autoscaling, rollouts and more.

The worker nodes do the every-day hard work of executing user applications.

Kubernetes as an orchestrator

Orchestrator is just a fancy word for a system that takes care of deploying and managing applications.

Let's look at a quick analogy.

In the real world, a football (soccer) team is made of individuals. Every individual is different and has a different role to play in the team – some defend, some attack, some are great at passing, some tackle, some shoot... Along comes the coach, and she or he gives everyone a position and organizes them into a team with a purpose. Figure 2.1 shows things in a mess without a coach, and then organised with a coach.

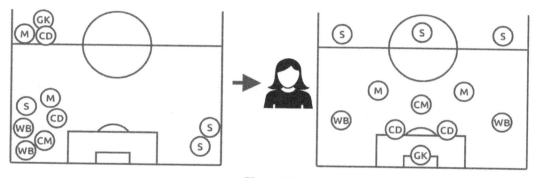

Figure 2.1

The coach also makes sure the team keeps its formation, sticks to the game-plan, and deals with any injuries and other realtime events.

Well guess what, microservices apps on Kubernetes are the same.

You start out with lots of individual specialised microservices. Some serve web pages, some do authentication, some perform searches, others persist data. Kubernetes comes along – like the coach in the football analogy – organizes everything into a useful app and keeps things running smoothly. It even responds to realtime events such as node failures and network issues.

In the sports world this is called *coaching*. In the application world it's called *orchestration*. Kubernetes *orchestrates* cloud-native microservices applications.

How it works

You start out with an app, package it as a container, then give it to the cluster (Kubernetes). The cluster is made up of one or more *control plane nodes* and a bunch of *worker nodes*.

As already stated, control plane nodes implement the cluster intelligence and worker nodes are where user applications run.

You follow this simple process to run applications on a Kubernetes cluster:

1. Design and write the application as small independent microservices in your favourite languages.
2. Package each microservice as its own container.
3. Wrap each container in a Kubernetes Pod.
4. Deploy Pods to the cluster via higher-level controllers such as *Deployments, DaemonSets, StatefulSets, CronJobs etc.*

Now then... this is the beginning of the book and you're not expected to know what all of this means yet. However, at a high-level, Kubernetes has several *controllers* that augment apps with important features such as self-healing, scaling, rollouts, and more. Some controllers are for stateless apps and others are for stateful apps. You'll learn all about them as you progress through the book.

Kubernetes likes to manage applications *declaratively*. This is a pattern where you describe what you want in a set of configuration files, post them to Kubernetes, then sit back and relax while Kubernetes makes it all happen.

However, it doesn't stop there. Because the declarative model tells Kubernetes how an application should look, Kubernetes can watch it and make sure it doesn't vary from what you asked for. If something isn't as it should be, Kubernetes attempts to fix it.

That's the big picture. Let's dig a bit deeper.

Control plane and worker nodes

As previously mentioned, a Kubernetes cluster is made of *control plane nodes* and *worker nodes*. These are Linux hosts that can be virtual machines (VM), bare metal servers in your datacenters, or instances in a private or public cloud. You can even run Kubernetes on ARM and IoT devices.

The control plane

A Kubernetes *control plane node* runs a collection of system services that make up the control plane of the cluster. Sometimes we call them *Masters*, *Heads* or *Head nodes*. However, the term "master" is no longer used.

The simplest setups run a single control plane node. However, this is only suitable for labs and test environments. For production environments, multiple control plane nodes configured for high availability (HA) are vital. Generally speaking, 3 or 5 is recommended, and you should spread them across availability zones.

It's also considered a good practice not to run user applications on control plane nodes. This allows them to concentrate entirely on managing the cluster.

Let's take a quick look at the different services making up the control plane. All of these services run on every control plane node.

The API server

The *API server* is the Grand Central station of Kubernetes. **All communication, between all components, must go through the API server**. We'll get into the detail later, but it's important to understand that internal system components, as well as external user components, **all** communicate through the API server – *all roads lead to the API Server*.

It exposes a RESTful API that you POST YAML configuration files to over HTTPS. These YAML files, which we sometimes call *manifests*, describe the desired state of an application. This desired state includes things like which container images to use, which ports to expose, and how many Pod replicas to run.

All requests to the API server are subject to authentication and authorization. Once these are done, the config in the YAML file is validated, persisted to the cluster store, and changes are scheduled to the worker nodes.

The cluster store

The cluster store is the only *stateful* part of the control plane and persistently stores the entire configuration and state of the cluster. As such, it's a vital component of every Kubernetes cluster – no cluster store, no cluster.

The cluster store is currently based on etcd, a popular distributed database. As it's the *single source of truth* for a cluster, you should run between 3-5 etcd replicas for high-availability, and you should provide adequate ways to recover when things go wrong. A default installation of Kubernetes installs a replica of the cluster store on every control plane node and automatically configures HA.

On the topic of *availability*, etcd prefers consistency over availability. This means it doesn't tolerate *split-brains* and will halt updates to the cluster in order to maintain consistency. However, if this happens, user applications should continue to work, you just won't be able to update the cluster config.

As with all distributed databases, consistency of writes to the database is vital. For example, multiple writes to the same value originating from different places need to be handled. etcd uses the popular RAFT consensus algorithm to accomplish this.

The controller manager and controllers

The controller manager implements all the background controllers that monitor cluster components and respond to events.

Architecturally, the controller manager is a *controller of controllers*, meaning it spawns all the core controllers and monitors them.

Some of the core controllers include the Deployment controller, the StatefulSet controller, and the ReplicaSet controller. Each one is responsible for a small subset of cluster intelligence and runs as a background watch-loop constantly watching the API Server for changes.

The goal of each controller is to ensure the *observed state* of the cluster matches the *desired state*. More on this soon.

The following logic, implemented by each controller, is at the heart of Kubernetes and declarative design patterns:

1. Obtain desired state
2. Observe current state
3. Determine differences
4. Reconcile differences

Each controller is also extremely specialized and only interested in its own little corner of the Kubernetes cluster. No attempt is made to over-complicate design by implementing awareness of other parts of the system. This is key to the distributed design of Kubernetes and adheres to the Unix philosophy of building complex systems from small specialized parts.

> **Terminology:** Throughout the book we'll use terms like *controller*, *control loop*, *watch loop*, and *reconciliation loop* to mean the same thing.

The scheduler

At a high level, the scheduler watches the API server for new work tasks and assigns them to appropriate healthy worker nodes. Behind the scenes, it implements complex logic that filters out nodes incapable of running tasks, and then ranks the nodes that are capable. The ranking system is complex, but the node with the highest-ranking score is selected to run the task.

When identifying nodes capable of running a task, the scheduler performs various predicate checks. These include; is the node tainted, are there any affinity or anti-affinity rules, is the required network port available on the node, does it have sufficient available resources etc. Any node incapable of running the task is ignored, and those remaining are ranked according to things such as does it already have the required image, how much free resource does it have, how many tasks is it currently running. Each is worth points, and the node with the most points is selected to run the task.

If the scheduler doesn't find a suitable node, the task isn't scheduled and gets marked as pending.

The scheduler is only responsible for picking the nodes to run tasks, it isn't responsible for *running* them. A *task* is normally a Pod/container. You'll learn about Pods and containers in later chapters.

The cloud controller manager

If you're running your cluster on a supported public cloud platform, such as AWS, Azure, GCP, or Linode, your control plane will be running a *cloud controller manager*. This facilitates integrations with cloud services, such as instances, load-balancers, and storage. For example, if your application asks for an internet-facing load-balancer, the cloud controller manager works with the underlying cloud to provision a load-balancer and connect it to your app.

Control Plane summary

Kubernetes control plane nodes run the cluster's control plane services. These services are the brains of the cluster where all the control and scheduling decisions happen. Behind the scenes, these services include the API server, the cluster store, scheduler, and core controllers.

The API server is the front-end into the control plane and all instructions and communication pass through it. By default, it exposes a RESTful endpoint on port 443.

Figure 2.2 shows a high-level view of a Kubernetes control plane node.

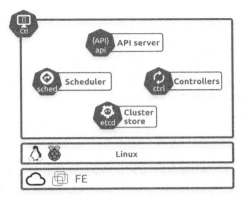

Figure 2.2 - control plane node

Worker nodes

Worker nodes are where user applications run.

At a high-level they do three things:

1. Watch the API server for new work assignments
2. Execute work assignments
3. Report back to the control plane (via the API server)

As you can see in Figure 2.3, they're a bit simpler than *control plane nodes*.

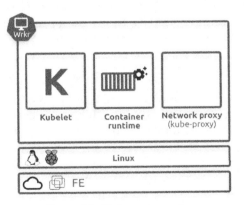

Figure 2.3 - Kubernetes node

Let's look at the three major components of a worker node.

Kubelet

The kubelet is the main Kubernetes agent and runs on every worker node.

When you join a node to a cluster, the process installs the kubelet, which is then responsible for registering it with the cluster. This registers the node's CPU, memory, and storage into the wider cluster pool.

One of the main jobs of the kubelet is to watch the API server for new work tasks. Any time it sees one, it executes the task and maintains a reporting channel back to the control plane.

If a kubelet can't run a task, it reports back to the control plane and lets the control plane decide what actions to take. For example, if a kubelet cannot execute a task, it is **not** responsible for finding another node to run it on. It simply reports back to the control plane and the control plane decides what to do.

Container runtime

The kubelet needs a *container runtime* to perform container-related tasks. This includes pulling images and starting and stopping containers.

In the early days, Kubernetes had native support for Docker. More recently, it's moved to a plugin model called the Container Runtime Interface (CRI). At a high-level, the CRI masks the internal machinery of Kubernetes and exposes a clean documented interface for 3rd-party container runtimes to plug into.

> **Note:** `containerd` (pronounced "container-dee") is the container supervisor and runtime logic stripped out from Docker – basically just the bits of Docker that Kubernetes needs. It was donated to the CNCF by Docker, Inc. and has a lot of community support. It fully supports images created by Docker. Other CRI container runtimes exist.

Kube-proxy

The last piece of the worker node puzzle is the kube-proxy. This runs on every node and is responsible for local cluster networking. It ensures each node gets its own unique IP address, and it implements local iptables or IPVS rules to handle routing and load-balancing of traffic.

Kubernetes DNS

As well as the various control plane and worker components, every Kubernetes cluster has an internal DNS service that is vital to service discovery.

The cluster's DNS service has a static IP address that is hard-coded into every Pod on the cluster. This ensures every app can locate it and use it for discovery. Service registration is also automatic. This means apps don't need to be coded with the intelligence to register with Kubernetes service discovery.

Cluster DNS is based on the open-source CoreDNS project (https://coredns.io/).

Now that you understand the fundamentals of control plane nodes and worker nodes, let's switch gears and see how to package applications to run on Kubernetes.

Packaging apps for Kubernetes

An application needs to tick a few boxes to run on a Kubernetes cluster. These include:

1. Wrapped in a Pod
2. Deployed via a declarative manifest file

It goes like this…

You write an application microservice in a language of your choice. You then build it into a container image and store it in a registry. At this point it's *containerized*.

Next, you define a Kubernetes Pod to run the containerized application. At the kind of high level we're at, a Pod is just a wrapper that allows a container to run on Kubernetes. Once you've defined the Pod, you're ready to deploy the app to Kubernetes.

While it's possible to run static Pods like this, the preferred model is to deploy all Pods via higher-level controllers. The most common controller is the *Deployment*. It offers scalability, self-healing, and rolling updates for stateless apps. You define *Deployments* in YAML manifest files that specify things like how many replicas to deploy and how to perform updates.

Figure 2.4 shows application code packaged as a *container*, running inside a *Pod*, managed by a *Deployment* controller.

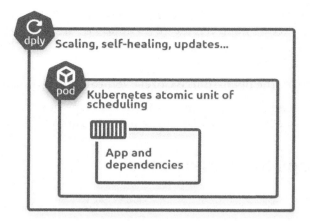

Figure 2.4

Once everything is defined in the *Deployment* YAML file, you can use the Kubernetes command-line tool to post it to the API server as the *desired state* of the application, and Kubernetes will implement it.

Speaking of desired state…

The declarative model and desired state

The *declarative model* and the concept of *desired state* are at the very heart of Kubernetes. So, it's vital you understand them.

In Kubernetes, the declarative model works like this:

1. Declare the desired state of an application microservice in a manifest file
2. Post it to the API server
3. Kubernetes stores it in the cluster store as the application's *desired state*
4. Kubernetes implements the desired state on the cluster
5. A controller makes sure the *observed state* of the application doesn't vary from the *desired state*

Let's look at each step in a bit more detail.

Manifest files are written in simple YAML and tell Kubernetes what an application should look like. This is called *desired state*. It includes things such as which image to use, how many replicas to run, which network ports to listen on, and how to perform updates.

Once you've created the manifest, you post it to the API server. A simple way to do this is with the kubectl command-line utility. This sends the manifest to the API Server over HTTPS.

Once the request is authenticated and authorized, Kubernetes inspects the manifest, identifies which controller to send it to (e.g., the *Deployments controller*), and records the config in the cluster store as part of overall *desired state*. Once this is done, any required work tasks get scheduled to worker nodes where the node components take care of pulling images, starting containers, attaching to networks, and starting application processes.

Finally, controllers run as background reconciliation loops that constantly monitor the state of the cluster. If the *observed state* varies from *desired state*, Kubernetes performs the tasks necessary to reconcile the issue.

It's important to understand that what we've described is the opposite of the traditional *imperative model*. The imperative model is where you write long scripts of platform-specific commands to build and monitor things. Not only is the declarative model a lot simpler, it also enables self-healing, scaling, and lends itself to version control and self-documentation. It does all of this by telling the cluster *how things should look*. If they start to look different, the appropriate controller notices the discrepancy and does all the hard work to reconcile the situation.

> **Terminology:** *observed state, actual state* and *current state* all mean the same thing.

Let's consider an example.

Declarative example

Assume you have an app with a desired state that includes 10 replicas of a web front-end Pod. If a node running two replicas fails, the *observed state* will be reduced to 8 replicas, but *desired state* will still be 10. This will be observed by a controller and two new replicas will be scheduled to bring the total back up to 10.

The same thing will happen if you intentionally scale the desired number of replicas up or down. You could even change the image you want to use (this is called a rollout). For example, if the app is currently using v2.00 of an image, and you update the desired state to specify v2.01, the relevant controller will notice the difference and go through the process of updating the cluster so all 10 replicas are running the new version.

To be clear. Instead of writing a complex script to step through the entire process of updating every replica to the new version, you simply tell Kubernetes you want the new version, and Kubernetes does the hard work for you.

Despite how simple this might seem, it's extremely powerful and at the very heart of how Kubernetes operates.

Pods

In the VMware world, the atomic unit of scheduling is the virtual machine (VM). In the Docker world, it's the container. Well... in the Kubernetes world, it's the *Pod*.

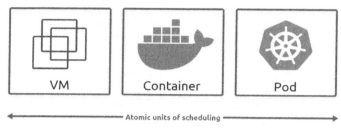

Figure 2.5

It's true that Kubernetes runs containerized apps. However, Kubernetes demands that every container runs inside a Pod.

> **Note:** Pods are objects in the Kubernetes API, so we capitalize the first letter. This might annoy you if you're passionate about language and proper use of capitalization. However, it adds clarity and the official Kubernetes docs are moving towards this standard.

Pods and containers

The very first thing to understand is that the term *Pod* comes from a *pod of whales* – in the English language we call a group of whales a *pod of whales*. As the Docker logo is a whale, Kubernetes ran with the whale concept and that's why we have *"Pods"*.

The simplest model is to run a single container in every Pod. This is why we often use the terms "Pod" and "container" interchangeably. However, there are advanced use-cases that run multiple containers in a single Pod. Powerful examples of multi-container Pods include:

- Service meshes
- Web containers supported by a *helper* container pulling updated content
- Containers with a tightly coupled log scraper

The point is, a Kubernetes Pod is a construct for running one or more containers. Figure 2.6 shows a multi-container Pod.

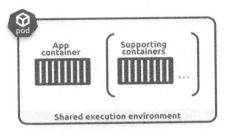

Figure 2.6

Pod anatomy

Pods themselves don't actually run applications – applications always run in containers. The Pod is just an execution environment to run one or more containers. Keeping it high level, Pods ring-fence an area of the host OS and run one or more containers.

If you're running multiple containers in a Pod, they all share the same Pod environment. This includes the network stack, volumes, IPC namespace, shared memory, and more. As an example, all containers in the same Pod will share the same IP address (the Pod's IP). This is shown in Figure 2.7.

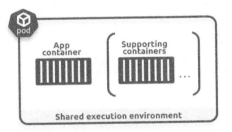

Figure 2.7

If two containers in the same Pod need to talk to each other (container-to-container within the Pod) they can use the Pod's localhost interface as shown in Figure 2.8.

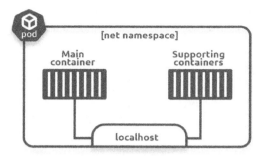

Figure 2.8

Multi-container Pods are ideal when you have requirements for tightly coupled containers that may need to share memory and storage. However, if you don't *need* to tightly couple containers, you should put them in their own Pods and loosely couple them over the network. This keeps things clean by having every Pod dedicated to a single task. However, it creates a lot of potentially un-encrypted east-west network traffic. You should seriously consider using a service mesh to secure traffic between Pods and provide better network observability.

Pods as the unit of scaling

Pods are also the minimum unit of scheduling in Kubernetes. If you need to scale an app, you add or remove Pods. You **do not** scale by adding more containers to existing Pods. Figure 2.9 shows how to scale the nginx front-end of an app using Pods as the unit of scaling.

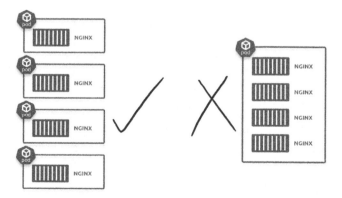

Figure 2.9 - Scaling with Pods

Pods - atomic operations

The deployment of a Pod is an atomic operation. This means a Pod is only ready for service when all its containers are up and running. The entire Pod either comes up and is put into service, or it doesn't.

A single Pod can only be scheduled to a single node - Kubernetes cannot schedule a single Pod across multiple nodes. This is also true of multi-container Pods – all containers in the same Pod run on the same node.

Pod lifecycle

Pods are mortal – they're created, they live, and they die. If they die unexpectedly, you don't bring them back to life. Instead, Kubernetes starts a new one in its place. This new one looks, smells, and feels like the old one. However, it's a shiny new Pod with a shiny new ID and IP address.

This has implications on how you design your applications. Don't design them to be tightly coupled to a particular instance of a Pod. Instead, design them so that when Pods fail, a totally new one (with a new ID and IP address) can pop up somewhere else in the cluster and seamlessly take its place.

Pod immutability

Pods are immutable. This means you don't change them once they're running.

For example, once a Pod is running, you never log on to it and change or update its configuration. If you need to change or update it, you replace it with a new one running the new configuration. Whenever we talk about *updating Pods*, we really mean delete the old one and replace it with a new one.

Deployments

Most of the time you'll deploy Pods indirectly via higher-level controllers. Examples of higher-level controllers include *Deployments*, *DaemonSets*, and *StatefulSets*.

As an example, a Deployment is a higher-level Kubernetes object that wraps around a Pod and adds features such as self-healing, scaling, zero-downtime rollouts, and versioned rollbacks.

Behind the scenes, Deployments, DaemonSets and StatefulSets are implemented as controllers that run as watch loops constantly observing the cluster making sure observed state matches desired state.

Service objects and stable networking

You've just learned that Pods are mortal and can die. However, if they're managed via higher level controllers, when they fail they get replaced with new ones with totally different IP addresses. This also happens with rollouts and scaling operations. Rollouts replace old Pods with new ones with new IPs. Scaling up adds new Pods with new IP addresses, whereas scaling down deletes existing Pods. Events like these cause a lot of *IP churn*.

The point is, **Pods are unreliable**, and this poses challenges.

Assume you've got a microservices app with a bunch of Pods performing video rendering. How can this work if clients of the rendering service can't rely on rendering Pods being there when needed?

This is where *Services* come in to play. They provide reliable networking for a set of Pods.

Figure 2.10 shows uploader Pods talking to the renderer Pods via a Kubernetes Service object. The Service (capital "S" because it's a Kubernetes API object) is providing a reliable name and IP. It's also load-balancing requests to the two renderer Pods behind it.

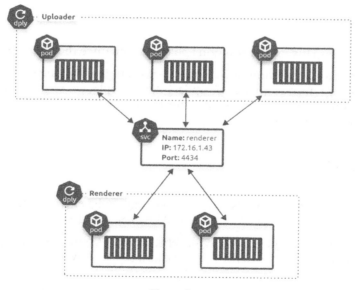

Figure 2.10

Digging into a bit more detail. Services have a front-end consisting of a stable DNS name, IP address, and port. On the back-end, they load-balance traffic across a dynamic set of Pods. As Pods come and go, the Service observes this, automatically updates itself, and continues to provide that stable networking endpoint.

The same applies if you scale the number of Pods up or down. New Pods are seamlessly added to the Service and will receive traffic. Terminated Pods are seamlessly removed and will not receive traffic.

That's the job of a Service – it's a stable network abstraction point that provides TCP and UDP load-balancing across a dynamic set of Pods.

However, Services don't possess *application intelligence*. This means they cannot provide application-layer host and path routing. For that, you need an *Ingress*, which understands HTTP and provides host and path-based routing. A later chapter is dedicated to Ingress.

In summary, Services bring stable IP addresses and DNS names to the unstable world of Pods.

Chapter summary

In this chapter, we introduced some of the major components of a Kubernetes cluster.

Control plane nodes are servers where the control plane components run. They can be physical servers, VMs, cloud instances and more.

Under-the-hood, the control-plane comprises several services. These include the API server that exposes a public REST interface, the scheduler, and various controllers. Running multiple control plane nodes for high availability (HA) is vital for production environments.

Worker nodes are servers where user applications run. They can also be physicals, virts, cloud instances and other platforms.

Every worker node runs a service called the kubelet that registers it with the cluster and communicates with the API server. This watches the API server for new work tasks and maintains a reporting channel. They also have a container runtime and the kube-proxy service. The container runtime is responsible for low-level container-related operations. The kube-proxy is responsible for networking on the node.

We also talked about some of the major Kubernetes API objects such as Pods, Deployments, and Services. The Pod is the basic building-block that application containers run in. Deployments add self-healing, scaling, and updates. Services add stable networking and basic load-balancing.

3: Getting Kubernetes

This chapter shows you a few of the different ways to create a Kubernetes environment, as well as how to get kubectl (the Kubernetes command line utility).

The chapter is divided as follows:

1. Creating a Kubernetes cluster on your laptop
2. Creating a hosted Kubernetes cluster in the cloud
3. Getting and working with **kubectl**

Not all of the clusters we'll show you how to create will work with all of the examples in the book. The GKE example will work with most of the examples but costs money to run.

Creating a Kubernetes cluster on your laptop

There are lots of easy ways to get a development Kubernetes environment on your laptop or other local machine. We'll look at the following:

- Docker Desktop
- K3d
- KinD

You will need Docker Desktop to be able to work with the K3d and KinD examples.

Docker Desktop

Docker Desktop is a great way to get a local development cluster on your Mac or Windows laptop. In just a few easy steps you get a single-node Kubernetes cluster that you can develop and test with. It automatically installs and configures kubectl and you get a GUI that simplifies common operations such as switching between *kubectl contexts*.

> **Note:** A *kubectl context* is a collection of settings that tells kubectl which cluster to issue commands to and which credentials to authenticate with. You'll learn more about them later.

1. Go to docker.com and follow the links to download Docker Desktop. Alternatively, search for "download docker desktop" in your favorite search engine and follow the links to download the installer for Mac or Windows.

2. Open the installer and follow the simple instructions.

   When the installer completes, you'll get a Docker whale icon on the Windows task bar or the menu bar on your Mac.

3. Right-click the whale icon, go to Preferences, and enable Kubernetes from the Kubernetes tab.

You may have to click Apply & Restart and it'll take a few minutes while Docker Desktop fires up your Kubernetes cluster.

When the process finishes, open a terminal to see your cluster.

```
$ kubectl get nodes
NAME              STATUS    ROLES              AGE    VERSION
docker-desktop    Ready     control-plane,etcd, 21d    v1.25.2
```

Congratulations, you've installed the Docker tools, a Kubernetes cluster, and kubectl. You can use this cluster to follow most of the examples in the book.

Creating a local multi-node Kubernetes cluster with K3d

K3d is a great tool for creating multi-node Kubernetes clusters on your laptop. Under the hood, it runs the stripped-down K3s Kubernetes distribution inside of Docker.

You'll need the following to build and work with a K3d cluster. If you've installed Docker Desktop you'll already have both:

- Docker
- kubectl

You may be asking yourself why you need K3d if you already have a local Kubernetes cluster with Docker Desktop. One reason is that K3d allows you to create multi-node Kubernetes clusters. These can feel a lot more like real-world clusters and are better for some of the demos later in the book.

You'll complete the following steps to build a multi-node cluster with K3d:

1. Install K3d
2. Create a K3d Kubernetes cluster
3. Check the cluster created properly

4. Test your kubectl config

Install K3d on macOS or Windows with either of the following commands. Up-to-date installation instructions can be found at `https://k3d.io`.

macOS

```
$ brew install k3d
```

Windows

You'll need the Chocolatey package manager installed for this to work.

```
> choco install k3d
```

Verify the installation.

```
$ k3d --version
k3d version v5.4.6
```

Create a 4-node K3d cluster called **tkb** with the following command.

```
$ k3d cluster create tkb \
  --servers 1 \
  --agents 3 \
  --image rancher/k3s:latest
```

The `--servers 1` flag creates a single control plane node, the `--agents 3` flag creates 3 worker nodes, and the `--image rancher/k3s:latest` creates the cluster based on the most recent Kubernetes image available.

Verify the cluster with this command.

```
$ k3d cluster list
NAME    SERVERS   AGENTS   LOADBALANCER
tkb     1/1       3/3      true
```

Run the following command to confirm your `kubectl context` has been updated to work with the new cluster. You'll need `kubectl` installed for this to work.

```
$ kubectl get nodes
NAME              STATUS   ROLES                  AGE     VERSION
k3d-tkb-server-0  Ready    control-plane,master   3m1s    v1.26.1+k3s1
k3d-tkb-agent-2   Ready    <none>                 2m59s   v1.26.1+k3s1
k3d-tkb-agent-1   Ready    <none>                 2m57s   v1.26.1+k3s1
k3d-tkb-agent-0   Ready    <none>                 2m57s   v1.26.1+k3s1
```

At the time of writing, there's a bug with K3d clusters on macOS with Docker Desktop that causes kubectl commands to timeout. This is because the host.docker.internal interface is unreachable. I fixed this by editing the kubeconfig file and replacing https://host.docker.internal with https://127.0.0.1 under the k3d-tkb cluster block. Hopefully this will be resolved when you're reading this. The kubeconfig file is called "config" and located in a hidden ".kube" directory in your home folder.

You can use this cluster for most of the hands-on examples in the book.

Creating a local multi-node Kubernetes cluster with KinD

KinD is an acronym for Kubernetes in Docker and is a great way to create multi-node clusters.

You'll need Docker and kubectl to use it. If you've already installed Docker Desktop you'll already have these.

You'll complete the following steps to build a multi-node cluster with KinD:

1. Install KinD
2. Create a KinD Kubernetes cluster
3. Check the cluster is running
4. Test your kubectl config

Install KinD on macOS or Windows with either of the following commands. Up-to-date installation instructions can be found at https://kind.sigs.k8s.io/.

macOS

```
$ brew install kind
```

Windows

You'll need the Chocolatey package manager installed for this to work.

```
> choco install kind
```

Verify the installation.

```
$ kind --version
kind version 0.17.0
```

You need a YAML configuration file to build multi-node clusters with KinD. The following YAML creates a new 4-node cluster called **tkb** with dual-stack networking enabled. It creates 1 control plane node and 3 worker nodes. The file is called `kind.yml` and it's in the `installation` folder of the book's GitHub repo.

```
kind: Cluster
apiVersion: kind.x-k8s.io/v1alpha4
name: tkb                              <<==== Cluster name
networking:
  ipFamily: dual                       <<==== Enable IPv4 and IPv6 networking
nodes:
- role: control-plane
  image: kindest/node:v1.26.0          <<==== Find the latest image versions on Docker Hub
- role: worker                         <<==== under the 'kindest/node' repo
  image: kindest/node:v1.26.0
- role: worker
  image: kindest/node:v1.26.0
- role: worker
  image: kindest/node:v1.26.0
```

At the time of writing there is no image with the `latest` tag. Go to Docker Hub and search the `kindest/node` repo for the latest versions available.

Run the following command to create the cluster. You'll need to run the command from the folder where the `kind.yml` file is located.

```
$ kind create cluster --config=kind.yml

Creating cluster "tkb" ...
  Ensuring node image (kindest/node:v1.26.0)
  Preparing nodes
  Writing configuration
  Starting control-plane
  Installing CNI
  Installing StorageClass
  Joining worker nodes
Set kubectl context to "kind-tkb"
...
```

Notice that your `kubectl context` has been set to **kind-tkb** and not just **tkb**. This is because KinD prefixes your cluster name with "kind-" for use with external tools.

Verify the cluster was created successfully.

```
$ kind get clusters
tkb
```

Check that your kubectl context is correctly set to you KinD **tkb** cluster.

```
$ kubectl get nodes
NAME                 STATUS    ROLES           AGE     VERSION
tkb-control-plane    Ready     control-plane   96s     v1.26.0
tkb-worker           Ready     <none>          76s     v1.26.0
tkb-worker2          Ready     <none>          76s     v1.26.0
tkb-worker3          Ready     <none>          76s     v1.26.0
```

You can use this cluster for most of the hands-on examples in the book, including dual-stack networking examples.

Creating a hosted Kubernetes cluster in the cloud

All the major cloud platforms offer a *hosted Kubernetes* service. This is a model where the cloud provider builds the Kubernetes cluster and ensures things such as high-availability (HA), performance, and updates.

Not all hosted Kubernetes services are equal, but they're usually as close as you'll get to a zero-effort *production-grade* Kubernetes cluster. For example, Google Kubernetes Engine (GKE) is a hosted Kubernetes service that creates high-performance highly-available clusters, with security best-practices out-of-the-box, Anthos service mesh, and more. All with just a few simple clicks.

Other popular hosted Kubernetes services include:

- AWS: Elastic Kubernetes Service (EKS)
- Azure: Azure Kubernetes Service (AKS)
- Civo Cloud Kubernetes
- DigitalOcean: DigitalOcean Kubernetes (DOKS)
- Google Cloud Platform: Google Kubernetes Engine (GKE)
- Linode: Linode Kubernetes Engine (LKE)

We'll create the following hosted Kubernetes clusters:

- Google Kubernetes Engine (GKE)
- Linode Kubernetes Engine (LKE)

Google Kubernetes Engine (GKE)

GKE is a *hosted Kubernetes* service that runs on the Google Cloud Platform (GCP). Like most *hosted Kubernetes* services, it provides:

- A fast and easy way to get a "production-grade" cluster
- A managed control plane
- Itemized billing
- Integration with additional services such as load-balancers, volumes, service meshes, and more…

Creating a cluster with GKE

To build a GKE cluster you'll need a Google Cloud account with billing configured and a blank project. These are simple to setup, so the remainder of this section assumes you already have them.

You'll also need the **gcloud** and **kubectl** command line utilities installed. Both can be installed from here – `https://cloud.google.com/sdk/`.

1. Go to `https://console.cloud.google.com/` and select `Kubernetes Engine > Clusters` from the navigation pane on the left. You may have to click the three horizontal bars (hamburger) in the top left corner to make the navigation pane visible.
2. Select the option to create a cluster and choose the option to create a standard cluster that you manage.
3. Give your cluster a meaningful name.
4. Choose a `Regional` cluster as some of the examples later in the book will only work with *regional* clusters.
5. Select a Region for your cluster.
6. Click `Release channel` and select the latest version available from the **Rapid channel**.
7. Click the `default pool` from the left menu and under the `Size` section be sure to set `Number of nodes (per zone)` to **1**.
8. Other settings exist, but some might cause issues with examples later in the book.
9. Once you're happy with your configuration and the estimated monthly cost, click `Create`.

It'll take a couple of minutes to create your cluster.

The "clusters" page shows a high-level overview of the Kubernetes clusters in your project. Feel free to poke around and familiarise yourself with some of the settings.

Clicking the three dots to the right of your new cluster reveals a Connect option. It gives you a long gcloud command that configures kubectl to talk to your cluster. Copy the command to your clipboard and run it in a terminal.

When the command completes, run the following kubectl get nodes command to list the nodes in the cluster.

```
$ kubectl get nodes
NAME                         STATUS      ROLES       VERSION
gke-gke-tkb-default...h2gp   Ready       <none>      v1.26.0-gke.2000
gke-gke-tkb-default...l29b   Ready       <none>      v1.26.0-gke.2000
gke-gke-tkb-default...qzv6   Ready       <none>      v1.26.0-gke.2000
```

The node names and Kubernetes version should relate to the GKE cluster you just created.

Notice how all of the nodes have **<none>** under the ROLES column. This is because GKE is a hosted platform and only lets you see worker nodes. Control plane nodes are managed by GKE and hidden from you.

If you get a warning about auth plugin deprecation, follow the instructions in the linked article.

Congratulations! You have a "production-grade" Kubernetes cluster and can continue with the exercises in the rest of the book.

> **Warning.** Be sure to delete the cluster as soon as you're finished using it. GKE is a cloud service and may incur costs even when you're not using it.

Linode Kubernetes Engine (LKE)

Linode Kubernetes Engine (LKE) is a *hosted Kubernetes* service that runs on the Linode cloud. It provides a hosted control plane and integrations with volumes, load-balancers and more.

You'll need to install kubectl separately. You'll already have this if you installed Docker Desktop.

Creating a cluster with LKE

1. Point your browser to linode.com and sign-up for an account.
2. Login to the Linode Cloud Console, click Kubernetes from the navigation pane on the left and choose Create a Cluster.
3. Give your cluster a meaningful name in the cluster label box, select an appropriate Region, and choose the most recent version.
4. Add 2 or 3 Linode 4GB Shared CPU instances to your Node Pool.
5. You can optionally enable the *HA Control Plane* but this isn't necessary to follow the examples.
6. Once you're happy with your configuration and the monthly costs, click Create Cluster.

It may take a minute or two for your cluster to build.

When it's ready, the console will show your nodes as Running and will display their IP addresses. It will also show your Kubernetes *API Endpoint* in URL format.

At this point, your LKE cluster is running. However, you'll have to install kubectl and manually configure your kubectl context.

If you're unsure whether you have kubectl installed, run the following command. Your output will be similar if it's installed.

```
$ kubectl version --client -o yaml
clientVersion:
  buildDate: "2023-01-18T15:58:16Z"
  <Snip>
  major: "1"
  minor: "26"
  platform: darwin/arm64
```

If you don't have it installed, run a brew install kubectl on macOS or a choco install kubectl on Windows (you'll need Chocolatey installed on Windows for that to work).

Once it's installed, go back to Linode and download your cluster's kubeconfig file and copy it to the appropriate folder for your OS:

- Windows: C:\Users\<username>\.kube\
- macOS: /Users/<username>/.kube/

You may have to enable hidden folders. On macOS type Command + Shift + period. On Windows 10 or 11, type "folder" into the Windows search bar and select File Explorer Options. Select the View tab and click the Show hidden files, folders, and drives button and click Apply.

If you already have a file in **kube** directory called **config**, rename it to **config.old**. Finally, rename the LKE kubeconfig file to **config**.

Run a kubectl get nodes to verify your kubectl context is correctly set and you're talking to your new LKE cluster.

```
$ kubectl get nodes
NAME                          STATUS    ROLES     AGE       VERSION
lke47224-75467-61c34614cbae   Ready     <none>    2m49s     v1.25.1
lke47224-75467-61c34615230e   Ready     <none>    100s      v1.25.1
```

The output shows an LKE cluster with two worker nodes. You know it's an LKE cluster because the node names start with lke. Control plane nodes are not displayed as they are managed by LKE and hidden from view.

At this point, your LKE cluster is up and running and you can use it to follow the examples in the book.

> **Warning.** LKE is a cloud service and costs money. Be sure to delete your cluster when you no longer need it. Forgetting to do this will incur unwanted costs.

Install and work with kubectl

kubectl is the main Kubernetes command-line tool. It's what you'll use for day-to-day Kubernetes management, and we use it extensively in the examples. It's available for most operating systems and architectures.

It's important that your kubectl version is no more than one minor version higher or lower than your cluster. For example, if your cluster is running Kubernetes 1.26.x, your kubectl should be no lower than 1.25.x and no higher than 1.27.x.

At a high-level, kubectl converts user-friendly commands into HTTP REST requests with JSON payloads required by the API server. It uses a configuration file to know which cluster and API server endpoint to send commands to, and it takes care of sending authentication tokens with commands.

The kubectl configuration file is called config and lives in a hidden directory called .kube in your home directory ($HOME/.kube/config). We normally call it the *"kubeconfig"* file and it contains definitions for:

- Clusters
- Users (credentials)
- Contexts

Clusters is a list of Kubernetes clusters that kubectl knows about. It allows a single kubectl installation to manage multiple clusters. Each cluster definition has a name, certificate info, and API server endpoint.

Users let you define users with different levels of access. For example, you might have a *dev* user and an *ops* user, each with different permissions. Each *user* has a friendly name, a username, and a set of credentials. If you're using X.509 certificates, the username and group info is embedded in the certificate.

Contexts group together clusters and users under a friendly name. For example, you might have a context called ops-prod that combines the ops user credentials with the prod cluster. If you use kubectl with this context, you'll be sending commands to the API server of the prod cluster as the ops user.

The following is a simple kubeconfig file with a single cluster called shield, a single user called coulson, and a single context called director. The director context combines the coulson user and the shield cluster and is also set as the default context.

```
apiVersion: v1
kind: Config
clusters:                                       <<==== Cluster definitions in this block
- cluster:
  name: shield
    certificate-authority: C:\Users\nigel\.minikube\ca.crt
    server: https://192.168.1.77:8443
users:                                          <<==== User definitions in this block
- name: coulson
  user:
    client-certificate: C:\Users\nigel\.minikube\client.crt
    client-key: C:\Users\nigel\.minikube\client.key
contexts:                                       <<==== Contexts in this block
- context:
    cluster: shield
    user: coulson
  name: director
current-context: director
```

You can view your kubeconfig using the kubectl config view command. Sensitive data will be redacted.

You can use kubectl config current-context to see your current context. The following example shows a system where kubectl is configured to use the cluster and user defined in a context called k8sbook_eks.

```
$ kubectl config current-context
k8sbook_eks
```

You can change the current active context with `kubectl config use-context`. The following command sets the current context to `docker-desktop` so that future commands will be sent to the cluster defined in the `docker-desktop` context. It will only work if your kubeconfig file has a valid context called `docker-desktop`.

```
$ kubectl config use-context docker-desktop
Switched to context "docker-desktop".

$ kubectl config current-context
docker-desktop
```

Chapter summary

This chapter showed you a few ways to get a Kubernetes cluster. However, lots of other options exist.

Options like *Docker Desktop, K3d,* and *KinD* are great for local development clusters on a laptop or other personal device.

Docker Desktop ships with the full suite of Docker development tools, creates a single-node Kubernetes cluster, and installs `kubectl`. K3d and KinD both rely on a local Docker installation and allow you to build multi-node clusters.

You learned how to spin up hosted Kubernetes clusters in the Google Cloud (GKE) and Linode Cloud (LKE).

The chapter finished with an overview of `kubectl`, the Kubernetes command-line tool.

You'll be able to follow most of the examples in the book with the clusters we've shown you how to create. The storage examples, as well as some of the networking and Ingress examples, will only work if you're following along on a GKE cluster.

4: Working with Pods

Pods are fundamental to running apps on Kubernetes. As such, this chapter goes into quite a bit of detail.

The chapter is divided into two main parts:

- Theory
- Hands-on

Before getting started, it's difficult to talk about Pods without referring to workload controllers such as Deployments, DaemonSets, and StatefulSets. However, this is the start of the book and we haven't covered any of those yet. So, we'll take a quick minute here to set the scene and give you a basic idea of what they are.

You'll almost always deploy Pods via higher-level workload controllers – from now on, we'll just call them *controllers*.

Controllers infuse Pods with super-powers such as self-healing, scaling, rollouts, and rollbacks. You'll see this later, but every controller has a *PodTemplate* defining the Pods it deploys and manages. So, even though you'll rarely interact directly with Pods, it's absolutely vital you have a solid understanding of them.

For these reasons, we'll cover quite a lot of Pod detail. It won't be wasted time and it'll be very useful as you progress to controllers and other more advanced objects. Also, a deep understanding of Pods is vital if you want to master Kubernetes.

With that out of the way, let's crack on.

This chapter builds on some of the concepts introduced in Chapter 2. I've tried to minimise the repetition, but if you've read Chapter 2 you may notice a minor amount of repetition.

Pod theory

The *atomic unit of scheduling* in Kubernetes is the Pod. This is just a fancy way of saying apps deployed to Kubernetes always run inside Pods.

Some quick examples... If you deploy an app, you deploy it in a Pod. If you terminate an app, you terminate its Pod. If you scale an app up or down, you add or remove Pods.

Why Pods

The process of building and running an app on Kubernetes is roughly as follows:

1. Write your app/code
2. Package it as a container image
3. Wrap the container image in a Pod
4. Run it on Kubernetes

This begs the question, *why not just run the container on Kubernetes?*

The short answer is *you just can't.* Kubernetes doesn't allow containers to run directly on a cluster, they always have to be wrapped in a Pod.

There are three main reasons for Pods:

1. Pods augment containers
2. Pods assist in scheduling
3. Pods enable resource sharing

Let's look closer at each.

Pods augment containers

Pods augment containers in all the following ways:

- Labels and annotations
- Restart policies
- Probes (startup probes, readiness probes, liveness probes, and potentially more)
- Affinity and anti-affinity rules
- Termination control
- Security policies
- Resource requests and limits

Run a `kubectl explain pods` command to list all possible Pod attributes. Beware, the command returns over 1,000 lines and the following output has been trimmed.

```
$ kubectl explain pods --recursive
KIND:      Pod
VERSION:   v1

DESCRIPTION:
     Pod is a collection of containers that can run on a host. This resource is
     created by clients and scheduled onto hosts.

FIELDS:
   apiVersion              <string>
   kind                    <string>
   metadata                <Object>
      annotations          <map[string]string>
      labels               <map[string]string>
      name                 <string>
      namespace            <string>
<Snip>
```

It's a useful command for finding which properties any object supports. It also shows the format of properties, such as whether it's a string, map, object, or something else.

Even more useful, is the ability to drill into specific attributes. The following command drills into the restart policy attribute of a Pod object.

```
$ kubectl explain pod.spec.restartPolicy
KIND:      Pod
VERSION:   v1
FIELD:     restartPolicy <string>
DESCRIPTION:
     Restart policy for all containers within the pod. One of Always, OnFailure, Never.
     Default to Always.
     More info: https://kubernetes.io/docs/concepts/workloads/pods/pod-lifecycle/...

     Possible enum values:
     - `"Always"`
     - `"Never"`
     - `"OnFailure"`
```

You'll see a lot of Pod features as you progress through the book. However, it's worth a quick introduction to some of them right now.

Labels let you group Pods and associate them with other objects in powerful ways. *Annotations* let you add experimental features and integrations with 3rd-party tools and services. *Probes* let you test the health and status of Pods and the apps they run. This enables advanced scheduling, updates, and more. *Affinity* and *anti-affinity* rules give you control over where in a cluster Pods are allowed to run. *Termination control* lets you gracefully terminate Pods and the applications they run. *Security policies* let you enforce security features. *Resource requests and limits* let you specify minimum and maximum values for things like CPU, memory, and disk IO.

Despite bringing so many features to the party, Pods are super-lightweight and add very little overhead.

Figure 4.1 shows a Pod wrapping one or more containers.

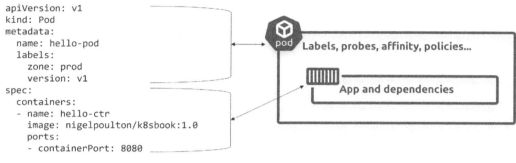

```
apiVersion: v1
kind: Pod
metadata:
  name: hello-pod
  labels:
    zone: prod
    version: v1
spec:
  containers:
  - name: hello-ctr
    image: nigelpoulton/k8sbook:1.0
    ports:
    - containerPort: 8080
```

Figure 4.1

Pods assist in scheduling

On the scheduling front, every container in a Pod is guaranteed to be scheduled to the same worker node. This in turn guarantees they'll be in the same region and zone in your cloud or datacenter. We call this *co-scheduling* and *co-locating*.

Labels, affinity and anti-affinity rules, as well as resource requests and limits give you fine-grained control over which worker nodes Pods can run on.

> **Note:** Remember that *worker nodes* are host servers that can be physical servers, virtual machines, or cloud instances. *Pods* are a thin wrapper around application containers and execute on worker nodes.

Pods enable resource sharing

On the sharing of resources front, Pods provide a *shared execution environment* for one or more containers. This shared execution environment includes things such as:

- Shared filesystem
- Shared network stack (IP address, routing table, ports...)
- Shared memory
- Shared volumes

This means that if a Pod has two containers, both will share the Pod's IP address and can access any of the Pod's volumes to share data.

We'll cover all these features throughout the book, but hopefully you understand some of the advantages of using Pods.

Static Pods vs controllers

There are two ways to deploy Pods:

1. Directly via a Pod manifest
2. Indirectly via a controller

Pods deployed directly from a Pod manifest are called *static Pods* and have no super-powers such as self-healing, scaling, or rolling updates. This is because they're only monitored and managed by the worker node's *kubelet* process which is limited to attempting restarts on the local worker node. If the worker node they're running on fails, there's no control-plane process watching and capable of starting a new one on a different node.

Pods deployed via controllers have all the benefits of being monitored and managed by a highly-available controller running on the control-plane. The local kubelet can still attempt local restarts, but if restart attempts fail, or the node itself fails, the observing controller can start a replacement Pod on a different worker node.

Just to be clear, it's vital to understand that Pods are *mortal*. When they die, they're gone. There's no fixing them and bringing them back from the dead. This firmly places them in the *cattle* category of the *pets vs cattle* paradigm. Pods are *cattle*, and when they die, they get replaced by another. There's no tears and no funeral. The old one is gone, and a shiny new one – with the same config, but a different IP address and UID – magically appears and takes its place.

This is why applications should always store *state* and *data* outside the Pod. It's also why you shouldn't rely on individual Pods – they're ephemeral, here today, gone tomorrow…

In the real world, you'll almost always deploy and manage Pods via controllers.

Single-container and multi-container Pods

Pods can run one or more containers. The single-container model is the simplest, but multi-container Pods are important in real-world production environments and vital for service meshes. You'll learn more about multi-container Pods later in the chapter.

Deploying Pods

The process of deploying a Pod to Kubernetes is as follows:

1. Define it in a YAML *manifest file*
2. Post the YAML to the API server

3. The API server authenticates and authorizes the request

4. The configuration (YAML) is validated

5. The scheduler deploys the Pod to a healthy worker node with enough available resources

6. The local kubelet monitors it

If the Pod is deployed via a controller, the configuration will be added to the cluster store as part of overall desired state and a controller will monitor it.

Let's dig a bit deeper.

The anatomy of a Pod

At the highest level, a Pod is an execution environment shared by one or more containers:

- **net namespace:** IP address, port range, routing table…
- **pid namespace:** isolated process tree
- **mnt namespace:** filesystems and volumes…
- **UTS namespace:** Hostname
- **IPC namespace:** Unix domain sockets and shared memory

As a quick example, let's look at how the Pod shared execution environment model affects networking.

Pods and shared networking

Every Pod has its own network *namespace*. This means every Pod has its own IP address, its own range of TCP and UDP ports, and its own routing table. If it's a single-container Pod, the container has full access to the IP, port range and routing table. If it's a multi-container Pod, all containers share the IP, port range and routing table.

Figure 4.2 shows two Pods, each with its own IP. Even though one of them is a multi-container Pod, it still only gets a single IP.

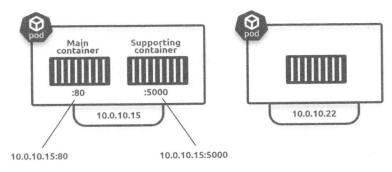

Figure 4.2

In Figure 4.2, external access to the containers in the Pod on the left is achieved via the IP address of the Pod coupled with the port of the container you're trying to reach. For example, `10.0.10.15:80` will get you to the main application container, but `10.0.10.15:5000` will get you to the supporting container.

Container-to-container communication within the same Pod happens via the Pod's `localhost` adapter and a port number. For example, the main container in Figure 4.2 can reach the supporting container on `localhost:5000`.

The pod network

On the topic of networking, every Pod gets its own unique IP address that's fully routable on an internal Kubernetes network called the *pod network*. This is a flat overlay network that allows every Pod to talk directly to every other Pod even if the worker nodes are all on different *underlay* networks.

Figure 4.3 shows five Kubernetes nodes on different physical networks. As long as the networks are connected by routers, the network plugin for the cluster creates the flat *pod network* that spans all nodes. Pods connect to this network.

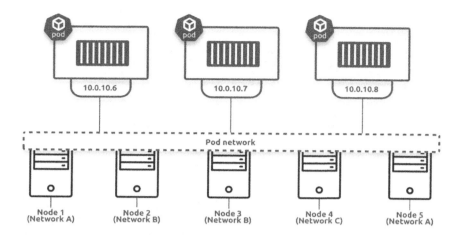

Figure 4.3 Inter-Pod communication

In a default out-of-the-box cluster, the pod network is wide open from a security perspective. You should use Kubernetes Network Policies to lock down access.

Atomic deployment of Pods

Pod deployment is an *atomic operation*. This means it's all-or-nothing – deployment either succeeds or it fails. You'll never have a scenario where a partially deployed Pod is servicing requests. Only after all a Pod's containers and resources are running and ready will it start servicing requests.

Pod lifecycle

The lifecycle of a typical Pod is something like this...

You define it in a declarative YAML object. This gets posted to the API server and the Pod enters the pending phase. It's then scheduled to a healthy worker node with enough resources and the local kubelet instructs the container runtime to pull all required images and start all containers. Once all containers are pulled and running, the Pod enters the *running* phase. If it's a short-lived Pod, as soon as all containers terminate successfully the Pod enters the *succeeded* state. If it's a long-lived Pod, it remains indefinitely in the running phase.

Shorted-lived and long-lived Pods

Pods can run all different types of applications. Some, such as web servers, are intended to be long-lived and should remain in the running phase indefinitely. If any containers in a long-lived Pod fail, the local kubelet may attempt to restart them.

We say the kubelet *"may"* attempt to restart them. This is based on the container's restart policy which is defined in the Pod config. Options include *Always*, *OnFailure*, and *Never*. *Always* is the default restart policy and appropriate for most long-lived Pods.

Other workload types, such as batch jobs, are designed to be short-lived and only run until a task completes. Once all containers in a short-lived Pod successfully terminate, the Pod terminates and its status is set to successful. Appropriate container restart policies for short-lived Pods will usually be *Never* or *OnFailure*.

Kubernetes has several controllers for different types of long-lived and short-lived workloads. *Deployments*, *StatefulSets*, and *DaemonSets* are examples of controllers designed for long-lived Pods. *Jobs* and *CronJobs* are examples designed for short-lived Pods.

Pod immutability

Pods are immutable objects. This means you can't modify them after they're deployed.

This can be a big mindset change, especially if you come from a background of deploying servers and regularly logging on to them to patch and update them.

The immutable nature of Pods is a key aspect of *cloud-native microservices* design patterns and forces the following behaviors:

- When updates are needed, replace all old Pods with new ones
- When failures occur, replace failed Pods with new ones

To be clear, you never actually update a running Pod, you always replace it with a new Pod running the updates. You also never log onto failed Pods and attempt fixes; you build fixes into an updated Pod and replace failed ones with the updated ones.

Pods and scaling

All Pods run a single application container instance, making them an ideal unit of scaling – if you need to scale the app, you add or remove Pods. This is called *horizontal scaling*.

You never scale an app by adding more of the same application containers to an existing Pod. Multi-container Pods are only for co-scheduling and co-locating containers that need tight coupling, they're not a way to scale an app.

Multi-container Pods

Multi-container Pods are a powerful pattern and heavily used in real-world environments.

At a very high-level, every container should have a single clearly defined responsibility. For example, an application that pulls content from a repository and serves it as a web page has two distinct responsibilities:

1. Pull the content
2. Serve the web page

In this example, you should design two containers, one responsible for pulling the content and the other responsible for serving the web page. We call this *separation of concerns* or *separation of responsibilities*.

This design approach keeps each container small and simple, encourages re-use, and makes troubleshooting simpler.

However, there are scenarios where it's a good idea to tightly couple two or more functions. Consider the same example app that pulls content and serves it via a web page. A simple design would have a "sync" container and a "web" container. The "sync" container can pull the updates and put them in a volume shared with the "web" container to serve them. For this to work, both containers need to run in the same Pod so they have access to the same shared volume in the Pod's shared execution environment.

Co-locating multiple containers in the same Pod allows containers to be designed with a single responsibility but co-operate closely with others.

Kubernetes offers several well-defined multi-container Pod patterns:

• Sidecar pattern
• Adapter pattern
• Ambassador pattern
• Init pattern

Each one is an example of the *one-container-one-responsibility* model.

Sidecar multi-container Pods

The sidecar pattern is probably the most popular and most generic multi-container pattern. It has a main application container and a *sidecar* container. It's the job of the sidecar to perform a secondary task for the main application container. The previous example of a main application web container, plus a helper pulling up-to-date content is a classic example of the sidecar pattern – the "sync" container pulling the content from the external repo is the *sidecar*.

An increasingly important user of the sidecar model is the service mesh. At a high level, service meshes inject sidecar containers into application Pods. The sidecars then do things like encrypt traffic and expose telemetry and metrics.

Adapter multi-container Pods

The *adapter pattern* is a specific variation of the sidecar pattern where the helper container takes non-standardized output from the main container and rejigs it into a format required by an external system.

A simple example is NGINX logs being sent to Prometheus. Out-of-the-box, Prometheus doesn't understand NGINX logs, so a common approach is to put an adapter container into the NGINX Pod that converts NGINX logs into a format accepted by Prometheus.

Ambassador multi-container Pods

The *ambassador pattern* is another variation of the sidecar pattern. This time, the helper container brokers connectivity to an external system. For example, the main application container can just dump its output to a port the ambassador container is listening on and sit back while the *ambassador container* does the hard work of getting it to the external system.

It acts a lot like political ambassadors that interface with foreign nations on behalf of a government. In Kubernetes, ambassador containers interface with external systems on behalf of the main app container.

Init multi-container Pods

The init pattern is not a form of sidecar. It runs a special *init container* that's guaranteed to start and complete <u>before</u> the main app container. It's also guaranteed to only run once.

As the name suggests, its job is to run tasks that *initialise* the environment for the main application container. For example, a main app container may need permissions setting, an external API to be up and accepting connections, or a remote repository cloning to a local volume. In these cases, an init container can do that prep work and will only exit when the environment is ready for the main app container. The main app container will not start until the init container completes.

Pod theory summary

1. Pods are the atomic unit of scheduling in Kubernetes
2. Single-container Pods are the simplest
3. Multi-container Pods are ideal for co-locating tightly coupled workloads and are fundamental to many service meshes
4. Pods get scheduled on worker nodes and you can't schedule a single Pod to span multiple nodes
5. Pods are defined declaratively in manifest files you post to the API server
6. You almost always deploy Pods via higher-level controllers

Hands-on with Pods

If you're following along, be sure to clone the book's GitHub repo and run all commands from within the pods folder.

```
$ git clone https://github.com/nigelpoulton/TheK8sBook.git
Cloning into 'TheK8sBook'...
```

If you don't have git, or are uncomfortable using it, you can just visit the repo and copy the file contents into files with the same name on your local machine.

You can follow along with any of the Kubernetes clusters you saw how to build in the "Getting Kubernetes" chapter.

Pod manifest files

You'll be using the following Pod manifest. It's available in the book's GitHub repo under the pods folder called pod.yml:

```
kind: Pod
apiVersion: v1
metadata:
  name: hello-pod
  labels:
    zone: prod
    version: v1
spec:
  containers:
  - name: hello-ctr
    image: nigelpoulton/k8sbook:1.0
    ports:
    - containerPort: 8080
```

Straight away you can see four top-level resources:

- `kind`
- `apiVersion`
- `metadata`
- `spec`

The `.kind` field tells Kubernetes the type of object being defined. This file is defining a Pod object.

`apiVersion` tells Kubernetes the schema version to use when creating the Pod.

The normal format for `apiVersion` is `<api-group>/<version>`. For example, StorageClass objects are defined in the `v1` schema of the `storage.k8s.io` API group and are described in YAML files as `storage.k8s.io/v1`. However, Pods are in the *core* API group which omits the API group name, so we describe them in YAML files as just `v1`.

So far, this file is describing a Pod object as defined in the `v1` schema in the *core API group*.

The `.metadata` section is where you attach things such as names, labels, annotations, and a Namespace. Names help you identify the object in the cluster, and labels let you create loose couplings with other objects. Annotations can help integrate with 3rd-party tools and services. We'll dig into all of these, including Namespaces, in future chapters.

The `.metadata` section of this manifest is naming the Pod "hello-pod" and assigning it two labels. You'll use the labels in a future chapter to couple it to a Service for stable networking. As it's not specifying a Namespace, it'll be deployed to the `default` Namespace.

The `.spec` section is where you define any containers in the Pod. This example is defining a single-container Pod based on the `nigelpoulton/k8sbook:1.0` image. It's calling the container `hello-ctr` and exposing it on port `8080`.

If this was a multi-container Pod, you'd define additional containers in the `.spec` section.

Manifest files: Empathy as Code

Quick side-step.

Configuration files, like Kubernetes manifests, are excellent sources of documentation. As such, they have a few secondary benefits. A couple of these include:

- Speeding-up on-boarding of new team members

- Bridging the gap between developers and operations

For example, if you need a new team member to understand the basic functions and requirements of an application, get them to read its Kubernetes manifest files.

Also, if your operations teams complain that developers don't give accurate application requirements and documentation, make your developers use Kubernetes. This forces them to describe applications in Kubernetes manifests, which can then be used by operations to understand the fundamentals of how the application works and what it requires from the environment. This is especially true in more advanced setups where you define things such as *resource requirements and limits* in manifest files.

These kinds of benefits were described as a form of *empathy as code* by Nirmal Mehta in his 2017 DockerCon talk entitled "A Strong Belief, Loosely Held: Bringing Empathy to IT".

Deploying Pods from a manifest file

You need to run the following commands from the pods folder.

```
$ kubectl apply -f pod.yml
pod/hello-pod created
```

Although the Pod is showing as created, it might not be fully deployed and available yet. This is because it takes time to pull the image.

Run a kubectl get pods to check the status.

```
$ kubectl get pods
NAME        READY     STATUS              RESTARTS    AGE
hello-pod   0/1       ContainerCreating   0           9s
```

In this example the Pod isn't ready yet.

This is a good time to mention that Kubernetes will pull (download) images from Docker Hub by default. To download from another registry, you need to specify the registry URL before the image name in the YAML file. The following image is in the Google Container Registry (k8s.gcr.io): k8s.gcr.io/git-sync:v3.1.6

You can add the --watch flag to the command to monitor it and see when the status changes to Running.

Congratulations. The Pod is running on a healthy node and is being monitored by the local kubelet process.

In future chapters, you'll see how to connect to the app in the Pod.

Introspecting running Pods

The two main commands for checking the status of Pods are `kubectl get` and `kubectl describe`.

kubectl get

You've already seen `kubectl get pods` and it's a bit light on detail. Not to worry though, there's plenty of options for deeper introspection.

First up, you can add a couple of flags that give you more information:

- `-o wide` gives a few more columns but is still a single line of output
- `-o yaml` takes things to the next level, returning a full copy of the Pod from the cluster store

The following command is the snipped output from a `kubectl get pods -o yaml`. The output is divided into two main parts:

- desired state (`.spec`)
- observed state (`.status`)

```
$ kubectl get pods hello-pod -o yaml
apiVersion: v1
kind: Pod
metadata:
  annotations:
    kubectl.kubernetes.io/last-applied-configuration: |
      ...
  name: hello-pod
  namespace: default
spec:                             <<==== Desired state is in this block
  containers:
  - image: nigelpoulton/k8sbook:1.0
    imagePullPolicy: IfNotPresent
    name: hello-ctr
    ports:
    ...
status:                           <<==== Observed state is in this block
  conditions:
  - lastProbeTime: null
    lastTransitionTime: "2022-02-02T18:21:51Z"
    status: "True"
    type: Initialized
 ...
```

The full output contains a lot more than the 13-line YAML file you posted. So, where does this extra information come from?

Two main sources:

- Pod objects have a lot of properties. Anything not explicitly set in the YAML file is automatically expanded with default values.
- The .status section is the current observed state of the Pod.

kubectl describe

Another great command for introspection is kubectl describe. This provides a nicely formatted multi-line overview of an object. It even includes important object lifecycle events.

```
$ kubectl describe pods hello-pod
Name:           hello-pod
Namespace:      default
Labels:         version=v1
                zone=prod
Status:         Running
IP:             10.42.1.28
Containers:
  hello-ctr:
    Container ID:   containerd://4f66e48e...
    Image:          nigelpoulton/k8sbook:1.0
    Port:           8080/TCP
    ...
Conditions:
  Type             Status
  Initialized      True
  Ready            True
  ContainersReady  True
  ...
Events:
  Type    Reason     Age     Message
  ----    ------     ----    -------
  Normal  Scheduled  5m30s   Successfully assigned ...
  Normal  Pulling    5m30s   Pulling image "nigelpoulton/k8sbook:1.0"
  Normal  Pulled     5m8s    Successfully pulled image ...
  Normal  Created    5m8s    Created container hello-ctr
  Normal  Started    5m8s    Started container hello-ctr
```

The output has been snipped to fit the page.

kubectl logs

Another useful command for introspecting Pods is `kubectl logs`. The format of the command is `kubectl logs <pod>`.

Each container in a multi-container Pod gets a name. The first Pod in the YAML object is the first container, and all commands will run against this unless you specify otherwise. If you need the command to run against another container, just add the `--container` flag and specify the container name.

The following YAML snippet is from a multi-container Pod called "multipod" that defines a container called `app` and another called `syncer`.

```
spec:
  containers:
  - name: app                    <<==== First container
    image: nginx
      ports:
        - containerPort: 8080
  - name: syncer                 <<==== Second container
    image: k8s.gcr.io/git-sync:v3.1.6
    volumeMounts:
    - name: html
<Snip>
```

The following command pulls logs from the `syncer` container.

```
$ kubectl logs multipod --container syncer
<Snip>
```

kubectl exec: running commands in Pods

Another way to introspect a running Pod is to execute commands inside it. You can do this with `kubectl exec` and the format is `kubectl exec <pod-name> -- <command>`.

The following example shows how to execute a `ps aux` command in the first container in the `hello-pod` Pod.

```
$ kubectl exec hello-pod -- ps
PID   USER      TIME  COMMAND
  1   root      0:00 node ./app.js
 17   root      0:00 ps aux
```

It's also possible to use `kubectl exec` to get shell access to a container running in a Pod. When you do this, your terminal prompt will change and you'll be able to execute commands from inside the Pod (as long as the command binaries are installed in it).

The following `kubectl exec` command will log-in to the first container in the hello-pod Pod. Once inside, install the `curl` utility and run a `curl` command to transfer data from the process listening on port 8080.

> **Note:** This example is just for demonstration purposes. Installing tools in running Pods and containers is an anti-pattern and should be avoided. If you need to make changes to a Pod, you should create a new Pod with the updates and replace old ones with the new one.

```
$ kubectl exec -it hello-pod -- sh

# apk add curl
<Snip>

# curl localhost:8080
<html><head><title>K8s rocks!</title><link rel="stylesheet" href="http://netdna....
```

The `-it` flags on the `kubectl exec` command make the session interactive and connect STDIN and STDOUT on your terminal to STDIN and STDOUT inside the first container in the Pod. Your shell prompt changes to indicate you're inside the container.

If you're running multi-container Pods, you'll need to pass the `--container` flag and give it the name of the container you want to create the exec session with. If you don't, commands will execute against the first container in the Pod. You can see the ordering and names of containers in a Pod with the `kubectl describe pods <pod>` command. You can also inspect the Pod's YAML file.

Pod hostnames

Every container in a Pod inherits its hostname from the name of the Pod. This means all containers in a multi-container Pod get the same hostname.

The Pod you deployed is named hello-pod in the `pod.yml` file.

```
kind: Pod
apiVersion: v1
metadata:
  name: hello-pod        <<==== Containers inherit it as their hostname
  labels:
  <Snip>
```

Run the following command from within the interactive exec session you already have to the Pod. The command is case-sensitive.

```
$ env | grep HOSTNAME
HOSTNAME=hello-pod
```

As you can see, the hostname of the container is set to the Pod's name. With this in mind, you should always set Pod names as valid DNS names (a-z and 0-9, the minus sign and the period sign).

Type exit to drop back to the terminal of your local machine.

Check Pod immutability

Pods are designed as immutable objects. You can use kubectl edit pod hello-pod to try and update some Pod attributes.

Try editing any of the following:

- Pod name
- Container port
- Container name

Kubernetes will prevent you from changing them.

Multi-container Pod example – init container

The following YAML defines a multi-container Pod with an init container and main app container.

```
apiVersion: v1
kind: Pod
metadata:
  name: initpod
  labels:
    app: initializer
spec:
  initContainers:
  - name: init-ctr
    image: busybox
    command: ['sh', '-c', 'until nslookup k8sbook; do echo waiting for k8sbook service;\
            sleep 1; done; echo Service found!']
  containers:
    - name: web-ctr
      image: nigelpoulton/web-app:1.0
      ports:
        - containerPort: 8080
```

The spec.initContainers block defines one or more containers that Kubernetes guarantees will run and complete before main app container starts.

This example has a single init container, called "init-ctr", that loops until a Kubernetes Service object called "k8sbook" is up and present.

Deploy it with the following command and then run a kubectl get pods with the --watch flag.

```
$ kubectl apply -f initpod.yml
pod/initpod created

$ kubectl get pods --watch
NAME       READY   STATUS     RESTARTS   AGE
initpod    0/1     Init:0/1   0          5s
```

The Init:0/1 status tells you that zero out of one init containers has completed successfully. The Pod will remain in this phase until a Service called "k8sbook" is created.

Press Ctrl-c to quit the current watch session, create the Service, and watch the Pod status change.

```
$ kubectl apply -f initsvc.yml
service/k8sbook created

$ kubectl get pods --watch
NAME       READY   STATUS           RESTARTS   AGE
initpod    0/1     Init:0/1         0          15s
initpod    0/1     PodInitializing  0          49s
initpod    1/1     Running          0          2m39s
```

As soon as the Service appears, the init container successfully completes and the main application container starts.

Multi-container Pod example – sidecar container

Sidecar containers are very different to init containers – they run alongside the main application container for the entire lifecycle of the Pod. They're commonly used to augment the main application container or provide a secondary support service.

The following YAML file defines a Pod with two containers mounting the same shared volume.

```
apiVersion: v1
kind: Pod
metadata:
  name: git-sync
  labels:
    app: sidecar
spec:
  containers:
  - name: ctr-web                  <<==== Start of first container
    image: nginx
    volumeMounts:
    - name: html                   <<==== shared volume
      mountPath: /usr/share/nginx/
  - name: ctr-sync                 <<==== Start of second container
    image: k8s.gcr.io/git-sync:v3.1.6
    volumeMounts:
    - name: html                   <<==== shared volume
      mountPath: /tmp/git
    env:
    - name: GIT_SYNC_REPO
      value: https://github.com/nigelpoulton/ps-sidecar.git
    - name: GIT_SYNC_BRANCH
      value: master
    - name: GIT_SYNC_DEPTH
      value: "1"
    - name: GIT_SYNC_DEST
      value: "html"
  volumes:
  - name: html
    emptyDir: {}
```

The first container is called "ctr-web" and is the main app container. It's a vanilla NGINX container and serves a static web page based on content loaded from the shared `html` volume.

The second container is called "ctr-sync" and is the sidecar. It watches a GitHub repo and syncs changes into the same shared `html` volume.

If the contents of the GitHub repo change, the "ctr-sync" sidecar will copy the new content into the shared volume where the "ctr-web" container will notice and serve an updated version of the web page.

You can complete the following steps to see it in action:

1. Fork the repo
2. Update the YAML file with the URL of your forked repo
3. Deploy the app
4. Connect to the app and see it display "This is version 1.0"

5. Make a change to the GitHub repo

6. Refresh your connection to the app and see it display the change you made

Fork the following GitHub repo. In a later step you'll update the repo and see your changes reflected by the app.

```
https://github.com/nigelpoulton/ps-sidecar
```

Edit the sidecarpod.yml and update the GIT_SYNC_REPO value with the URL of your forked repo and save your changes.

Run one of the following commands to deploy the application. This will deploy the multi-container Pod as well as a Service object you can use to connect to the app.

Run this command if you're running a Docker Desktop or other local cluster.

```
$ kubectl apply -f sidecar-local.yml
pod/git-sync created
service/svc-sidecar created
```

Run this command if you're running your Kubernetes cluster in the cloud.

```
$ kubectl apply -f sidecar-cloud.yml
pod/git-sync created
service/svc-sidecar created
```

Monitor the status of the Pod with a kubectl get pods command.

As soon as the Pod enters the running state, run a kubectl get svc to get the connection details.

If your cluster is in the cloud, copy the public IP of the svc-sidecar Service and paste it into your browser to see the web page. If your cluster is on your laptop, point your browser to localhost:30001 (the NodePort value of the Service). In both cases, the web page should display the content of your forked repo – "This is version 1.0".

Now make a change to the <h1> line in the index.html file *in your fork of the GitHub repo* and refresh your browser. The update should be reflected almost immediately in the app.

Congratulations. The sidecar container has successfully watched a GitHub repo and sync'd changes to your app.

Feel free to run the kubectl get pods and kubectl describe pod commands to see how multi-container Pods appear in the outputs.

There's obviously a lot more to Pods that we haven't covered. However, you've learned enough to get started.

Clean-up

Use kubectl delete pods and kubectl delete svc to delete any Pods and Services still running from this chapter. You'll need to provide the names of the Pods and Services you're deleting. For example, the following command deletes the git-sync Pod. It may take a few seconds for Pods to gracefully terminate.

```
$ kubectl delete pod git-sync
pod "git-sync" deleted
```

Be sure to delete the other Pods and Services deployed as part of the chapter.

Chapter Summary

In this chapter, you learned the atomic unit of deployment in Kubernetes is the *Pod*. Each Pod has one or more containers and gets deployed to a single node in the cluster as an all-or-nothing *atomic operation*.

Pods are defined and deployed declaratively using YAML manifest files, and it's normal to deploy them via higher-level controllers such as Deployments and DaemonSets. If a Pod is not deployed via a controller, it's called a *static Pod*.

You use kubectl apply to post the YAML manifests to the API server and Kubernetes picks a worker node to run the Pod on.

The kubelet daemon on the assigned worker node is responsible for pulling the strings to get the Pod started and then monitoring it and attempting local fixes.

If the node a static Pod is running on fails, the missing Pod doesn't get replaced.

5: Virtual clusters with Namespaces

Namespaces are a native way to divide a single Kubernetes cluster into multiple *virtual clusters*.

This chapter will set the scene for Namespaces, get you up-to-speed with creating and managing them, and familiarise you with use-cases. How they integrate with things like service discovery and resource quotas will be discussed in later chapters.

We'll split the chapter as follows:

- Use cases for Namespaces
- Inspecting Namespaces
- Creating and managing Namespaces
- Deploying to Namespaces

It's important to know that Kubernetes Namespaces are not the same as Linux kernel namespaces. *Kernel namespaces* are an integral part of slicing operating systems into virtual operating systems called **containers**. Kubernetes Namespaces divide Kubernetes clusters into virtual clusters called... you guessed it... **Namespaces**.

We'll capitalise the word "Namespace" when referring to Kubernetes Namespaces. This follows the pattern of capitalizing Kubernetes API objects and makes it obvious we're not referring to other types of "namespaces".

Use cases for Namespaces

Namespaces partition a Kubernetes cluster and are designed as an easy way to apply *quotas* and *policies* to groups of objects. They're **not** designed for strong workload isolation.

Before going any further, it's important to understand that most Kubernetes objects are deployed to a Namespace. These objects are said to be *namespaced* and include common objects such as Pods, Services and Deployments. Some objects exist outside of Namespaces and include nodes and PodSecurityPolicies.

If you don't explicitly define a target Namespace when deploying a *namespaced object*, it'll be deployed to the *default* Namespace.

You can run the following command to see all Kubernetes API resources (objects) supported by your cluster. The output displays whether an object is *namespaced* or not. The output is trimmed.

```
$ kubectl api-resources
NAME                        SHORTNAMES    ...    NAMESPACED    KIND
nodes                       no                   false         Node
persistentvolumeclaims      pvc                  true          PersistentVolumeClaim
persistentvolumes           pv                   false         PersistentVolume
pods                        po                   true          Pod
podtemplates                                     true          PodTemplate
replicationcontrollers      rc                   true          ReplicationController
resourcequotas              quota                true          ResourceQuota
secrets                                          true          Secret
serviceaccounts             sa                   true          ServiceAccount
services                    svc                  true          Service
...
```

Namespaces are a good way of sharing a single cluster among different departments and environments. For example, a single cluster might have the following Namespaces:

- Dev
- Test
- QA

Each one can have its own set of users, permissions, and unique resource quotas.

What they're **not** good for, is isolating hostile workloads. This is because a compromised container or Pod in one Namespace can wreak havoc in other Namespaces. Putting this into context, you shouldn't place competitors, such as Pepsi and Coke, in separate Namespaces on the same shared cluster.

If you need strong workload isolation, the current method is to use multiple clusters. There are projects and technologies aiming to provide better solutions, but at the time of writing, the safest and most common way of isolating workloads is putting them in their own clusters.

Inspecting Namespaces

Every Kubernetes cluster has a set of pre-created Namespaces.

Run the following command to list yours.

```
$ kubectl get namespaces
NAME              STATUS    AGE
default           Active    5d5h
kube-system       Active    5d5h
kube-public       Active    5d5h
kube-node-lease   Active    5d5h
```

The *default* Namespace is where newly created objects go if you don't specify a Namespace. *Kube-system* is where DNS, the metrics server, and other control plane components run. *Kube-public* is for objects that need to be readable by anyone. And last but not least, *kube-node-lease* is used for node heartbeat and managing node leases.

Run a kubectl describe to inspect one of the Namespaces on your cluster.

> **Note:** You can substitute namespace with ns when working with kubectl.

```
$ kubectl describe ns default
Name:         default
Labels:       kubernetes.io/metadata.name=default
Annotations:  <none>
Status:       Active
No resource quota.
No LimitRange resource.
```

You can also add -n or --namespace to regular kubectl commands to filter results based on a specific Namespace.

List all Service objects in the kube-system Namespace (your output might be different).

```
$ kubectl get svc --namespace kube-system
NAME                TYPE          CLUSTER-IP      EXTERNAL-IP    PORT(S)
kube-dns            ClusterIP     10.43.0.10      <none>         53/UDP,53/TCP,9153...
metrics-server      ClusterIP     10.43.4.203     <none>         443/TCP
traefik-prometheus  ClusterIP     10.43.49.213    <none>         9100/TCP
traefik             LoadBalancer  10.43.222.75    <pending>      80:31716/TCP,443:31...
```

You can also use the --all-namespaces flag to return objects from all Namespaces.

Creating and managing Namespaces

To follow along with these examples, you'll need a clone of the book's GitHub repo and run all commands from within the namespaces folder.

```
$ git clone https://github.com/nigelpoulton/TheK8sBook.git
<Snip>

$ cd TheK8sBook/namespaces
```

Namespaces are first-class resources in the core v1 API group. This means they're stable, well understood, and have been around for a long time. It also means you can create and manage them imperatively with kubectl, and declaratively with YAML manifests.

Create a new Namespace, called "hydra", with the following imperative command.

```
$ kubectl create ns hydra
namespace/hydra created
```

The following YAML is from the shield-ns.yml file and defines a Namespace called "shield".

```
kind: Namespace
apiVersion: v1
metadata:
  name: shield
  labels:
    env: marvel
```

Create it with the following command.

```
$ kubectl apply -f shield-ns.yml
namespace/shield created
```

List all Namespaces to see the two new ones you created.

```
$ kubectl get ns
NAME          STATUS    AGE
<Snip>
hydra         Active    51s
shield        Active    7s
```

If you know anything about the Marvel Cinematic Universe, you'll know Shield and Hydra are bitter enemies and should not be sharing the same cluster separated only by Namespaces.

Delete the "hydra" Namespace.

```
$ kubectl delete ns hydra
namespace "hydra" deleted
```

Configuring `kubectl` to use a specific Namespace

When you start using Namespaces, you'll quickly realise it's painful remembering to add the `-n` or `--namespace` flag on all `kubectl` commands. A better way might be to set your *kubeconfig* to automatically work with a particular Namespace.

The following command configures `kubectl` to run all future commands against the `shield` Namespace.

```
$ kubectl config set-context --current --namespace shield
Context "tkb" modified.
```

Run a few simple `kubectl get` commands to test it works. Your `shield` Namespace should currently be empty.

Deploying to Namespaces

As previously mentioned, most objects exist in the context of a Namespace. If you don't specify otherwise, new objects will be created in the `default` Namespace.

There are two ways to deploy objects to a specific Namespace:

- Imperatively
- Declaratively

The imperative method requires you to add the `-n` or `--namespace` flag to commands. The declarative method specifies the Namespace in the YAML manifest file.

We'll declaratively deploy a simple app to the `shield` Namespace and test it.

The application is defined in the `shield-app.yml` file in the `namespaces` folder. It defines a *ServiceAccount, Service*, and *Pod*. The following snipped content shows all three objects are declaratively configured for the `shield` Namespace. At this point in the book, you don't need to understand what everything else in the YAML is doing.

```
apiVersion: v1
kind: ServiceAccount
metadata:
  namespace: shield        <<==== Namespace
  name: default
---
apiVersion: v1
kind: Service
metadata:
  namespace: shield        <<==== Namespace
  name: the-bus
spec:
  ports:
  - nodePort: 31112
    port: 8080
    targetPort: 8080
  selector:
    env: marvel
---
apiVersion: v1
kind: Pod
metadata:
  namespace: shield        <<==== Namespace
  name: triskelion
<Snip>
```

Deploy it with the following command. You don't have to specify the Namespace on the command line.

```
$ kubectl apply -f shield-app.yml
serviceaccount/default configured
service/the-bus configured
pod/triskelion created
```

Run a few commands to verify all three objects were deployed to the `shield` Namespace. Remember to use the `-n` or `--namespace` flag if you haven't configured `kubectl` to automatically use the shield Namespace.

```
$ kubectl get pods -n shield
NAME         READY   STATUS    RESTARTS   AGE
triskelion   1/1     Running   0          48s

$ kubectl get svc -n shield
NAME      TYPE       CLUSTER-IP     EXTERNAL-IP   PORT(S)          AGE
the-bus   NodePort   10.43.30.174   <none>        8080:31112/TCP   52s
```

Use `curl` or your browser to connect to the app. If you're running a local Docker Desktop cluster, you can send requests to `localhost:31112`. If your cluster is in the cloud, send requests to the public IP of any of your worker nodes on port 31112. You'll learn more about Services in a later chapter.

Congratulations. You've created a Namespace and deployed an app to it. Connecting to the app was no different to connecting to an app in the default Namespace.

Clean-up

The following commands will clean-up your cluster and revert your kubeconfig to use the default Namespace.

Delete the shield app. Be sure to run the command from the directory where the shield-app.yml file is located.

```
$ kubectl delete -f shield-app.yml
serviceaccount "default" deleted
service "the-bus" deleted
pod "triskelion" deleted
```

Delete the shield Namespace.

```
$ kubectl delete ns shield
namespace "shield" deleted
```

Reset your kubeconfig so it uses the default Namespace. If you don't do this, future commands will automatically run against the deleted shield Namespace which you just deleted.

```
$ kubectl config set-context --current --namespace default
Context "tkb" modified.
```

Chapter Summary

In this chapter, you learned that Kubernetes has a technology called Namespaces that can divide a cluster for resource and accounting purposes. Each Namespace can have its own users and RBAC rules, as well as resource quotas. You also learned that Namespaces are not a strong workload isolation boundary.

You learned that many objects are namespaced and if you don't explicitly target an object at a Namespace, it'll be deployed to the default Namespace.

6: Kubernetes Deployments

In this chapter, you'll see how to use *Deployments* to bring cloud-native features such as self-healing, scaling, rolling updates, and versioned rollbacks to stateless apps on Kubernetes. Deployments are extremely useful and you'll use them all the time.

The chapter is divided as follows:

- Deployment theory
- Create a Deployment
- Perform scaling operations
- Perform a rollout
- Perform a rollback

Kubernetes offers several *controllers* that augment Pods with important capabilities. The Deployment controller is specifically designed for stateless apps. We'll cover other controllers later in the book.

Throughout the chapter, we'll use terms like *release, rollout,* and *rolling update* to mean the same thing – pushing a new version of an app.

Deployment theory

There are two major components to Deployments:

1. The spec
2. The controller

The *Deployment spec* is a declarative YAML object where you describe the desired state of a stateless app. You give it to Kubernetes where the *Deployment controller* implements and manages it. The controller element is highly-available and operates as a background loop on the control plane reconciling observed state with desired state.

The latest version of the Deployment object, including all features and attributes, is defined in the apps/v1 workloads API sub-group.

Note: The Kubernetes API is architecturally divided into smaller sub-groups to make it easier to manage and navigate. The apps sub-group is where Deployments, DaemonSets, StatefulSets, and other *workload*-related objects are defined. We sometimes call it the workloads API. If you're new to APIs, it's normal for the Kubernetes API to be confusing. Things will become clearer as you progress through the book, and we have an entire chapter devoted to explaining it.

You start with a stateless application, package it as a container, then define it in a Pod template. At this point you *could* run it on Kubernetes. However, static Pods like this don't self-heal, they don't scale, and they don't allow for easy updates and rollbacks. For these reasons, you'll almost always wrap them in a Deployment object.

Figure 6.1 shows a Pod template wrapped in a Deployment object. In fact, there are three levels of nesting. The container holds the application, the Pod augments the container with labels, annotations, and other metadata useful for Kubernetes, and the Deployment further augments things with scaling and updates.

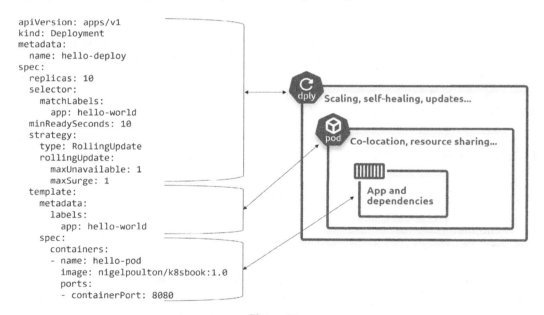

Figure 6.1

You post the Deployment object to the API server where Kubernetes implements it and the Deployment controller watches it.

Deployments and Pods

A Deployment object only manages a single Pod template. For example, an application with a front-end web service and a shopping basket service will have a different Pod template for each. As a result, it'll need two Deployment objects – one managing front-end web Pods, the other managing any shopping basket Pods. However, a Deployment can manage multiple replicas of the same Pod. For example, the front-end web Deployment might be managing 5 identical replicas of the front-end web Pod.

If you look at Figure 6.1 you'll see the YAML holds the *definition* of a single Pod. However, it's requesting 10 replicas of that Pod.

Deployments and ReplicaSets

Behind-the-scenes, Deployments rely heavily on another object called a ReplicaSet. While it's recommended not to manage ReplicaSets directly (let the Deployment controller manage them), it's important to understand the role they play.

At a high-level, containers are a great way to package applications and dependencies. Pods allow containers to run on Kubernetes and enable co-scheduling and a bunch of other good stuff. ReplicaSets manage Pods and bring self-healing and scaling. Deployments manage ReplicaSets and add rollouts and rollbacks. As a result, working with Deployments brings the benefits of everything else – the container, the Pod, the ReplicaSet.

Figure 6.2. is similar to 6.1 but adds a ReplicaSet into the relationship and shows which object is responsible for which features.

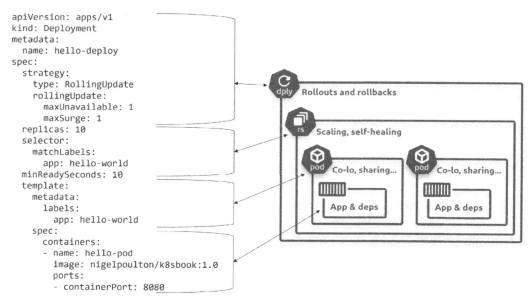

```
apiVersion: apps/v1
kind: Deployment
metadata:
  name: hello-deploy
spec:
  strategy:
    type: RollingUpdate
    rollingUpdate:
      maxUnavailable: 1
      maxSurge: 1
  replicas: 10
  selector:
    matchLabels:
      app: hello-world
  minReadySeconds: 10
  template:
    metadata:
      labels:
        app: hello-world
    spec:
      containers:
      - name: hello-pod
        image: nigelpoulton/k8sbook:1.0
        ports:
        - containerPort: 8080
```

Figure 6.2

Think of *Deployments* as managing *ReplicaSets*, and *ReplicaSets* as managing *Pods*. Put them together, and you've got a great way to deploy and manage stateless applications on Kubernetes.

Self-healing and scalability

Pods are great. They let you co-locate containers, share volumes, share memory, simplify networking, and a lot more. But they offer nothing in the way of self-healing and scalability – if the node a Pod is running on fails, the Pod is lost.

Enter Deployments…

- If Pods managed by a Deployment fail, they will be replaced – *self-healing*
- If Pods managed by a Deployment see increased or decreased load, they can be *scaled*

Remember though, hidden away behind-the-scenes, it's actually the ReplicaSets doing the self-healing and scalability. You'll see them in action soon.

It's all about the *state*

Before going any further, it's critical to understand three concepts that are fundamental to everything about Kubernetes:

- Desired state
- Observed state (sometimes called *actual state* or *current state*)
- Reconciliation

Desired state is what you **want**. *Observed state* is what you **have**. If they match, everybody's happy. If they don't match, a process of *reconciliation* attempts to bring observed state into sync with desired state.

The *declarative model* is a method for telling Kubernetes your *desired state*, while avoiding the detail of *how* to implement it. You leave the *how* up to Kubernetes.

A declarative vs imperative example

The declarative model is all about describing an end-goal – telling Kubernetes *what* you want. The imperative model is all about long lists of commands to reach an end-goal – telling Kubernetes *how* to do something.

The following is an extremely simple analogy that might help:

- **Declarative:** Make me a chocolate cake to feed 10 people.
- **Imperative:** Drive to store. Buy; eggs, milk, flour, cocoa powder… Drive home. Pre-heat oven. Mix ingredients. Place in baking tray. If a fan-assisted oven, place tray in oven for 30 minutes. If not a fan-assisted oven, place tray in oven for 40 minutes. Remove from oven and turn oven off. Leave to stand until cool. Add icing.

The declarative model is stating what you want (chocolate cake for 10). The imperative model is a long list of steps that will *hopefully* make a chocolate cake for 10.

Let's look at a more concrete example.

Assume an application with two microservices – front-end and back-end. You know you need 5 instances of the front-end Pod and 2 instances of the back-end Pod to meet expected demand.

Taking the declarative approach, you write a simple configuration file telling Kubernetes you want 5 replicas of the front-end Pod all listening externally on port 80. You also want 2 back-end Pods listening internally on port 27017. That's your desired state.

Once you've described this in a config file, you give it to Kubernetes and sit back while Kubernetes does the hard work of implementing and monitoring it. It's a beautiful thing.

The opposite of this is the imperative model. It has no concept of desired state, it's just a list of steps and instructions.

To make things worse, imperative instructions can have endless potential variations. For example, the commands to pull and start `containerd` containers are different from the commands to pull and start `cri-o` containers. This creates more work, is prone to more errors, and because it's not declaring a desired state, there's no self-healing. It's not so beautiful.

Kubernetes supports both models, but strongly prefers the declarative model.

> **Note:** *containerd* and *cri-o* are CRI container runtimes that run on worker nodes to perform low-level tasks such as starting and stopping containers.

Controllers and reconciliation

Fundamental to *desired state* is the process of *reconciliation*.

For example, ReplicaSets are implemented as a controller running as a background reconciliation loop checking the right number of Pod replicas are present on the cluster. If there aren't enough, it adds more. If there are too many, it terminates some.

Assume a scenario where desired state is 10 replicas, but only 8 are present. It makes no difference if this is due to a failure, or if it's because an autoscaler has requested an increase in desired state from 8 to 10. Either way, this is a red-alert condition for Kubernetes and the ReplicaSet controller brings up two more replicas. And the best part... it does all this without calling you at 4:20 am!

The exact same reconciliation process powers self-healing, scaling, rollouts, and rollbacks. Let's take a closer look.

Rolling updates with Deployments

Zero-downtime rolling-updates (rollouts) of stateless apps are what Deployments are all about. However, they require a couple of things from your microservices applications in order to work properly:

1. Loose coupling via APIs
2. Backwards and forwards compatibility

Both of these are hallmarks of modern cloud-native microservices apps and work as follows.

All microservices in an app should be decoupled and only communicate via well-defined APIs. This allows any microservice to be updated without having to think about clients and other microservices that interact with them – everything talks to formalised APIs that expose documented interfaces and hide specifics. Ensuring releases are backwards and forwards compatible means you can perform independent updates without having to factor in which versions of clients are consuming the service. A simple non-tech example is a car. You can swap the engine in a car, change the exhaust, get bigger brakes etc. However, as long as the driving API (steering wheel and foot pedals) doesn't change, drivers can still drive the car without having to learn any new skills.

With those points in mind, zero-downtime rollouts work like this.

Assume you're running 5 replicas of a stateless web front-end. As long as all clients communicate via APIs and are backwards and forwards compatible, it doesn't matter which of the 5 replicas a client connects to. To perform a rollout, Kubernetes creates a new replica running the new version and terminates an existing one running the old version. At this point, you've got 4 replicas on the old version and 1 on the new. This process repeats until all 5 replicas are on the new version. As the app is stateless, and there are always multiple replicas up and running, clients experience no downtime or interruption of service.

There's actually a lot that goes on behind the scenes, so let's look a bit closer.

You design applications with each discrete microservice as its own Pod. For convenience – self-healing, scaling, rolling updates and more – you wrap the Pods in their own higher-level controller such as a Deployment. Each Deployment describes all the following:

- How many Pod replicas
- What images to use for the Pod's containers
- What network ports to expose
- Details about how to perform rolling updates

In the case of Deployments, when you post the YAML file to the API server, the Pods get scheduled to healthy nodes and a Deployment and ReplicaSet work together to make the magic happen. The ReplicaSet controller sits in a watch loop making sure our old friends *observed state* and *desired state* are in agreement. A Deployment object sits above the ReplicaSet, governing its configuration and providing mechanisms for rollouts and rollbacks.

All good so far.

Now, assume you're exposed to a known vulnerability and need to rollout a newer version with the fix. To do this, you update the **same Deployment YAML file** with the new image version and re-post it to the API server. This updates the existing Deployment object with a new desired state requesting the same number of Pods but all running the newer image.

To make this happen, Kubernetes creates a second ReplicaSet to create and manage the Pods with the new image. You now have two ReplicaSets – the original one for the Pods with the old image, and a new one for the Pods with the new image. As Kubernetes increases the number of Pods in the new ReplicaSet it decreases the number of Pods in the old ReplicaSet. Net result, you get a smooth incremental rollout with zero downtime.

You can rinse and repeat the process for future updates – just keep updating the same Deployment manifest, which should be stored in a version control system.

Brilliant.

Figure 6.3 shows a Deployment that's been updated once. The initial release created the ReplicaSet on the left, and the update created the one on the right. You can see the ReplicaSet for the initial release has been wound down and no longer manages any Pods. The one for the update is active and owns all the Pods.

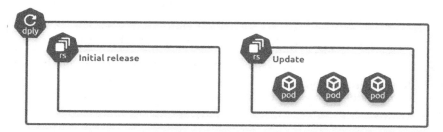

Figure 6.3

It's important that the old ReplicaSet from the initial release still exists with its configuration intact. You'll see why in the next section.

Rollbacks

As you saw in Figure 6.3, older ReplicaSets are wound down and no longer manage any Pods. However, their configurations still exist on the cluster, making them a great option for reverting to previous versions.

The process of a rollback is the opposite of a rollout – you wind one of the old ReplicaSets up while you wind the current one down. Simple.

Figure 6.4 shows the same app rolled back to the initial release.

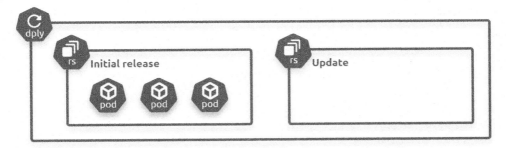

Figure 6.4

That's not the end though. Kubernetes gives you fine-grained control over how rollouts and rollbacks proceed. For example, you can insert delays, control the pace and cadence of releases, and you can even probe the health and status of updated replicas.

But talk is cheap, let's see it in action.

Create a Deployment

You'll need a Kubernetes cluster and the lab files from the book's GitHub repo if you want to follow along. If you haven't already cloned it, you can use the following command.

```
$ git clone https://github.com/nigelpoulton/TheK8sBook.git
Cloning into 'TheK8sBook'...
```

If you don't know how to use `git`, or can't install it, you can just go to the GitHub repo and copy the text from the relevant files into files with the same name on your local machine.

Be sure to run the following commands from within the `deployments` folder.

```
$ cd TheK8sBook/deployments
```

The following YAML snippet is from the `deploy.yml` file. It defines a single-container-Pod wrapped in a Deployment object. It's been annotated to highlight some important sections.

```
apiVersion: apps/v1
kind: Deployment
metadata:
  name: hello-deploy          <<==== Deployment name. Must be valid DNS name
spec:
  replicas: 10                <<==== Number of Pod replicas to deploy & manage
  selector:
    matchLabels:
      app: hello-world
  revisionHistoryLimit: 5
  progressDeadlineSeconds: 300
  minReadySeconds: 10
  strategy:                   <<==== This block controls how updates happen
    type: RollingUpdate
    rollingUpdate:
      maxUnavailable: 1
      maxSurge: 1
  template:                   <<==== Below here is the PodTemplate
    metadata:
      labels:
        app: hello-world
    spec:
      containers:
      - name: hello-pod
        image: nigelpoulton/k8sbook:1.0
        ports:
        - containerPort: 8080
```

Let's step through it and explain some of the important parts.

Right at the very top, you specify the API version to use. At the time of writing, the latest stable Deployment schema is defined in the apps/v1 API sub-group.

Next, the kind field tells Kubernetes this is defining a Deployment object.

The metadata section gives the Deployment a name. This should be a valid DNS name. So, alphanumerics, the dot and the dash are valid, and you should avoid exotic characters.

The spec section is where most of the action happens. Anything nested below .spec relates to the Deployment. Anything nested below .spec.template is the Pod template. In this example, the Pod template defines a single-container Pod based on the nigelpoulton/k8sbook:1.0 image.

spec.replicas is how many Pod replicas the Deployment should create and manage.

spec.selector is a list of labels that Pods must have in order for the Deployment to manage them. Notice how the Deployment selector matches the labels assigned to the Pod lower down in the Pod template (app=hello-world).

`spec.revisionHistoryLimit` tells Kubernetes how many older versions/ReplicaSets to keep. Keeping more gives you more rollback options but keeping too many can bloat the object. This can be a problem on large clusters with lots of software releases.

`spec.progressDeadlineSeconds` tells Kubernetes how long to wait during a rollout for each new replica to come online. The example sets a 5-minute deadline, meaning each new replica has 5 minutes to come up before Kubernetes considers the rollout to have stalled. To be clear, the clock is reset for each new replica, meaning each step in the rollout gets its own 5-minute window.

Finally, `spec.strategy` tells the Deployment controller how to update the Pods when a rollout occurs.

Use `kubectl apply` to deploy it on the cluster.

> **Note:** `kubectl apply` posts the YAML file to the Kubernetes API server and includes all necessary authentication tokens from your kubeconfig file.

```
$ kubectl apply -f deploy.yml
deployment.apps/hello-deploy created
```

At this point, the Deployment configuration is persisted to the cluster store as a record of intent and the 10 replicas will be scheduled to healthy worker nodes. In the background, Deployment and ReplicaSet controllers are watching the state of play and are eager to perform their reconciliation magic.

Inspecting Deployments

You can use the normal `kubectl get` and `kubectl describe` commands to see details of Deployments and ReplicaSets.

```
$ kubectl get deploy hello-deploy
NAME          READY   UP-TO-DATE   AVAILABLE   AGE
hello-deploy  10/10   10           10          4m17s

$ kubectl describe deploy hello-deploy
Name:                   hello-deploy
Namespace:              default
Annotations:            deployment.kubernetes.io/revision: 1
Selector:               app=hello-world
Replicas:               10 desired | 10 updated | 10 total | 10 available | 0 unavailable
StrategyType:           RollingUpdate
MinReadySeconds:        10
RollingUpdateStrategy:  1 max unavailable, 1 max surge
Pod Template:
```

```
    Labels:  app=hello-world
    Containers:
     hello-pod:
       Image:        nigelpoulton/k8sbook:1.0
       Port:         8080/TCP
<SNIP>
OldReplicaSets:  <none>
NewReplicaSet:   hello-deploy-67959776b5 (10/10 replicas created)
<Snip>
```

The command outputs have been trimmed for readability, but take a minute to look at them as they contain a lot of interesting information that can help you learn.

As mentioned earlier, Deployments automatically create associated ReplicaSets. Verify this with the following command.

```
$ kubectl get rs
NAME                       DESIRED   CURRENT   READY   AGE
hello-deploy-67959776b5    10        10        10      6m
```

Right now, you only have one ReplicaSet. This is because you've only performed an initial rollout. However, you can see the name of the ReplicaSet matches the name of the Deployment with a hash added to the end. This is a crypto-hash of the Pod template section of the Deployment manifest (everything below .spec.template). You'll see this shortly, but making changes to the Pod template section initiates a rollout and a new ReplicaSet with a hash of the updated Pod template.

You can get more detailed information about the ReplicaSet with the usual kubectl describe command. Your ReplicaSet will have a different name.

```
$ kubectl describe rs hello-deploy-67959776b5
Name:           hello-deploy-67959776b5
Namespace:      default
Selector:       app=hello-world,pod-template-hash=67959776b5
Labels:         app=hello-world
                pod-template-hash=67959776b5
Annotations:    deployment.kubernetes.io/desired-replicas: 10
                deployment.kubernetes.io/max-replicas: 11
                deployment.kubernetes.io/revision: 1
Controlled By:  Deployment/hello-deploy
Replicas:       10 current / 10 desired
Pods Status:    10 Running / 0 Waiting / 0 Succeeded / 0 Failed
Pod Template:
  Labels:   app=hello-world
            pod-template-hash=67959776b5
  Containers:
   hello-pod:
     Image:         nigelpoulton/k8sbook:1.0
```

```
    Port:          8080/TCP
<Snip>
```

Notice how the output is similar to the Deployment output. This is because the config of the ReplicaSet is dictated by the Deployment that created it. The status (observed state) of the ReplicaSet is also rolled up into the Deployment status.

As with the Deployment output, the ReplicaSet output tells us a lot about it and how it connects to Pods and its governing Deployment. Take a minute to explore the different fields of the output and work out how they link to the Pods and Deployment.

Accessing the app

As things stand, you've got 10 replicas of a web app running. In order to access it from a stable name or IP address, or even from outside the cluster, you need a Kubernetes *Service* object. We'll discuss these in detail in the next chapter, but for now, it's enough to know they provide reliable networking for a set of Pods.

The following YAML defines a Service that works with the Pod replicas previously deployed. It's included in the "deployments" folder of the book's GitHub repo called svc.yml.

```
apiVersion: v1
kind: Service
metadata:
  name: hello-svc
  labels:
    app: hello-world
spec:
  type: NodePort
  ports:
  - port: 8080
    nodePort: 30001
    protocol: TCP
  selector:
    app: hello-world
```

Deploy it with the following command. Be sure to run the command from the deployments directory.

```
$ kubectl apply -f svc.yml
service/hello-svc created
```

With the Service deployed, you can access the app by hitting any of the cluster nodes on port 30001.

If you're running Docker Desktop you should be able to use localhost:30001. Some older versions for Mac contain a bug and this doesn't work. It may be fixed in your version.

If you're running your cluster in the cloud, you need to hit the public IP or public DNS name of one of your cluster nodes on port 30001.

If you're using Minikube, get your Minikube IP ($ minikube ip) and append port 30001.

Figure 6.5 shows the Service being accessed from outside the cluster via a node called node1 on port 30001. It assumes node1 is resolvable via DNS, and port 30001 is allowed on any intervening firewalls.

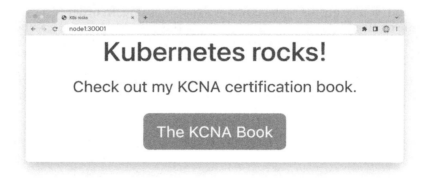

Figure 6.5

Perform scaling operations

Manually scaling the number of replicas in a Deployment is easy. You can do it imperatively with the kubectl scale command, or declaratively by updating the YAML file and re-posting it to the API server. You'll do it both ways, but the preferred way is the declarative way.

Verify the current number of replicas.

```
$ kubectl get deploy hello-deploy
NAME            READY    UP-TO-DATE    AVAILABLE    AGE
hello-deploy    10/10    10            10           104m
```

Run the following imperative commands to scale down to 5 and verify the operation.

```
$ kubectl scale deploy hello-deploy --replicas 5
deployment.apps/hello-deploy scaled

$ kubectl get deploy hello-deploy
NAME           READY   UP-TO-DATE   AVAILABLE   AGE
hello-deploy   5/5     5            5           105m
```

You've successfully scaled the Deployment down to 5 replicas, however, there's a potential problem. The current state of your environment no longer matches what is in your declarative manifest – the cluster has 5 replicas but the Deployment YAML still defines 10. This can cause issues in the future if you use the YAML file to update other properties of the Deployment. For example, if you update the image version in the YAML file and re-post it to the API server, you'll also increase the number of replicas back to 10. For this reason, you should always keep your YAML manifests in sync with your live environment, and the easiest way to do this is to make all changes to your live environment via your YAML manifests.

Let's re-post the YAML file and take the replica count back to 10.

You can edit the YAML file and set a different number of replicas, but the examples later in the chapter will assume you have 10.

```
$ kubectl apply -f deploy.yml
deployment.apps/hello-deploy configured

$ kubectl get deploy hello-deploy
NAME           READY   UP-TO-DATE   AVAILABLE   AGE
hello-deploy   10/10   10           10          109m
```

You may have noticed the scaling operations were almost instantaneous. This is different to rolling updates that you're going to see next.

Kubernetes also has autoscalers that scale Pods and infrastructure based on metrics and demand.

Perform a rolling update

In this section, you'll see how to perform a rolling update on the app already deployed. As previously mentioned, terms such as *rollout, release, zero-downtime update,* and *rolling update* all mean the same thing.

We'll assume the new version of the app has already been created and containerized as an image with the 2.0 tag. All that's left to do is perform the rollout. To simplify the process and keep the focus on Kubernetes, we'll ignore real-world CI/CD workflows and version control tools.

Before continuing, it's vital you understand that update operations are ***replacement operations***. When you "update" a Pod, you're actually terminating it and replacing it with a brand new one. Remember, Pods are designed as *immutable objects,* so you never change or update them after they're deployed.

Ok, let's crack on.

The first step is to update the image version in the Deployment's resource manifest. The initial release of the app is using the `nigelpoulton/k8sbook:1.0` image. Use your favorite editor to update the image to the newer `nigelpoulton/k8sbook:2.0` image and save your changes. This ensures next time the manifest is posted to the API server, all Pods managed by the Deployment will be replaced with new ones running the new `2.0` image.

The following trimmed output shows the updated file. The only change is to the container image line in the Pod template section.

```
apiVersion: apps/v1
kind: Deployment
metadata:
  name: hello-deploy
spec:
  replicas: 10
  <Snip>
  template:
    <Snip>
    spec:
      containers:
      - name: hello-pod
        image: nigelpoulton/k8sbook:2.0          <<==== The only line that changed
        ports:
        - containerPort: 8080
```

Before posting it to Kubernetes, let's look at the settings governing how the rollout will work.

The `.spec` section contains all the settings governing how updates will be performed.

```
<Snip>
revisionHistoryLimit: 5
progressDeadlineSeconds: 300
minReadySeconds: 10
strategy:
  type: RollingUpdate
  rollingUpdate:
    maxUnavailable: 1
    maxSurge: 1
<Snip>
```

revisionHistoryLimit tells Kubernetes to keep the configs of the previous 5 releases. This means the previous 5 ReplicaSet objects will be kept and you can easily rollback to any of them.

progressDeadlineSeconds governs how long each new Pod replica has to start before Kubernetes considers the rollout to have stalled. The config shown gives each Pod replica its own 5-minute window to come up.

.spec.minReadySeconds throttles the rate at which replicas are replaced. The one in the example tells Kubernetes that any new replica must be up and running for 10 seconds, without any issues, before it's allowed to start replacing the next one. Longer waits give you a chance to identify problems and avoid replacing all replicas with a broken version. In the real world, you should make the value large enough to trap common failures.

There is also a nested .spec.strategy map telling Kubernetes you want this Deployment to:

- Update using the RollingUpdate strategy
- Never have more than one Pod below desired state (maxUnavailable: 1)
- Never have more than one Pod above desired state (maxSurge: 1)

As the desired state of the app requests 10 replicas, maxSurge: 1 means you'll never have more than 11 replicas during the update process, and maxUnavailable: 1 means you'll never have less than 9. The net result is a rollout that updates two Pods at a time (the delta between 9 and 11 is 2).

What you've seen so far is great, but we haven't explained how Kubernetes knows which Pods to terminate and replace when performing the rollout.

The answer to this is simple but vital... label selectors!

If you look closely at the deploy.yml file, you'll see the Deployment spec has a selector block. This is a list of labels the Deployment controller looks for when finding Pods to update during rollout operations. In this example, it's looking for Pods with the app=hello-world label. If you look at the Pod template, you'll notice it creates Pods with this same label. Net result... the Pods created by this Deployment will be managed by it.

```
apiVersion: apps/v1
kind: Deployment
metadata:
  name: hello-deploy
spec:
  selector:                       <<==== The Deployment will manage all
    matchLabels:                  <<==== replicas on the cluster with
      app: hello-world            <<==== this label
      <Snip>
  template:
    metadata:
      labels:
        app: hello-world          <<==== Matches the label selector
<Snip>
```

The Deployment's label selector is immutable, so you cannot change it once it's created.

With the updated manifest ready and saved, you can initiate the update by re-posting it to the API server.

```
$ kubectl apply -f deploy.yml
deployment.apps/hello-deploy configured
```

The update may take some time to complete. This is because it's incrementing two Pods at a time, pulling the new image on each node, starting the new Pods, and then waiting 10 seconds before moving on to the next two.

You can monitor the progress with kubectl rollout status.

```
$ kubectl rollout status deployment hello-deploy
Waiting for deployment "hello-deploy" rollout... 4 out of 10 new replicas...
Waiting for deployment "hello-deploy" rollout... 4 out of 10 new replicas...
Waiting for deployment "hello-deploy" rollout... 6 out of 10 new replicas...
^C
```

If you press Ctrl+C to stop watching the progress, you can run kubectl get deploy commands while the update is in process. This lets you see the effect of some of the update-related settings in the manifest. For example, the following command shows that 6 of the replicas have been updated and you currently have 9. 9 is 1 less than the desired state of 10. This is a result of the maxUnavailable=1 value in the manifest.

```
$ kubectl get deploy hello-deploy
NAME           READY   UP-TO-DATE   AVAILABLE   AGE
hello-deploy   9/10    6            9           125m
```

Pausing and resuming rollouts

It's possible to pause and resume a rollout using kubectl.

If the rollout is still in progress, you can pause it with the following command.

```
$ kubectl rollout pause deploy hello-deploy
deployment.apps/hello-deploy paused
```

Running a kubectl describe provides some interesting info.

```
$ kubectl describe deploy hello-deploy
Name:                   hello-deploy
Namespace:              default
Annotations:            deployment.kubernetes.io/revision: 2
                        kubernetes.io/change-cause: kubectl apply --filename=deploy.yml
                        --record=true
Selector:               app=hello-world
Replicas:               10 desired | 6 updated | 11 total | 9 available | 2 unavailable
StrategyType:           RollingUpdate
MinReadySeconds:        10
RollingUpdateStrategy:  1 max unavailable, 1 max surge
<Snip>
Conditions:
  Type          Status    Reason
  ----          ------    ------
  Available     True      MinimumReplicasAvailable
  Progressing   Unknown   DeploymentPaused
OldReplicaSets: hello-deploy-67959776b5 (3/3 replicas created)
NewReplicaSet:  hello-deploy-7975c755b6 (6/6 replicas created)
```

The deployment.kubernetes.io annotation shows the object is on revision 2 (revision 1 was the initial rollout and this update is revision 2). Replicas shows the rollout is incomplete. The third line from the bottom shows the Deployment condition as "progressing" but paused. Finally, you can see the ReplicaSet for the initial release is wound down to 3 replicas and the one for the new release is up to 6.

If a scale-up operation occurs during a rollout, the additional replicas will be balanced across both ReplicaSets. In this example, if the Deployment was increased to 20 by adding 10 new replicas, Kubernetes would assign 3 of the new replicas to the old ReplicaSet and 6 to the new. This happens even if the rollout is not paused.

You can resume the rollout with the following command.

```
$ kubectl rollout resume deploy hello-deploy
deployment.apps/hello-deploy resumed
```

Once it completes, you can verify with `kubectl get deploy`.

```
$ kubectl get deploy hello-deploy
NAME           READY    UP-TO-DATE    AVAILABLE    AGE
hello-deploy   10/10    10            10           136m
```

The output shows the rollout as complete – 10 Pods are up-to-date and available.

If you've been following along with the examples, you'll be able to hit `refresh` in your browser and see the updated app (Figure 6.6). The old version displayed "Kubernetes Rocks!", the new one displays "WebAssembly is coming!".

Figure 6.6

Perform a rollback

As previously mentioned, Kubernetes maintains a documented revision history of rollouts. The following command shows the Deployment with two revisions.

```
$ kubectl rollout history deployment hello-deploy
deployment.apps/hello-deploy
REVISION   CHANGE-CAUSE
1          <none>
2          kubectl apply --filename-deploy.yml --record=true
```

Revision 1 was the initial release that used the 1.0 image tag. Revision 2 is the rolling update you just performed to the 2.0 image. The command that invoked the update has even been recorded in the object's history.

You know that rolling updates create new ReplicaSets, and that old ReplicaSets aren't deleted. The fact the old ones still exist makes them ideal for executing rollbacks, which are the same as rollouts, just in reverse.

The following commands show the two ReplicaSet objects. The second command shows the config of the old one and that it still references the old image version. The output is trimmed to fit the book.

```
$ kubectl get rs
NAME                      DESIRED   CURRENT   READY   AGE
hello-deploy-7975c755b6   10        10        10      13m
hello-deploy-67959776b5   0         0         0       136m

$ kubectl describe rs hello-deploy-65cbc9474c
Name:           hello-deploy-67959776b5
Namespace:      default
Selector:       app=hello-world,pod-template-hash=67959776b5
Labels:         app=hello-world
                pod-template-hash=67959776b5
Annotations:    deployment.kubernetes.io/desired-replicas: 10
                deployment.kubernetes.io/max-replicas: 11
                deployment.kubernetes.io/revision: 1
Controlled By:  Deployment/hello-deploy
Replicas:       0 current / 0 desired
Pods Status:    0 Running / 0 Waiting / 0 Succeeded / 0 Failed
Pod Template:
  Containers:
   hello-pod:
    Image:      nigelpoulton/k8sbook:1.0   <<==== Still configured with old version
    Port:       8080/TCP
```

The line you're interested in is the one shown second-from-last in the book as it shows the old image version. Therefore, flipping the Deployment back to this ReplicaSet will automatically replace all Pods with the original version.

> **Note:** Don't get confused if you hear rollbacks referred to as "updates". That's exactly what they are. A rollback follows exactly the same logic and rules as

an update/rollout – terminate Pods with the current image and replace them with Pods running the new image. Just in the case of a rollback, the "new" image is actually an "older" one.

The following example uses kubectl rollout to revert the application to revision 1. This is an imperative operation and not recommended. However, it's convenient for quick rollbacks, just make sure you remember to update your source YAML files to reflect the changes you make.

```
$ kubectl rollout undo deployment hello-deploy --to-revision=1
deployment.apps "hello-deploy" rolled back
```

Although it might look like the operation is instantaneous, it isn't. Like we said before, rollbacks follow the same rules defined in the strategy block of the Deployment object. You can verify this and track the progress with the following kubectl get deploy and kubectl rollout commands.

```
$ kubectl get deploy hello-deploy
NAME            READY    UP-TO-DATE   AVAILABLE   AGE
hello-deploy    9/10     6            9           140m

$ kubectl rollout status deployment hello-deploy
Waiting for deployment "hello-deploy"... 6 out of 10 new replicas have been updated...
Waiting for deployment "hello-deploy"... 7 out of 10 new replicas have been updated...
Waiting for deployment "hello-deploy"... 8 out of 10 new replicas have been updated...
Waiting for deployment "hello-deploy"... 1 old replicas are pending termination...
Waiting for deployment "hello-deploy"... 9 of 10 updated replicas are available...
^C
```

Congratulations. You've performed a rolling update and a successful rollback.

Just a quick reminder. The rollback operation you performed was an imperative one. This means the current state of the cluster no longer matches your source YAML files – the latest version of the YAML file lists the 2.0 image, but you rolled the app back to 1.0. This is a fundamental flaw with the imperative approach and a major reason why you should only update your cluster declaratively by updating your YAML files and re-posting them to Kubernetes.

Rollouts and labels

You've already seen that Deployments and ReplicaSets use labels and selectors to find the Pods they own.

In earlier versions of Kubernetes, it was possible for Deployments to take over management of existing static Pods if they had the same labels. However, recent versions use the system-generated `pod-template-hash` label so only Pods that were originally created by the Deployment/ReplicaSet will be managed.

Assume a quick example. You already have 5 static Pods on a cluster with the `app=front-end` label. At a later date, you create a Deployment that requests 10 Pods with the same `app=front-end` label. Older versions of Kubernetes would notice there were already 5 Pods with that label, seize control of them, and only create 5 new ones. The net result would be 10 Pods with the `app=front-end` label all owned by the Deployment. However, newer versions of Kubernetes tag all Pods created by a Deployment with the `pod-template-hash` label. This stops higher-level controllers seizing ownership of existing static Pods.

The following extremely snipped outputs show how this `pod-template-hash` label connects everything.

```
$ kubectl describe deploy hello-deploy
Name:        hello-deploy
<Snip>
NewReplicaSet:    hello-deploy-5445f6dcbb

$ kubectl describe rs hello-deploy-5445f6dcbb
Name:        hello-deploy-5445f6dcbb
<Snip>>
Selector:        app=hello-world,pod-template-hash=5445f6dcbb

$ kubectl get pods --show-labels
NAME                         READY   STATUS    LABELS
hello-deploy-5445f6dcbb..    1/1     Running   app=hello-world,pod-template-hash=5445f6dcbb
hello-deploy-5445f6dcbb..    1/1     Running   app=hello-world,pod-template-hash=5445f6dcbb
hello-deploy-5445f6dcbb..    1/1     Running   app=hello-world,pod-template-hash=5445f6dcbb
hello-deploy-5445f6dcbb..    1/1     Running   app=hello-world,pod-template-hash=5445f6dcbb
<Snip>
```

You shouldn't mess about with the `pod-template-hash` label or selector.

Clean-up

Use `kubectl delete -f deploy.yml` and `kubectl delete -f svc.yml` to delete the Deployment and Service created in the examples.

Chapter summary

In this chapter, you learned that *Deployments* are a great way to manage stateless apps on Kubernetes. They augment Pods with *self-healing, scalability, rolling updates,* and *rollbacks.*

Behind-the-scenes, Deployments use ReplicaSets to do most of the work with Pods –
it's actually a ReplicaSet that creates, terminates, and otherwise manages Pods, but the
Deployment tells the ReplicaSet what to do.

Like Pods, Deployments are objects in the Kubernetes API and you should work with
them declaratively. They're defined in the apps/v1 workloads API sub-group and
implement a controller architecture running as a reconciliation loop on the control
plane.

When you perform updates with the kubectl apply command, previous versions of
ReplicaSets get wound down, but they stick around making it easy to perform rollbacks.

7: Kubernetes Services

When Pods fail, they get replaced by new ones with new IPs. Scaling-up introduces new Pods with new IP addresses. Scaling down removes Pods. Rolling updates delete existing Pods and replace them with new ones with new IPs. All of this creates massive *IP churn* and demonstrates why you should never connect directly to any Pod. This is where *Services* come to the rescue by providing a stable and reliable network endpoint for groups of unreliable Pods.

The chapter is divided as follows:

- Theory
- Hands-on

Second, every Service gets its own **stable IP address**, its own **stable DNS name**, and its own **stable port**.

Third, Services use *labels* and *selectors* to dynamically select the Pods they send traffic to.

Service Theory

When talking about *Services* with a capital "S", we're talking about the Service object in Kubernetes that provides stable networking for Pods. Just like a *Pod*, *ReplicaSet*, or *Deployment*, a Kubernetes *Service* is a REST object in the API that you define in a manifest file and post to the API server.

Figure 7.1 shows a simple application managed by a Deployment controller. There's a client (which could be another Pod) that needs a reliable network endpoint to access the applications. Remember, it's a bad idea to talk directly to individual Pods because scaling operations, rollouts, rollbacks, and even failures can make them disappear.

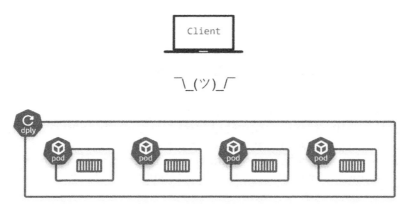

Figure 7.1

Figure 7.2 shows the same application with a Service thrown into the mix. The Service fronts the Pods with a **stable IP**, **stable DNS name**, and **stable port**. It also load-balances traffic to Pods with the right labels.

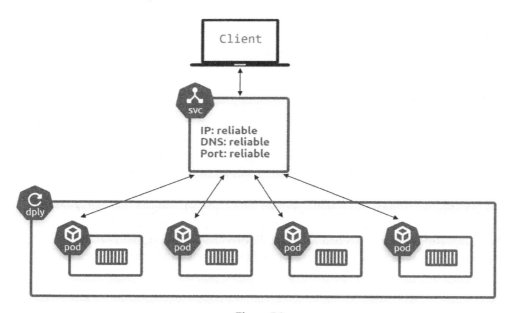

Figure 7.2

With a Service in place, the Pods can scale up and down, they can fail, and they can be updated and rolled back. Despite all of this, client access is still possible via the Service. This is because the Service observes changes and maintains an up-to-date list of healthy Pods and sends traffic to them. ***But it never changes its stable IP, DNS, and port.***

Think of Services as having a static front-end and a dynamic back-end. The front-end consists of the IP, DNS name, and port that never changes. The back-end comprises the list of healthy Pods and can be constantly changing.

Labels and loose coupling

Services are loosely coupled with Pods via *labels* and *selectors*. This is the same technology that loosely couples Deployments to Pods and is key to the flexibility of Kubernetes. Figure 7.3 shows an example where 3 Pods are labelled as zone=prod and ver=v1, and the Service has a *selector* that matches.

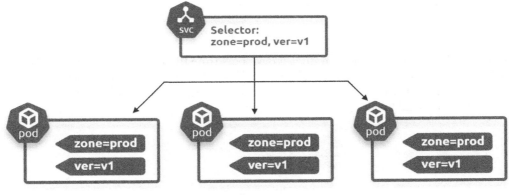

Figure 7.3

In Figure 7.3, the Service is providing stable networking to all three Pods – you send requests to the Service and it forwards them to the Pods. In doing this, it also provides basic load-balancing across the three Pods.

For a Service to send traffic to a Pod, the Pod needs *every* label the Service is selecting on. It can also have additional labels the Service isn't looking for. If that's confusing, the examples in Figures 7.4 and 7.5 will help.

Figure 7.4 shows an example where none of the Pods match. This is because the Service is looking for Pods with both labels. The logic is a Boolean AND.

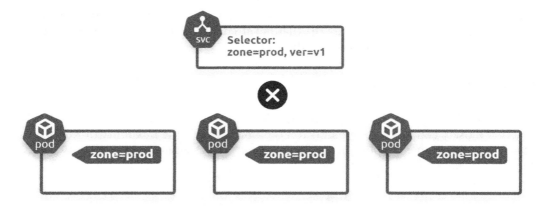

Figure 7.4

Figure 7.5 shows an example that does work. This time the Pods have all the labels the Service is selecting on. It makes no difference if the Pods have additional labels – the Service is looking for Pods with two specific labels, it finds them and ignores the fact they have additional labels.

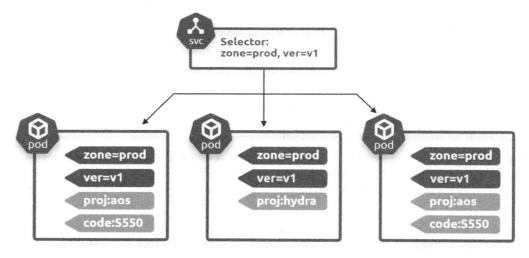

Figure 7.5

The following YAML defines a Service and Deployment and shows how the label selector and labels work.

```
apiVersion: v1
kind: Service
metadata:
  name: hello-svc
spec:
  ports:
  - port: 8080
  selector:
    app: hello-world        <<==== Send to Pods with these labels
    env: tkb                <<==== Send to Pods with these labels
---
apiVersion: apps/v1
kind: Deployment
metadata:
  name: hello-deploy
spec:
  replicas: 10
  <Snip>
  template:
    metadata:
      labels:
        app: hello-world    <<====  Pod labels
        env: tkb            <<====  Pod labels
    spec:
      containers:
  <Snip>
```

In the example, the Service is selecting on Pods with the `app=hello-world` and `env=tkb` labels. The Deployment has a Pod template with the same two labels. This means any Pods it deploys will match the Service's selector and receive traffic from it. This loose coupling is how Services know which Pods to send traffic to and allows Pods to be added and removed from the network.

Services and EndpointSlices

As Pods come-and-go, Services maintain an up-to-date list in one or more *EndpointSlice* objects that are created automatically for every Service with a label selector.

Every time you create a Service, Kubernetes automatically creates an associated *Endpoints* object. This Endpoints object is used to store a dynamic list of healthy Pods matching the Service's label selector.

It works like this…

Kubernetes is constantly evaluating the Service's label selector against all healthy Pods on the cluster. Any new Pods that match the selector get added to one of the Service's EndpointSlice objects, whereas any Pods that disappear get removed. This means the Services EndpointSlice objects are always up to date.

When sending traffic to Pods via a Service, the cluster's internal DNS resolves the Service name to an IP address. It then sends the traffic to this stable IP address and the traffic gets routed to one of the Pods. However, a *Kubernetes-native* application (that's a fancy way of saying an application that understands Kubernetes and can query the Kubernetes API) can query EndpointSlices directly, bypassing the DNS lookup and use of the Service's IP.

> **Note:** Recent versions of Kubernetes are replacing older monolithic *Endpoints* objects with more efficient *EndpointSlices*. The functionality is identical, but *EndpointSlices* achieve better performance and are more efficient on large busy clusters.

Dual stack networking (IPv4 and IPv6)

Kubernetes 1.23 promoted IPv4/IPv6 dual-stack networking to stable. This means Pods and Services can have IPv4 and IPv6 addresses. It's a major step forward in general Kubernetes networking and may be a game-changer for Kubernetes on IoT where there are potentially thousands of devices needing their own IP addresses.

For this to work, you need all cluster nodes to have routable IPv4 and IPv6 addresses and your CNI plugin needs to support dual stack networking.

Accessing Services from inside the cluster

Kubernetes supports several *types* of Service. The default type is *ClusterIP*.

A *ClusterIP* Service has a stable virtual IP address that is **only accessible from inside the cluster**. It's programmed into the internal network fabric and guaranteed to be stable for the life of the Service. *Programmed into the network fabric* is a fancy way of saying the network *just knows about it* and you don't need to bother with the details.

Anyway, every Service you create gets a ClusterIP that's registered, along with the name of the Service, in the cluster's internal DNS service. All Pods in the cluster are pre-programmed to use the cluster's DNS service, meaning all Pods can convert Service names to ClusterIPs.

Let's look at a simple example.

Creating a new Service called "skippy" will dynamically assign a stable ClusterIP. This name and ClusterIP are automatically registered with the cluster's DNS service. These are all guaranteed to be long-lived and stable. As all Pods in the cluster send service discovery requests to the internal DNS, they can all resolve "skippy" to the ClusterIP. iptables or IPVS rules are distributed across all cluster nodes to ensure traffic sent to the ClusterIP gets routed to Pods with the label the Service is selecting on.

Net result… if a Pod knows the name of a Service, it can resolve it to a ClusterIP address and connect to the Pods behind it.

This only works for Pods and other objects on the cluster, as it requires access to the cluster's DNS service. It does not work for clients outside of the cluster.

Accessing Services from outside the cluster

Kubernetes has two types of Service for requests originating from outside the cluster:

- NodePort
- LoadBalancer

NodePort Services build on top of the ClusterIP type and allow external clients to hit a dedicated port on every cluster node and reach the Service. We call this dedicated port the "NodePort".

You already know the default Service type is ClusterIP and it registers a DNS name, virtual IP, and port with the cluster's DNS. NodePort Services build on this by adding an additional *NodePort* that can be used to reach the Service from outside the cluster.

The following YAML shows a NodePort Service called "skippy".

```
apiVersion: v1
kind: Service
metadata:
  name: skippy
spec:
  type: NodePort
  ports:
  - port: 8080
    nodePort: 30050
  selector:
    app: hello-world
```

Pods **inside** the cluster can access this Service by its name (skippy) on port 8080. Clients connecting from **outside** the cluster can send traffic to any cluster node on port 30050.

Figure 7.6 shows a NodePort Service where 3 Pods are exposed externally on port 30050 on every cluster node. In step 1, an external client hits **node2** on port 30050. In step 2 it's redirected to the Service object. Step 3 shows the associated Endpoint object with an always-up-to-date list of Pods matching the label selector. Step 4 shows the client being directed to a healthy Pod on **node1**.

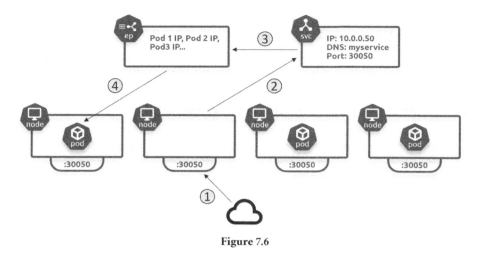

Figure 7.6

The Service could just as easily have directed the client to a Pod on node 3 or 4. In fact, future requests may go to other Pods as the Service performs basic load-balancing.

LoadBalancer Services make external access even easier by integrating with an internet-facing load-balancer on your cloud platform. You get a high-performance highly-available public IP or DNS name that external clients can use to access the Service. You can even register friendly DNS names to make access even simpler – you don't need to know cluster node names or IPs.

You'll create and use a LoadBalancer Service in the hands-on section later.

Summary of Service theory

The front-end of a Service provides an IP, DNS name and port that is guaranteed not to change for the entire life of the Service. The back-end of a Service uses labels and selectors to load-balance traffic across a potentially dynamic set of application Pods.

Hands-on with Services

In this section, you'll test Services for internal and external access and take a closer look at EndpointSlices.

The remainder of the chapter is divided as follows:

- Dual stack networking primer
- Managing Services the imperative way (not recommended)

- Managing Services the declarative way

To follow along, you'll need the lab files from the book's GitHub repo. You can clone the repo with the following command, or you can manually copy the file contents into files on your local machine.

```
$ git clone https://github.com/nigelpoulton/TheK8sBook.git
Cloning into 'TheK8sBook'...
```

Run all commands from the `services` sub-folder.

Dual stack networking primer

This section of the chapter introduces and demonstrates dual stack networking. To follow along with the examples, you'll need a cluster with the following configuration:

- All cluster nodes need a routable IPv4 and IPv6 addresses
- Your CNI network plugin must support dual stacks

If you're desperate to try dual stack networking, you can follow the instructions in the `kindlab.md` file in the `Services` folder of the GitHub repo. It shows you how to build a simple development cluster using KinD (Kubernetes in Docker).

Assuming you meet the requirements and are running Kubernetes 1.23 or later, all Pods and Services can have a single IPv4 and IPv6 address.

The majority of the hands-on examples in this edition of the book use IPv4 single stack networking to ensure they work on as many clusters as possible. However, the following examples show dual stack networking and you can use what you learn to manually adjust other examples in the book. You'll obviously need a cluster with dual stack networking configured.

The following Service config is from the `dual-stack-svc.yml` file in the `svc` folder of the book's GitHub repo. It's annotated to show the important line.

```
apiVersion: v1
kind: Service
metadata:
  name: dual-stack-svc
spec:
  ipFamilyPolicy: PreferDualStack          <<==== Assign IPv4 and IPv6 ClusterIPs
  type: ClusterIP
  ports:
  - port: 8080
    protocol: TCP
  selector:
    app: hello-world
```

The field of interest is `.spec.ipFamilyPolicy` which can be set to any of the following three values:

- SingleStack
- PreferDualStack
- RequireDualStack

`PreferDualStack` and `RequireDualStack` tell Kubernetes to allocate the Service an IPv4 and an IPv6 address. However, if it's set to `RequireDualStack` on a cluster that doesn't support dual stack networking, the Service will fail to create. If it's set to `PreferDualStack` and the cluster doesn't support dual stack networking, the creation will succeed but the Service will only have an IPv4 address.

Deploy it with the following command.

```
$ kubectl apply -f dual-stack-svc.yml
service/dual-stack-svc created
```

List it and describe it with the following commands.

```
$ kubectl get svc
NAME             TYPE        CLUSTER-IP     EXTERNAL-IP   PORT(S)    AGE
dual-stack-svc   ClusterIP   10.96.18.55    <none>        8080/TCP   5s

$ kubectl describe svc dual-stack-svc
Name:              dual-stack-svc
Namespace:         default
Labels:            <none>
Annotations:       <none>
Selector:          app=hello-world
Type:              ClusterIP
IP Family Policy:  PreferDualStack
IP Families:       IPv4,IPv6                        <<==== IPv4 and IPv6 families
```

```
IP:                 10.96.18.55
IPs:                10.96.18.55,fd00:10:96::4053   <<==== IPv4 and IPv6 addresses
Port:               <unset>  8080/TCP
TargetPort:         8080/TCP
Endpoints:          <none>
Session Affinity:   None
Events:             <none>
```

If you look closely at the output for the describe command, you'll notice both IP families are configured and a single IPv4 and a single IPv6 address have been allocated. However, the kubectl get output only shows the IPv4 ClusterIP. This is interesting and brings us to the point of "ClusterIP" and "ClusterIPs".

Dual stack networking means Service objects can have multiple ClusterIPs – one IPv4 and one IPv6. With this in mind, the object spec is updated to list multiple values under the new .spec.clusterIPs property. The first item in the list is considered the primary ClusterIP and is listed under the .spec.clusterIP field and is the value returned by kubectl get svc commands.

You can control whether the IPv4 or IPv6 address is the primary ClusterIP by specifying the order in spec.ipFamilies. The first family in the list will be the primary ClusterIP and therefore the value returned by kubectl get.

Delete the dual-stack-svc Service and edit the dual-stack-svc.yml file to include the following three lines. Listing IPv6 first in the ipFamilies list will make it the primary ClusterIP.

```
apiVersion: v1
kind: Service
metadata:
  name: dual-stack-svc
spec:
  ipFamilyPolicy: PreferDualStack
  ipFamilies:          <<==== Add this line
  - IPv6               <<==== Add this line
  - IPv4               <<==== Add this line
  type: ClusterIP
  ports:
  - port: 8080
    protocol: TCP
  selector:
    app: hello-world
```

Save your changes and re-post it to the API server and then run another kubectl get svc command.

```
$ kubectl apply -f dual-stack-svc.yml
service/dual-stack-svc created

$ kubectl get svc dual-stack-svc
NAME             TYPE        CLUSTER-IP          EXTERNAL-IP    PORT(S)     AGE
dual-stack-svc   ClusterIP   fd00:10:96::8f5c    <none>         8080/TCP    5s
```

The ClusterIP is now showing the IPv6 address.

The examples you've seen have been for ClusterIP Services, however, LoadBalancer Services can also be dual stack and support the same .spec.ipFamilyPolicy and .spec.ipFamilies fields. They obviously require your cloud's internet-facing load-balancers to support IPv6.

One last thing on dual stack networking... IPv4 isn't going away, so don't panic if you don't need or use IPv6 yet.

The rest of the examples focus on IPv4 single stack networking to give them the best chance of working on most clusters. If your cluster supports dual stack networking, you should feel free to manually edit the following examples to work with IPv6.

The imperative way

Managing resources the imperative way is not the Kubernetes way. It moves your cluster and apps out of sync with your YAML files. However, it can be useful for demonstration purposes.

Use kubectl to declaratively deploy the following Deployment (later steps will be done imperatively). Be sure to run the command from within the services folder.

```
$ kubectl apply -f deploy.yml
deployment.apps/svc-test created
```

Now the "svc-test" Deployment is running, it's time to *imperatively* deploy a Service for it.

The following command imperatively creates a new Service that will provide networking and load-balancing for the Pods created and managed by the svc-test Deployment.

```
$ kubectl expose deployment svc-test --type=NodePort
service/hello-svc exposed
```

Run a kubectl get to ensure it was created.

```
$ kubectl get svc -o wide
NAME         TYPE       CLUSTER-IP    EXTERNAL-IP   PORT(S)          SELECTOR
kubernetes   ClusterIP  10.43.0.1     <none>        443/TCP          <none>
svc-test     NodePort   10.43.56.24   <none>        8080:30013/TCP   chapter=services
```

The first line is a system Service that exposes the Kubernetes API on the cluster. Your Service is on the second line, and you can see the imperative command was clever enough to read the Deployment spec and configure the correct label selector and container port. It also gave the Service the same name as the Deployment.

You can get more detailed info with the kubectl describe command.

```
$ kubectl describe svc svc-test
Name:                    svc-test
Namespace:               default
Labels:                  <none>
Annotations:             <none>
Selector:                chapter=services
Type:                    NodePort
IP Family Policy:        SingleStack
IP Families:             IPv4
IP:                      10.43.56.24
IPs:                     10.43.56.24
Port:                    <unset>  8080/TCP
TargetPort:              8080/TCP
NodePort:                <unset>  30013/TCP
Endpoints:               10.42.0.19:8080,10.42.0.20:8080,10.42.0.21:8080 + 7 more...
Session Affinity:        None
External Traffic Policy: Cluster
Events:                  <none>
```

If your cluster is running dual stack networking your output may also list IPv6 addresses.

Let's look at some of the interesting values:

- Selector is the list of labels the Service looks for when building its list of Pods to load-balance traffic to
- ipFamilyPolicy configures the Service as either single stack or dual stack (IPv4 and IPv6)
- IP is the permanent internal ClusterIP (VIP) of the Service
- IP Families lists which IP address types and can be IPv4 or IPv6
- Port is the port the Service listens on inside the cluster
- TargetPort is the port the application is listening on
- NodePort is the cluster-wide port that can be used for external access

- `Endpoints` is the dynamic list of healthy Pod IPs currently matching the selector

Now that you know the cluster-wide NodePort (`30013`) you can open a web browser and access the app. To do this, you need to know the IP address of at least one of your cluster nodes, and you need to be able to reach it from your browser – e.g. a publicly routable IP if you're accessing via the internet.

Figure 7.7 shows a web browser accessing a node with an IP address of `54.246.255.52` on the cluster-wide NodePort `30013`.

Figure 7.7

The app you've deployed is a simple web app. It's built to listen on port `8080`, and you've configured a Kubernetes *Service* to map port `30013` on every cluster node back to port `8080` on the app. By default, cluster-wide NodePorts are between 30,000 - 32,767. In this example it was dynamically assigned, but you can also explicitly choose a port if using a YAML file.

Coming up next, you'll see how to do the same thing the proper way – the declarative way. To do that, you need to clean up by deleting the Service you just created. You can do this with the following `kubectl delete svc` command.

```
$ kubectl delete svc svc-test
service "svc-test" deleted
```

The declarative way

Time to do things the proper way… the Kubernetes way.

A Service manifest file

You'll use the following resource manifest to deploy the same Service you deployed in the previous section. However, this time you'll specify a value for the cluster-wide NodePort.

```
apiVersion: v1
kind: Service
metadata:
  name: svc-test
spec:
  type: NodePort
  ports:
  - port: 8080
    nodePort: 30001
    targetPort: 8080
    protocol: TCP
  selector:
    chapter: services
```

Let's step through it.

Services are mature objects defined in the v1 core API group (apiVersion).

The kind field tells Kubernetes you're defining a Service object.

The metadata block defines a name for the Service. This is the name registered with DNS. You can also apply labels and annotations here. Any labels you add here are used to identify the Service and are not related to selecting Pods.

The spec section is where you actually define the Service. This example is telling Kubernetes to deploy a NodePort Service. The port value tells Kubernetes to listen internally on port 8080, and the NodePort value tells it to listen externally on 30001. The targetPort value is part of the back-end configuration and tells Kubernetes to forward traffic to the application Pods on port 8080. Then you're explicitly telling it to use TCP (default). Finally, spec.selector tells the Service to send traffic to all healthy Pods on the cluster with the chapter=services label.

Deploy it with the following command.

```
$ kubectl apply -f svc.yml
service/svc-test created
```

Inspecting Services

Now the Service is deployed, you can inspect it with the usual kubectl get and kubectl describe commands.

```
$ kubectl get svc svc-test
NAME       TYPE       CLUSTER-IP     EXTERNAL-IP   PORT(S)          AGE
svc-test   NodePort   10.43.206.49   <none>        8080:30001/TCP   11s
```

The Service is up and exposed via every cluster node on port 30001. This means you can point a web browser to the name or IP of any node on that port and reach the Service. You'll need to use the IP address of a node you can reach, and you'll need to ensure any firewalls and security rules allow the traffic to flow. If you're running a local cluster, such as Docker Desktop, you can use localhost:30001.

EndpointSlice objects

Earlier in the chapter, you learned every Service gets its own *EndpointSlice* objects. These hold the list of Pods that match the Service's label selector and are dynamically updated as matching Pods come and go. You can inspect them with the normal kubectl commands.

The examples show the output for dual stack IPv4 and IPv6 networking. Notice how two EndpointSlice objects are created, one for the IPv4 mappings and the other for IPv6.

```
$ kubectl get endpointslices
NAME             ADDRESSTYPE   PORTS   ENDPOINTS                               AGE
svc-test-n7jg4   IPv4          8080    10.42.1.16,10.42.1.17,10.42.0.19  + 7 more...   2m1s
svc-test-9s6sq   IPv6          8080    fd00:10:244:1::c,fd00:10:244:1::9 + 7 more...   2m1s

$ kubectl describe endpointslice svc-test-n7jg4
Name:          svc-test-n7jg4
Namespace:     default
Labels:        chapter=services
               endpointslice.kubernetes.io/managed-by=endpointslice-controller.k8s.io
               kubernetes.io/service-name=svc-test
Annotations:   endpoints.kubernetes.io/last-change-trigger-time: 2022-01-10T16:20:46Z
AddressType:   IPv4
Ports:
  Name     Port   Protocol
  ----     ----   --------
  <unset>  8080   TCP
Endpoints:
  - Addresses:   10.42.1.16
    Conditions:
      Ready:     true
    Hostname:    <unset>
    TargetRef:   Pod/svc-test-9d7b4cf9d-hnvbf
    NodeName:    k3d-tkb-agent-2
    Zone:        <unset>
  - Addresses:   10.42.1.17
<Snip>
Events:          <none>
```

The full output of the kubectl describe command has a block for each healthy Pod containing useful info.

LoadBalancer Services

Now for the best type of Service. And it's also the easiest...

If your cluster is on a cloud platform, deploying a Service with type=LoadBalancer will provision one of your cloud's internet-facing load-balancers and configure it to send traffic to your Service.

The following YAML is from the lb.yml file. It defines a new Service called "clou-lb" that will provision a cloud load-balancer listening on port 9000 and forward traffic on port 8080 to all Pods with the chapter=services label. Basically, one of your cloud's load-balancers sending traffic to the Pods you already deployed through the "svc-test" Deployment.

```
apiVersion: v1
kind: Service
metadata:
  name: cloud-lb
spec:
  type: LoadBalancer
  ports:
  - port: 9000
    targetPort: 8080
  selector:
    chapter: services
```

Deploy it with the following command.

```
$ kubectl apply -f lb.yml
service/cloud-lb created
```

Now list it.

```
$ kubectl get svc --watch
NAME          TYPE           CLUSTER-IP      EXTERNAL-IP    PORT(S)          AGE
cloud-lb      LoadBalancer   10.43.128.113   172.21.0.4     9000:32688/TCP   47s
<Snip>
```

The EXTERNAL-IP column shows the public address assigned to the Service by your cloud. On some cloud platforms it may be a DNS name instead of an IP, and it may take a minute or two to populate. The delay is while your cloud platform provisions the internet-facing load-balancer.

Copy the value in the EXTERNAL-IP column and paste it into your browser with port 9000 to get to the app.

Congratulations, you just configured a high performance highly-available internet-facing load-balancer to front your Service.

Clean-up

Clean-up the lab with the following command. This will delete the Deployment and Services. Endpoints and EndpointSlices are automatically deleted with their associated Service.

```
$ kubectl delete -f deploy.yml -f svc.yml -f lb.yml
deployment.apps "svc-test" deleted
service "svc-test" deleted
service "cloud-lb" deleted
```

If you built the temporary KinD cluster for dual stack testing, you can delete it with the following command.

```
$ kind delete cluster tkb-dual-stack
```

Chapter Summary

In this chapter, you learned that *Services* bring stable and reliable networking to apps deployed on Kubernetes. On the front end, they provide a stable DNS name that's automatically registered with the cluster DNS. They also provide a stable IP. On the back end, they load-balance traffic across a dynamic set of Pods that match a label selector. They also let you expose elements of your application to the outside world, including integrating with cloud load-balancers.

Finally, Services are first-class objects in the Kubernetes API and should be managed declaratively through version-controlled YAML manifest files.

8: Ingress

Ingress is all about accessing multiple web applications through a single LoadBalancer Service.

A working knowledge of Kubernetes Services is recommended before reading this chapter. If you don't have this, consider reading the previous chapter first.

The chapter is divided as follows:

- Setting the scene for Ingress
- Ingress architecture
- Hands-on with Ingress

We'll be capitalising the word "Ingress" as it's a resource in the Kubernetes API. This adds clarity and is in-line with recent updates to the official style guide for the Kubernetes docs. We'll also be using the terms *LoadBalancer* and *load-balancer* as follows:

- `LoadBalancer` refers to a Kubernetes Service object of `type=LoadBalancer`
- `load-balancer` refers to the internet-facing load-balancer on your cloud

As an example, *when you create a Kubernetes LoadBalancer Service, Kubernetes talks to your cloud platform and provisions a cloud load-balancer.*

Setting the Scene for Ingress

In the previous chapter, you saw how Service objects provide stable networking for Pods. You also saw how to expose applications to external consumers via NodePort Services and LoadBalancer Services. However, both of these have limitations.

NodePorts only work on high port numbers (30000-32767) and require knowledge of node names or IPs. LoadBalancer Services fix this but require a 1-to-1 mapping between an internal Service and a cloud load-balancer. This means a cluster with 25 internet-facing apps will need 25 cloud load-balancers, and cloud load-balancers aren't cheap. Your cloud may also place a limit on how many load-balancers you can provision in a region.

Ingress fixes this by exposing multiple Services through a single cloud load-balancer.

To do this, Ingress creates a single LoadBalancer Service, on port 80 or 443, and uses *host-based* and *path-based* routing to send traffic to the correct *backend* Service. This is shown in Figure 8.1, and don't worry if it's unclear at this point. We'll keep building the picture, and the hands-on bits should clarify any doubts.

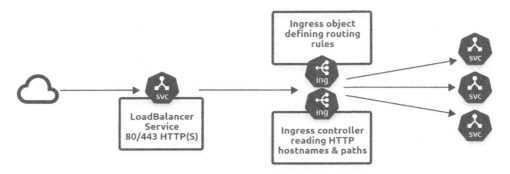

Figure 8.1

Ingress architecture

Ingress is a stable resource in the Kubernetes API. It went GA in Kubernetes 1.19 after being in beta for over 15 releases. During the 3+ years it was in alpha and beta, service meshes increased in popularity and there's some overlap in functionality. As a result, if you plan to run a service mesh, you may not need Ingress.

Ingress is defined in the `networking.k8s.io` API sub-group as a `v1` object and is based on the usual two constructs:

1. A controller
2. An object spec

The object spec defines rules to govern traffic routing, whereas the controller implements the rules.

However, a lot of Kubernetes clusters don't ship with a built-in Ingress controller – you have to install your own. This is the opposite of other API resources, such as Deployments and ReplicaSets, which have a built-in pre-configured controller. However, some hosted Kubernetes clusters give you the option to pre-install one.

Once you have an *Ingress controller*, you deploy *Ingress objects* with rules that tell the controller how to route requests.

On the topic of routing, Ingress operates at layer 7 of the OSI model, also known as the "application layer". This means it can inspect HTTP headers and forward traffic based on hostnames and paths.

> **Note:** A quick side-step. The "OSI model" is *the* reference model for TCP/IP networking. It comprises seven layers numbered 1-7, with the lowest layers concerned with things like signalling and electronics, the middle layers dealing with reliability through things like acks and retries, and the higher layers adding awareness of user apps such as HTTP services. Ingress operates at layer 7, also known as the *application layer*, and implements HTTP intelligence.

The following table shows how hostnames and paths can route to backend ClusterIP Services.

Host-based example	Path-based example	Backend K8s Service
shield.mcu.com	mcu.com/shield	svc-shield
hydra.mcu.com	mcu.com/hydra	svc-hydra

Figure 8.2 shows two different hostnames (URLs) configured to hit the same load-balancer. An Ingress object is watching and uses the hostnames in the HTTP headers to route traffic to the appropriate backend Service. This is an example of the HTTP *host-based* routing pattern, and it's almost identical for path-based routing.

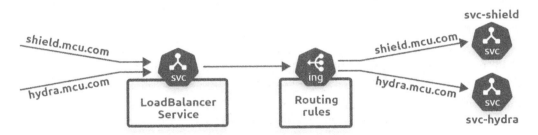

Figure 8.2 Host-based routing

For this to work, name resolution needs to point the appropriate DNS names to the public endpoint of the Ingress load-balancer. In the example in Figure 8.2 you'll need shield.mcu.com and hydra.mcu.com to resolve to the public IP of the Ingress load-balancer.

In summary, Ingress exposes multiple ClusterIP Services through a single cloud load-balancer. You create and deploy Ingress objects that are rules governing how traffic reaching the load-balancer is routed to backend Services. The Ingress controller, which you usually have to install yourself, inspects hostnames and paths to make intelligent routing decisions.

Now that you know the basics, let's see it in action.

Hands-on with Ingress

The following examples require a Kubernetes cluster running on a cloud platform that supports load-balancer integration. All the major clouds will work. The examples are tweaked for the NGINX Ingress controller, which you'll see how to install, but we'll point out things you'll need to change if you want to run with a different Ingress controller.

If you're following along, you'll need a clone of the book's GitHub repo and you'll need to run all commands from within the ingress folder.

```
$ git clone https://github.com/nigelpoulton/TheK8sBook.git
Cloning from...

$ cd ingress
```

Installing the NGINX Ingress controller

It's possible to skip this step if your cluster has a built-in Ingress controller. Run a kubectl get ing to find out.

The NGINX Ingress controller is installed from a YAML file hosted in the Kubernetes GitHub repo. It installs a bunch of Kubernetes constructs including a Namespace, ServiceAccounts, ConfigMap, Roles, RoleBindings, and more.

Install it with the following command. I've split the command over two lines because the URL is so long. If you're following along, you'll have to run it on a single line. You should also make sure you're installing the latest release (see https://github.com/kubernetes/ingress-nginx/releases).

```
$ kubectl apply -f https://raw.githubusercontent.com/kubernetes/ingress-nginx/
controller-v1.5.1/deploy/static/provider/cloud/deploy.yaml

namespace/ingress-nginx created
serviceaccount/ingress-nginx created
ingressclass.networking.k8s.io/nginx created
<Snip>
job.batch/ingress-nginx-admission-patch created
```

Check the `ingress-nginx` Namespace to make sure the controller Pod is running. It may take a few moments to enter the running phase.

```
$ kubectl get pods -n ingress-nginx \
  -l app.kubernetes.io/name=ingress-nginx

NAME                                        READY   STATUS      RESTARTS   AGE
ingress-nginx-admission-create--1-4w5ps     0/1     Completed   0          87s
ingress-nginx-admission-patch--1-9hg7t      0/1     Completed   1          87s
ingress-nginx-controller-54bfb9bb-cbgh6     1/1     Running     0          88s
```

Don't worry about the `Completed` Pods. These were short-lived to initialise the environment.

Once the controller Pod is running, you've got an NGINX Ingress controller, and you're ready to create some Ingress objects. However, before doing that, let's see how to use *Ingress classes* in case your cluster has multiple Ingress controllers.

Configure Ingress classes for clusters with multiple Ingress controllers

Ingress classes allow you to run multiple Ingress controllers on a single cluster. The process is simple:

1. You assign each Ingress controller to an Ingress class
2. When you create Ingress objects, you assign them to an Ingress class

If you've been following along, you'll have at least one Ingress class, called "nginx", that was created when you installed the NGINX controller.

```
$ kubectl get ingressclass
NAME    CONTROLLER             PARAMETERS   AGE
nginx   k8s.io/ingress-nginx   <none>       9m23s
```

You may have multiple classes if your cluster already had an Ingress controller.

Take a closer look at your Ingress class with the following command. There is currently no shortname for Ingress class objects, so you'll have to use "ingressclass".

```
$ kubectl describe ingressclass nginx
Name:          nginx
Labels:        app.kubernetes.io/component=controller
               app.kubernetes.io/instance=ingress-nginx
               app.kubernetes.io/managed-by=Helm
               app.kubernetes.io/name=ingress-nginx
               app.kubernetes.io/version=1.5.1
               helm.sh/chart=ingress-nginx-4.0.10
Annotations:   <none>
Controller:    k8s.io/ingress-nginx
Events:        <none>
```

With an Ingress controller and Ingress class in place, you're ready to configure and create Ingress objects.

Configuring host-based and path-based routing

This section deploys two apps and a single Ingress object. The Ingress will be configured to route traffic to both apps via a single load-balancer.

You'll complete all the following steps:

1. Deploy an app called shield and front it with a ClusterIP Service (backend) called svc-shield

2. Deploy an app called hydra and front it with a ClusterIP Service (backend) called svc-hydra

3. Deploy an Ingress object to route the following hostnames and paths

   • Host-based: shield.mcu.com >> svc-shield
   • Host-based: hydra.mcu.com >> svc-hydra
   • Path-based: mcu.com/shield >> svc-shield
   • Path-based: mcu.com/hydra >> svc-hydra

4. A cloud load-balancer will be created and the Ingress controller will monitor it for traffic

5. Configure DNS name resolution to point shield.mcu.com, hydra.mcu.com, and mcu.com to the cloud load-balancer

The overall architecture is shown in Figure 8.3.

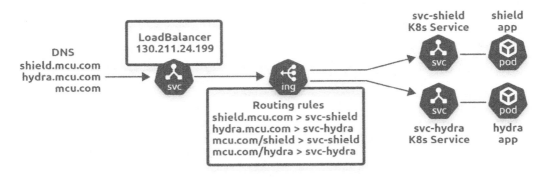

Figure 8.3 Host-based routing

Traffic flow to the `shield` app using host-based routing will be as follows:

1. A client will send traffic to `shield.mcu.com`
2. DNS name resolution will send the traffic to the load-balancer's public endpoint
3. Ingress will read the HTTP headers for the hostname (`shield.mcu.com`)
4. An Ingress rule will trigger, and the traffic will be routed to the `svc-shield` ClusterIP backend
5. The ClusterIP Service will ensure the traffic reaches the `shield` Pod

Deploy the apps

The `shield` and `hydra` apps, as well as associated ClusterIP Services, are defined in the `app.yml` file in the `ingress` folder. It defines the following:

- Two Pods. One called `shield` and one called `hydra`, both listening on port 8080
- Two ClusterIP Services. One called `svc-shield` and the other called `svc-hydra`

Deploy it with the following command.

```
$ kubectl apply -f app.yml
service/svc-shield created
service/svc-hydra created
pod/shield created
pod/hydra created
```

Check them with `kubectl get` and `kubectl describe` commands.

Create the Ingress object

You'll deploy the ingress object defined in `ig-all.yml`. It describes an Ingress object called "mcu-all" with four rules.

```
apiVersion: networking.k8s.io/v1
kind: Ingress
metadata:
  name: mcu-all
  annotations:
    nginx.ingress.kubernetes.io/rewrite-target: /
spec:
  ingressClassName: nginx
  rules:
  - host: shield.mcu.com
    http:
      paths:
      - path: /
        pathType: Prefix
        backend:
          service:
            name: svc-shield
            port:
              number: 8080
  - host: hydra.mcu.com
    http:
      paths:
      - path: /
        pathType: Prefix
        backend:
          service:
            name: svc-hydra
            port:
              number: 8080
  - host: mcu.com
    http:
      paths:
      - path: /shield
        pathType: Prefix
        backend:
          service:
            name: svc-shield
            port:
              number: 8080
      - path: /hydra
        pathType: Prefix
        backend:
          service:
            name: svc-hydra
            port:
              number: 8080
```

Let's step through it.

The first 4 lines define normal stuff such as the type of object and which schema version to use.

The annotation tells the controller to make a best-effort attempt to re-write paths to the path expected by your app. This example will re-write incoming paths to "/". For example, traffic hitting the load-balancer via the /shield path will have the path re-written to "/". You'll see an example shortly. Also, this annotation is specific to the NGINX Ingress controller and you'll have to comment it out if you're using a different one.

The spec.ingressClassName field tells Kubernetes to target this Ingress object at the NGINX controller you installed earlier. You'll have to change this line, or comment it out, if you're using a different Ingress controller.

The rules are a little more complex, so let's look at an example of a host-based rule and then a path-based rule.

The following *host-based* rule triggers on traffic arriving via shield.mcu.com at the root "/" path and forwards it to a backend Service called svc-shield. "svc-shield" is one of the ClusterIP Services you just deployed via the app.yml file.

```
- host: shield.mcu.com            <<==== Traffic arriving via this hostname
  http:
    paths:
    - path: /                     <<==== Arriving at root (no subpath specified)
      pathType: Prefix
      backend:                    <<==== This block references an existing
        service:                  <<==== "backend" ClusterIP Service
          name: svc-shield        <<==== called "svc-shield"
          port:                   <<==== that's listening on
            number: 8080          <<==== port 8080
```

The following *path-based* rule triggers when traffic arrives from mcu.com/shield. It gets routed to the same svc-shield backend Service.

```
- host: mcu.com                   <<==== Traffic arriving via this hostname
  http:
    paths:
    - path: /shield               <<==== Arriving on this subpath
      pathType: Prefix
      backend:                    <<==== This block references an existing
        service:                  <<==== "backend" ClusterIP Service
          name: svc-shield        <<==== called "svc-shield"
          port:                   <<==== that's listening on
            number: 8080          <<==== port 8080
```

Deploy it with the following command.

```
$ kubectl apply -f ig-all.yml
ingress.networking.k8s.io/mcu-all created
```

Inspecting Ingress objects

List the Ingress objects in the default Namespace. It may take a minute or so for yours to acquire an address. This is while Kubernetes provisions a load-balancer on your cloud.

```
$ kubectl get ing
NAME      CLASS   HOSTS                                     ADDRESS          PORTS
mcu-all   nginx   shield.mcu.com,hydra.mcu.com,mcu.com      34.159.139.235   80
```

The CLASS field shows which Ingress class is handling this set of rules. It may show as <None> if you only have a single Ingress controller and didn't configure classes. The HOSTS field shows it's configured to handle traffic based on three hostnames. The ADDRESS column is the public endpoint of the cloud load-balancer. In this example it's an IP address, but some clouds provide a URL. This one is configured for port 80.

On the topic of ports, Ingress is an HTTP/HTTPS solution.

Describe the Ingress. The output is trimmed to fit the page.

```
$ kubectl describe ing mcu-all
Name:            mcu-all
Namespace:       default
Address:         34.159.139.235
Default backend: default-http-backend:80...
Rules:
  Host            Path  Backends
  ----            ----  --------
  shield.mcu.com  /    svc-shield:8080 (10.36.1.5:8080)
  hydra.mcu.com   /    svc-hydra:8080 (10.36.0.7:8080)
  mcu.com         /shield   svc-shield:8080 (10.36.1.5:8080)
                  /hydra    svc-hydra:8080 (10.36.0.7:8080)
Annotations:     nginx.ingress.kubernetes.io/rewrite-target: /
Events:          <none>
  Type    Reason  Age              From                      Message
  ----    ------  ----             ----                      -------
  Normal  Sync    42s (x2 over 66s) nginx-ingress-controller  Scheduled for sync
```

Let's step through the output.

The Address line is the public IP of the cloud load-balancer associated with the Ingress.

Default backend is where the controller sends traffic arriving from an unknown host or path. Not all Ingress controllers implement a default backend.

The rules define the mappings between *hosts*, *paths*, and *backends*. Remember that "backends" are usually ClusterIP Services pre-configured to send traffic to application Pods.

The annotations often define integrations with your cloud back-end as well as controller-specific features. This example's telling the controller to re-write all paths to look like they arrived on root "/". This is a *best effort* approach, and as you'll see later, it doesn't work with all apps.

You should also be able to view the Ingress and load-balancer on your cloud backend. Figure 8.4 shows how it looks on the Google Cloud at the time of writing.

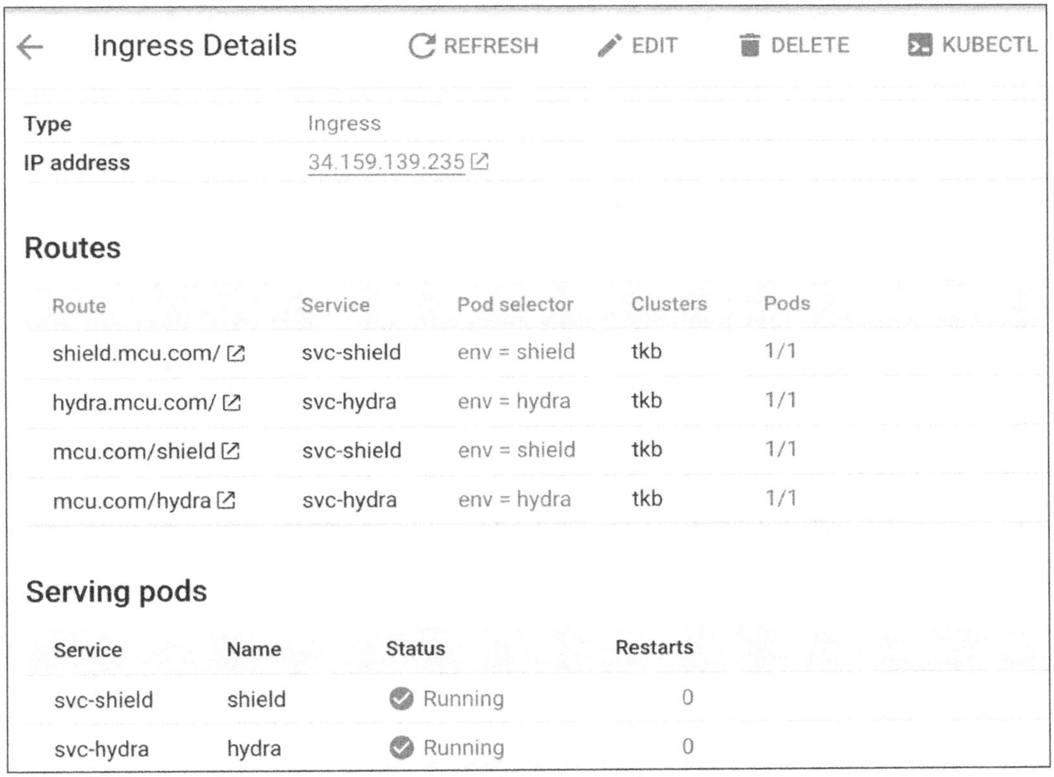

←	Ingress Details	⟳ REFRESH	✎ EDIT	🗑 DELETE	⊠ KUBECTL

Type Ingress
IP address 34.159.139.235 ☑

Routes

Route	Service	Pod selector	Clusters	Pods
shield.mcu.com/ ☑	svc-shield	env = shield	tkb	1/1
hydra.mcu.com/ ☑	svc-hydra	env = hydra	tkb	1/1
mcu.com/shield ☑	svc-shield	env = shield	tkb	1/1
mcu.com/hydra ☑	svc-hydra	env = hydra	tkb	1/1

Serving pods

Service	Name	Status	Restarts
svc-shield	shield	✔ Running	0
svc-hydra	hydra	✔ Running	0

Figure 8.4 Host-based routing

At this point, the application and backend Services are running and Ingress is configured to route traffic. The only thing left to configure is DNS name resolution so that `shield.mcu.com`, `hydra.mcu.com` and `mcu.com` resolve to the public endpoint of the Ingress.

Configure DNS name resolution

In the real world, you'll configure your internal DNS or internet DNS to point host-names to the Ingress load-balancer. How you do this varies depending on your environment and who your internet DNS is with.

If you're following along, it's possible to edit the hosts file on your local computer as a temporary solution.

On Mac and Linux, edit the /etc/hosts file and add the following lines. The example uses the public IP of the Ingress retrieved from the kubectl get ing command. Yours will be different.

```
$ sudo vi /etc/hosts

# Host Database
<Snip>
34.159.139.235 shield.mcu.com
34.159.139.235 hydra.mcu.com
34.159.139.235 mcu.com
```

On Windows the file is located at C:\Windows\System32\drivers\etc\hosts.

Make sure you've used the public IP from your environment and save your changes.

With this done, any traffic you send to shield.mcu.com, hydra.mcu.com, or mcu.com will be sent to the Ingress load-balancer.

Test the Ingress

Open a web browser and try the following URLs:

- shield.mcu.com
- hydra.mcu.com
- mcu.com

Figure 8.5 shows what happens to each request. Notice the traffic for the mcu.com request is routed to the *default backend*. This is because there's no ingress rule for mcu.com. Depending on your Ingress controller, the message returned will be different, and your Ingress may not even implement a default backend. The default backend configured by the GKE built-in Ingress returns a helpful message saying "response 404 (backend NotFound), service rules for [/] non-existent ".

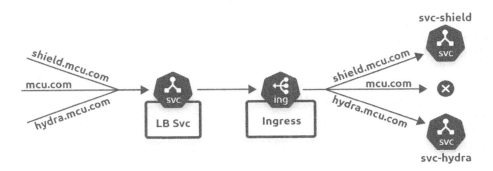

Figure 8.5

Now try connecting to either of the following:

- mcu.com/shield
- mcu.com/hydra

The Ingress uses the *re-write targets* feature with path-based routing to handle these connections. Notice how the image doesn't display for either. This is because not all apps work correctly with path rewrites.

Congratulations, you've successfully configured Ingress for host-based and path-based routing – you've got two applications running on a Kubernetes cluster, fronted by a couple of internal ClusterIP Services, and they're both exposed through a single cloud-based internet-facing load-balancer managed by Kubernetes Ingress!

Clean-up

If you've been following along, you'll have several things running on you Kubernetes cluster. Most importantly, the cloud load-balancer created by the Ingress controller costs money, so be sure to delete it when you're finished.

Delete the Ingress object.

```
$ kubectl delete ingress mcu-all
ingress.networking.k8s.io "mcu-all" deleted
```

Delete the apps and Services by referencing the YAML file. It may take a few seconds for the applications inside the Pods to gracefully terminate.

```
$ kubectl delete -f app.yml
service "svc-shield" deleted
service "svc-hydra" deleted
pod "shield" deleted
pod "hydra" deleted
```

If you want to, you can delete the NGINX Ingress controller with the following three commands.

```
$ kubectl delete namespace ingress-nginx
namespace "ingress-nginx" deleted

$ kubectl delete clusterrole ingress-nginx
clusterrole.rbac.authorization.k8s.io "ingress-nginx" deleted

$ kubectl delete clusterrolebinding ingress-nginx
clusterrolebinding.rbac.authorization.k8s.io "ingress-nginx" deleted
```

Finally, **don't forget to reset your `/etc/hosts` file if you added manual entries earlier**.

```
$ sudo vi /etc/hosts

# Host Database
<Snip>
34.159.139.235 shield.mcu.com       <<==== Delete this entry
34.159.139.235 hydra.mcu.com        <<==== Delete this entry
34.159.139.235 mcu.com              <<==== Delete this entry
```

Chapter summary

In this chapter, you learned that Ingress is a way to expose multiple applications and Kubernetes Services via a single cloud load-balancer. They're stable objects in the API but have feature overlap with a lot of service meshes – if you're running a service mesh you may not need Ingress.

Most Kubernetes clusters require you to install an Ingress controller and lots of options exist. However, some hosted Kubernetes services make things easy by shipping with a built-in Ingress controller.

Once you have an Ingress controller up and running, you create and deploy Ingress objects that are sets of rules governing how incoming traffic is routed to applications and Services on your Kubernetes cluster. It supports host-based and path-based HTTP routing.

9: Service discovery deep dive

In this chapter, you'll learn what service discovery is, why it's important, and how it's implemented in Kubernetes. You'll also learn some troubleshooting tips.

To get the most from this chapter, you should know what Kubernetes Services are and how they work.

The chapter is split into the following sections:

- Quick background
- Service registration
- Service discovery
- Service discovery and Namespaces
- Troubleshooting service discovery

> **Note:** The word "service" has a lot of meanings. So, for clarity, we capitalise the first letter when referring to the Service resource in the Kubernetes API.

Quick background

Here's the outrageously high-level... finding stuff on a crazy-busy platform like Kubernetes is hard. Service discovery makes it simple.

Let's paint a bit more of a picture.

Kubernetes runs *cloud-native microservices* apps that scale up and down, self-heal from failures, and regularly get replaced by newer releases. All of this makes individual application Pods unreliable. To solve this, Kubernetes has a super-stable Service object that fronts unreliable application Pods with a stable IP, DNS name, and port. All good so far, but in a big bustling environment like many Kubernetes clusters, apps need a way to find the other apps they work with. This is where *service discovery* comes into play.

There are two major components to service discovery:

- Registration
- Discovery

Service registration

Service registration is the process of an application listing its connection details in a *service registry* so other apps can find it and consume it.

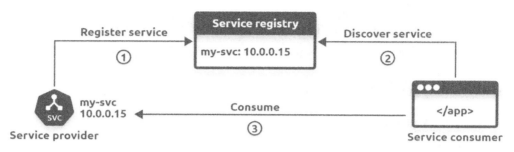

Figure 9.1

Two important things to note about service discovery in Kubernetes:

1. Kubernetes operates its internal DNS as a *service registry*
2. All Kubernetes Services are automatically registered with DNS

Kubernetes provides a *well-known* internal DNS service that we usually call the "cluster DNS". It's *well known* because every Pod in the cluster is automatically configured to know where to find it. It's implemented in the kube-system Namespace as a set of Pods managed by a Deployment called coredns and fronted by a Service called kube-dns. Behind the scenes, it's based on a DNS technology called CoreDNS and runs as a *Kubernetes-native application*.

The previous paragraph contains a lot of detail and buzzwords, so the following commands show how it's implemented. You can run them on your own Kubernetes cluster.

This command lists the Pods providing the cluster DNS.

```
$ kubectl get pods -n kube-system -l k8s-app=kube-dns
NAME                        READY   STATUS    RESTARTS   AGE
coredns-5644d7b6d9-fk4c9    1/1     Running   0          31d
coredns-5644d7b6d9-s5zlr    1/1     Running   0          31d
```

The next command lists the Deployment managing the CoreDNS Pods.

```
$ kubectl get deploy -n kube-system -l k8s-app=kube-dns
NAME      READY   UP-TO-DATE   AVAILABLE   AGE
coredns   2/2     2            2           31d
```

This command lists the Service fronting them. The ClusterIP is the *well known* IP configured on every Pod/container.

```
$ kubectl get svc -n kube-system -l k8s-app=kube-dns
NAME       TYPE        CLUSTER-IP       EXTERNAL-IP   PORT(S)                  AGE
kube-dns   ClusterIP   192.168.200.10   <none>        53/UDP,53/TCP,9153/TCP   31d
```

The process of service registration looks like this (exact flow might slightly differ):

1. You post a new Service manifest to the API server
2. The request is authenticated, authorized, and subjected to admission policies
3. The Service is allocated a stable virtual IP address called a *ClusterIP*
4. EndpointSlice objects are created to hold the list of healthy Pods matching the Service's label selector
5. The *Pod network* is configured to handle traffic sent to the ClusterIP (more on this later)
6. The Service's name and IP are registered with the cluster DNS

Step 6 is the secret sauce.

We mentioned earlier that cluster DNS is a *Kubernetes-native application.* This means it knows it's running on Kubernetes and implements a controller that watches the API server for new Service objects. Any time it observes one, it automatically creates the DNS records mapping the Service name to its ClusterIP. This means apps, and even Services, don't need to perform their own service registration – the cluster DNS does it for them.

It's important to understand that the name registered in DNS for the Service is the value stored in its `metadata.name` property. This is why it's important that Service names are valid DNS names and don't include exotic characters. The ClusterIP is dynamically assigned by Kubernetes.

```
apiVersion: v1
kind: Service
metadata:
  name: ent              <<==== this name is registered with the cluster DNS
spec:
  selector:
    app: web
  ports:
    ...
```

At this point, the Service's *front-end* configuration (name, IP, port) is registered with DNS and the Service can be discovered by apps and clients.

The Service back-end

Now that the Service's front-end is registered and can be discovered by other apps, the back-end needs building so there's something to send traffic to. This involves maintaining a list of healthy Pod IPs the Service will load-balance traffic to.

As explained in the chapter on Services, every Service has a `label selector` that determines which Pods it will load-balance traffic to. See Figure 9.2.

Figure 9.2

To help with backend operations, such as knowing which Pods to send traffic to and how traffic is routed, Kubernetes builds EndpointSlice objects for every Service.

The following command shows an EndpointSlice object for a Service called `ent`. It has the IP address and port of two Pods matching the corresponding Service's label selector.

```
$ kubectl get endpointslice ent-48vnx
NAME          ADDRESSTYPE    PORTS    ENDPOINTS                                      AGE
ent-48vnx     IPv4           8080     192.168.129.46:8080,192.168.130.127:8080       14m
```

Figure 9.3 shows the same `ent` Service that will load-balance traffic to two Pods. It also shows the EndpointSlice object with the IPs of the two Pods matching the Service's label selector. For simplicity it only shows IPv4, but IPv6 is also supported.

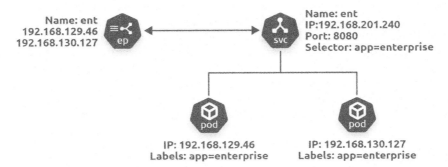

Figure 9.3

The kube-proxy agent on every node is also watching the API server for new End-pointSlice objects. When it sees one, it creates local networking rules on all worker nodes to redirect ClusterIP traffic to Pod IPs. In modern Linux-based Kubernetes clusters, the technology used to create these rules is the Linux IP Virtual Server (IPVS). Older versions used iptables.

At this point the Service is fully registered and ready to be used:

- Its front-end configuration is registered with DNS
- Its back-end label selector is created
- Its EndpointSlice objects are created
- kube-proxies have created the necessary local routing rules on worker nodes

Summarising service registration

Let's summarise the service registration process with the help of a simple flow diagram.

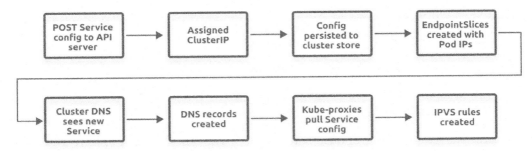

Figure 9.4

You post a new Service resource manifest to the API server where it's authenticated and authorized. The Service is allocated a ClusterIP and its configuration is persisted to the cluster store. Associated EndpointSlice objects are created to hold the list of healthy Pod IPs matching the label selector. The cluster DNS is running as a Kubernetes-native application and watching the API server for new Service objects. It observes it and registers the appropriate DNS A and SRV records. Every node is running a kube-proxy that observes the new objects and creates local IPVS/iptables rules so traffic to the Service's ClusterIP is routed to the Pods matching the Service's label selector.

Service discovery

Let's assume there are two microservices apps on the same Kubernetes cluster – enterprise and cerritos. The Pods for enterprise sit behind a Service called ent and the Pods for cerritos sit behind another Service called cer. They've been assigned ClusterIPs, registered with DNS, and things are as follows.

App	Service name	ClusterIP
Enterprise	ent	192.168.201.240
Cerritos	cer	192.168.200.217

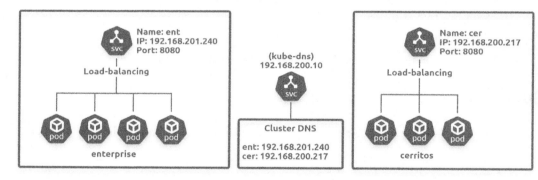

Figure 9.5

For service discovery to work, apps need to know both of the following:

1. The **name** of the Service fronting the apps they want to connect to
2. How to convert the **name** to an IP address

Application developers are responsible for point 1. They need to code apps to know the names of other apps they want to consume. Actually, they need to code the names of Services fronting the remote apps. For example, if the cerritos app wants to connect to enterprise, it needs to send requests to the ent Service.

Kubernetes takes care of point 2, converting the name to an IP.

Converting names to IP addresses using the cluster DNS

Kubernetes automatically populates every container's /etc/resolv.conf file with the IP address of the cluster DNS Service. It also adds any search domains that should be appended to unqualified names.

An "unqualified name" is a short name such as ent. Appending a search domain converts it to a fully qualified domain name (FQDN) such as ent.default.svc.cluster.local.

The following snippet shows a container that is configured to send DNS queries to the cluster DNS at 192.168.200.10. It also lists three search domains to append to unqualified names.

```
$ cat /etc/resolv.conf
search svc.cluster.local cluster.local default.svc.cluster.local
nameserver 192.168.200.10          <<==== matches ClusterIP of internal cluster DNS service
options ndots:5
```

The following snippet proves that nameserver in the previous /etc/resolv.conf matches the IP address of the cluster DNS (the kube-dns Service). This means Service names will be sent to the cluster DNS for conversion to IP addresses.

```
$ kubectl get svc -n kube-system -l k8s-app=kube-dns
NAME       TYPE        CLUSTER-IP       PORT(S)                 AGE
kube-dns   ClusterIP   192.168.200.10   53/UDP,53/TCP,9153/TCP  3h53m
```

With what you've learned so far, let's talk through how the Pods in the enterprise app will send requests to the cerritos app.

The process is as follows:

1. Know the name of the remote app (Service name)
2. Name resolution (service discovery)
3. Network routing

First up, the enterprise app needs to know the cer Service is fronting the cerritos app. That's the job of the app developer. Next, it needs to convert cer into an IP address. Fortunately, all containers know how to do this and the request is sent to the cluster DNS where it's resolved to a ClusterIP (in this case, 192.168.200.217).

All good so far, but ClusterIPs are virtual IPs that require additional magic before traffic reaches the cerritos application Pods.

Some network magic

ClusterIPs are on a *"special"* network called the *service network*, and there are no routes to it! This means containers send all ClusterIP traffic to their *default gateway*.

> **Terminology:** A *default gateway* is where systems send traffic when there's no known route. Normally, the *default gateway* forwards traffic to another device with a larger routing table in the hope it will have a route to the destination. A simple analogy might be driving from City A to City Z. The local roads in City A probably don't have signs to City Z, so you follow signs to the major highway/motorway. Once on the highway/motorway there's more chance you'll find directions to City Z. If the first signpost doesn't have a route, you keep driving until you see one that does. Occasionally you don't find a sign and you get lost or run out of battery/fuel. Routing is similar, if a system doesn't have a route for the destination network, it sends it from one default gateway to the next until hopefully a system has a route. As with driving, it's also possible you never find a route and the request times out.

The container's default gateway sends the traffic to the node it's running on.

The node doesn't have a route to the *service network* either, so it sends it to its own default gateway. Doing this causes the traffic to be processed by the node's kernel, which is where the magic happens...

Every Kubernetes node runs a system service called `kube-proxy` that implements a controller watching the API server for new Services and EndpointSlice objects. When it sees them, it creates local IPVS rules telling the node to intercept traffic destined for the Service's ClusterIP and forward it to individual Pod IPs.

This means that every time a node's kernel processes traffic headed for an address on the *service network*, a trap occurs and the traffic is redirected to the IP of a healthy Pod matching the Service's label selector.

Summarising service discovery

Let's quickly summarise the service discovery process with the help of the flow diagram in Figure 9.6.

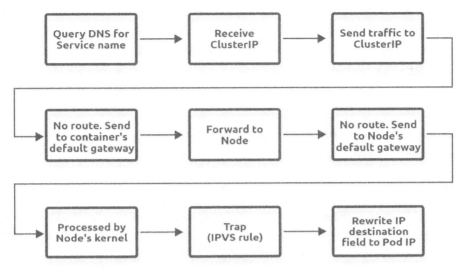

Figure 9.6

Assume the "enterprise" app is sending traffic to "cerritos". First up, it needs the name of the "cer" Service sitting in front of "cerritos". Like we said before, it's the responsibility of the application developer to make sure this is known.

An instance of the "enterprise" app tries to send traffic to the "cer" Service. However, networks work with numbers, not names. So, the container hosting the "enterprise" app sends the "cer" name to cluster DNS asking it to resolve it to an IP address. The container knows where to send this because it's pre-configured with the address of cluster DNS in its /etc/resolv.conf file. The cluster DNS replies with the ClusterIP and the "enterprise" container sends the traffic to the network. However, ClusterIPs are on the special *service network* and the container doesn't have a route to it. So, it sends it to its default gateway, which forwards it to the node it's running on. The node doesn't have a route either, so it sends it to its own default gateway. This causes the request to be processed by the node's kernel. A trap occurs and the request is redirected to the IP address of a Pod that matches the Service's label selector.

Service discovery and Namespaces

It's important to understand that every cluster has an *address space*, and we can use Namespaces to partition it.

Cluster *address spaces* are based on a DNS domain that we call the *cluster domain*. The domain name is usually cluster.local and objects have unique names within it.

For example, a Service in the default Namespace called `ent` will have a fully qualified domain name (FQDN) of `ent.default.svc.cluster.local`

The format is `<object-name>.<namespace>.svc.cluster.local`

Namespaces let you partition the address space below the cluster domain. For example, creating Namespaces called `dev` and `prod` will partition the cluster address space into the following two address spaces:

- **dev:** <service-name>.dev.svc.cluster.local
- **prod:** <service-name>.prod.svc.cluster.local

Object names have to be unique *within* a Namespace but not *across* Namespaces. For example, you can't have two Services called "ent" in the same Namespace, but you can if they're in different Namespaces. This is useful for parallel development and production configurations. For example, Figure 9.7 shows a single cluster divided into `dev` and `prod` Namespaces with identical configurations deployed to each.

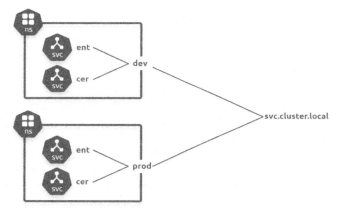

Figure 9.7

Objects can connect to Services in the local Namespace using short names such as `ent` and `cer`. But connecting to objects in a remote Namespace requires FQDNs such as `ent.dev.svc.cluster.local` and `cer.dev.svc.cluster.local`.

Service discovery example

Let's walk through a quick example.

The following YAML is called `sd-example.yml` and it's in the `service-discovery` folder of the book's GitHub repo. It defines two Namespaces, two Deployments, two

Services, and a standalone jump Pod. The two Deployments have identical names, as do the Services. This is OK as they're deployed to different Namespaces. The jump Pod is only deployed to the dev Namespace.

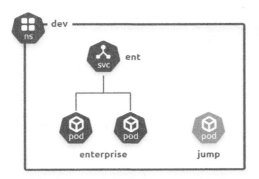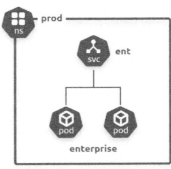

Figure 9.8

```
apiVersion: v1
kind: Namespace
metadata:
  name: dev
---
apiVersion: v1
kind: Namespace
metadata:
  name: prod
---
apiVersion: apps/v1
kind: Deployment
metadata:
  name: enterprise
  labels:
    app: enterprise
  namespace: dev
spec:
  selector:
    matchLabels:
      app: enterprise
  replicas: 2
  template:
    metadata:
      labels:
        app: enterprise
    spec:
      containers:
      - image: nigelpoulton/k8sbook:text-dev
        name: enterprise-ctr
```

```
      ports:
      - containerPort: 8080
---
apiVersion: apps/v1
kind: Deployment
metadata:
  name: enterprise
  labels:
    app: enterprise
  namespace: prod
spec:
  selector:
    matchLabels:
      app: enterprise
  replicas: 2
  template:
    metadata:
      labels:
        app: enterprise
    spec:
      containers:
      - image: nigelpoulton/k8sbook:text-prod
        name: enterprise-ctr
        ports:
        - containerPort: 8080
---
apiVersion: v1
kind: Service
metadata:
  name: ent
  namespace: dev
spec:
  selector:
    app: enterprise
  ports:
    - port: 8080
  type: ClusterIP
---
apiVersion: v1
kind: Service
metadata:
  name: ent
  namespace: prod
spec:
  selector:
    app: enterprise
  ports:
    - port: 8080
  type: ClusterIP
---
apiVersion: v1
```

```
kind: Pod
metadata:
  name: jump
  namespace: dev
spec:
  terminationGracePeriodSeconds: 5
  containers:
  - name: jump
    image: ubuntu
    tty: true
    stdin: true
```

Deploy the configuration to your cluster.

```
$ kubectl apply -f sd-example.yml
namespace/dev created
namespace/prod created
deployment.apps/enterprise created
deployment.apps/enterprise created
service/ent created
service/ent created
pod/jump-pod created
```

Check each object is correctly deployed to each Namespace. The outputs are trimmed to fit the page and don't show all objects.

```
$ kubectl get all --namespace dev
NAME            TYPE        CLUSTER-IP       EXTERNAL-IP   PORT(S)    AGE
service/ent     ClusterIP   192.168.202.57   <none>        8080/TCP   43s

NAME                          READY   UP-TO-DATE   AVAILABLE   AGE
deployment.apps/enterprise    2/2     2            2           43s
<snip>

$ kubectl get all --namespace prod
NAME            TYPE        CLUSTER-IP        EXTERNAL-IP   PORT(S)    AGE
service/ent     ClusterIP   192.168.203.158   <none>        8080/TCP   52s

NAME                          READY   UP-TO-DATE   AVAILABLE   AGE
deployment.apps/enterprise    2/2     2            2           52s
<snip>
```

You have an enterprise app and ent Service in both Namespaces (dev and prod). You also have a jump Pod in the dev Namespace. Let's test how service discovery works **within** a Namespace and **across** Namespaces.

The next steps will:

1. Log on to the jump Pod in the dev Namespace
2. Check its /etc/resolv.conf file
3. Connect to ent in the **local** dev Namespace
4. Connect to ent in the **remote** prod Namespace

To help with the demo, the apps used in each Namespace return different messages.
Connect to the jump Pod.

```
$ kubectl exec -it jump --namespace dev -- bash
root@jump:/#
```

Your terminal prompt will change to indicate you are attached to the jump Pod.

Inspect the contents of the /etc/resolv.conf file and verify the search domains
listed include the dev Namespace (search dev.svc.cluster.local) and not the prod
Namespace.

```
# cat /etc/resolv.conf
search dev.svc.cluster.local svc.cluster.local cluster.local default.svc.cluster.local
nameserver 192.168.200.10
options ndots:5
```

The search domains lists the dev Namespace, and the nameserver is set to the IP of the
cluster DNS.

Install the curl utility.

```
# apt-get update && apt-get install curl -y
<snip>
```

Use curl to connect to the version of the app running in dev by using the ent short
name. The app listens on port 8080.

```
# curl ent:8080
Hello from the DEV Namespace!
Hostname: enterprise-7d49557d8d-k4jjz
```

The "Hello from the DEV Namespace" response proves the connection reached the
instance in the dev Namespace.

When the curl command was issued, the container automatically appended
dev.svc.cluster.local to the ent name and sent the query to the cluster DNS
specified in /etc/resolv.conf. DNS returned the ClusterIP for the ent Service in the
local dev Namespace and the app

sent the traffic to that address. En-route to the node's default gateway the traffic caused a trap in the node's kernel and was redirected to one of the Pods hosting the app.

Run the curl command again, however, this time append the domain name of the prod Namespace. This will cause the cluster DNS to return the ClusterIP for the instance in the prod Namespace and traffic will eventually reach a Pod running in prod.

```
# curl ent.prod.svc.cluster.local:8080
Hello from the PROD Namespace!
Hostname: enterprise-5464d8c4f9-v7xsk
```

This time the response comes from a Pod in the prod Namespace.

The test proves that short names are automatically resolved to the local Namespace, and FQDNs are required to connect across Namespaces.

Remember to detach your terminal from the jump Pod by typing exit.

Troubleshooting service discovery

Service registration and discovery involves a lot of moving parts. If any of them stops working, the whole process can break. Let's quickly run through what needs to be working and how to check.

As previously mentioned, Kubernetes uses the cluster DNS as its *service registry*. This runs as one or more Pods in the kube-system Namespace with a Service object providing a stable endpoint. The important components are:

- Pods: Managed by the coredns Deployment
- Service: A ClusterIP Service called kube-dns listening on port 53 TCP/UDP
- EndpointSlice objects: Names pre-fixed with kube-dns

All objects relating to the cluster DNS are in the kube-system Namespace and tagged with the k8s-app=kube-dns label. This is helpful when filtering kubectl output.

Make sure the coredns Deployment and its managed Pods are up and running.

```
$ kubectl get deploy -n kube-system -l k8s-app=kube-dns
NAME      READY   UP-TO-DATE   AVAILABLE   AGE
coredns   2/2     2            2           28d

$ kubectl get pods -n kube-system -l k8s-app=kube-dns
NAME                       READY   STATUS    RESTARTS   AGE
coredns-5644d7b6d9-74pv7   1/1     Running   0          28d
coredns-5644d7b6d9-s759f   1/1     Running   0          28d
```

Check the logs from each of the coredns Pods. You'll need to substitute the names of the Pods in your environment. The following output is typical of a working DNS Pod.

```
$ kubectl logs coredns-5644d7b6d9-74pv7 -n kube-system
2022-01-3T21:31:01.456Z [INFO] plugin/reload: Running configuration...
CoreDNS-1.6.2
linux/amd64, go1.12.8, 795a3eb
```

Assuming the Pods and Deployment are working, you should also check the Service and associated Endpoints object. The output should show the service is up, has an IP address in the ClusterIP field, and is listening on port 53 TCP/UDP.

The ClusterIP address for the kube-dns Service should match the IP address in the /etc/resolv.conf files of all containers on the cluster. If the IP addresses are different, containers will send DNS requests to the wrong place.

```
$ kubectl get svc kube-dns -n kube-system
NAME       TYPE        CLUSTER-IP       EXTERNAL-IP   PORT(S)                  AGE
kube-dns   ClusterIP   192.168.200.10   <none>        53/UDP,53/TCP,9153/TCP   28d
```

The associated kube-dns EndpointSlice object should also be up and have the IP addresses of the coredns Pods listening on port 53.

```
$ kubectl get endpointslice -n kube-system -l k8s-app=kube-dns
NAME             ADDRESSTYPE   PORTS        ENDPOINTS        AGE
kube-dns-m5rg6   IPv4          9153,53,53   192.168.128.24   28d
```

Once you've verified the fundamental DNS components are up and working, you can perform more detailed and in-depth troubleshooting. Here are some simple tips.

Start a *troubleshooting Pod* that has your favourite networking tools installed (ping, traceroute, curl, dig, nslookup etc.). The standard gcr.io/kubernetes-e2e-test-images/dnsutils:1.3 image is a popular choice if you don't have your own custom image with your tools installed. Unfortunately, there's no image tagged as latest in the repo, meaning you have to specify a version. At the time of writing, 1.3 has been the latest version for a very long time.

The following command starts a new standalone Pod called dnsutils based on the dnsutils image just mentioned. It will also connect your terminal to it.

```
$ kubectl run -it dnsutils \
  --image gcr.io/kubernetes-e2e-test-images/dnsutils:1.3
```

A common way to test DNS resolution is to use nslookup to resolve the kubernetes Service fronting the API server. The query should return an IP address as well as the name kubernetes.default.svc.cluster.local.

```
# nslookup kubernetes
Server:         192.168.200.10
Address:        192.168.200.10#53
Name:   kubernetes.default.svc.cluster.local
Address: 192.168.200.1
```

The first two lines should return the IP address of your cluster DNS. The last two lines should show the FQDN of the kubernetes Service and its ClusterIP. You can verify the ClusterIP of the kubernetes Service by running a kubectl get svc kubernetes command.

Errors such as "nslookup: can't resolve kubernetes" are possible indicators that DNS isn't working. A possible solution is to recreate the coredns Pods. The easiest way to do this is just to delete them and let the owning Deployment recreate them.

The following command deletes the DNS Pods and must be ran from a terminal with kubectl installed. If you're still logged on to the dnsutils Pod, you'll need to type exit to disconnect.

```
$ kubectl delete pod -n kube-system -l k8s-app=kube-dns
pod "coredns-5644d7b6d9-2pdmd" deleted
pod "coredns-5644d7b6d9-wsjzp" deleted
```

Run a kubectl get pod -n kube-system -l k8s-app=kube-dns to verify they've restarted, and then test DNS again.

Chapter summary

In this chapter, you learned that Kubernetes uses the internal cluster DNS for service registration and service discovery.

All new Service objects are automatically registered with the cluster DNS, and all containers are pre-configured to use the cluster DNS for service discovery.

The cluster DNS resolves Service names to ClusterIPs. These are stable virtual IPs on a special network called the *service network*. Although there are no routes to this network, the kube-proxy configures all cluster nodes to redirect traffic destined for the service network to Pod IPs on the Pod network.

10: Kubernetes storage

Storing and retrieving important data is critical to most real-world business applications. Fortunately, Kubernetes has a mature and feature-rich storage subsystem called the *persistent volume subsystem*. The 3rd-party ecosystem also extends this with products that provide data management services such as backup and recovery, remote replication, snapshots and more.

The chapter is divided as follows:

- The big picture
- Storage providers
- The Container Storage Interface (CSI)
- The Kubernetes persistent volume subsystem
- Dynamic provisioning with Storage Classes
- Hands-on

Kubernetes supports a variety of storage back-ends. These include enterprise-class storage systems from providers such as EMC and NetApp, as well as cloud storage back-ends. Each of these requires slightly different configuration. The examples in this chapter are designed to work on Google Kubernetes Engine (GKE) clusters and will not work on other cluster types. However, the principles and theory are applicable to the majority of Kubernetes environments.

The big picture

Kubernetes supports lots of types of storage from lots of different places. For example, block, file, and object storage from a variety of external systems that can be in the cloud or your on-premises datacenters. However, no matter what type of storage, or where it comes from, when it's exposed to Kubernetes it's called a *volume*. For example, Azure File resources surfaced in Kubernetes are called *volumes*, as are block devices from an HPE 3PAR array, or object storage from Alicloud.

Figure 10.1 shows the high-level architecture.

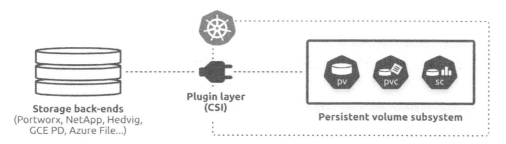

Figure 10.1

On the left are storage providers. They can be traditional enterprise storage arrays from established vendors like EMC and NetApp, or they can be cloud storage services such as AWS Elastic Block Store (EBS) and GCE Persistent Disks (PD). All that's required is a *plugin* allowing the storage resources to be surfaced as volumes in Kubernetes.

In the middle of the diagram is the plugin layer. In simple terms, this is the interface that connects external storage with Kubernetes. Modern plugins are be based on the **Container Storage Interface** *(CSI)* which is an open standard aimed at providing a clean storage interface for container orchestrators such as Kubernetes. If you're a developer writing storage plugins, the CSI abstracts the internal Kubernetes machinery and lets you develop *out-of-tree*.

> **Note:** Prior to the CSI, all storage plugins were implemented as part of the main Kubernetes code tree (*in-tree*). This meant they had to be open-source, and all updates and bug-fixes were tied to the main Kubernetes release-cycle. This was a problem for storage providers as well as the Kubernetes maintainers. However, now that we have the CSI, storage vendors no longer need to open-source their code, and they can release updates and bug-fixes against their own timeframes.

On the right of Figure 10.1 is the Kubernetes persistent volume subsystem. This is a set of API objects that make it easy for applications to consume storage. There are a growing number of storage-related API objects, but the core ones are:

- Persistent Volumes (PV)
- Persistent Volume Claims (PVC)
- Storage Classes (SC)

Throughout the chapter, we may refer to them by their PascalCase truncated API names – *PersistentVolume, PersistentVolumeClaim, and StorageClass*. We will also use their shortnames, PV, PVC, and SC.

PVs map to external storage assets, PVCs are like tickets that authorize applications (Pods) to use them, and SCs make it all automatic and dynamic.

Consider the quick example in Figure 10.2.

A Kubernetes cluster is running on AWS and the AWS administrator has created a 25GB EBS volume called "ebs-vol". She creates a PV called "k8s-vol" that maps back to the "ebs-vol" via the ebs.csi.aws.com CSI plugin. While that might sound complicated, it's not. The PV is simply a way of representing the external storage asset on the Kubernetes cluster. Finally, the Pod uses a PVC to claim access to the PV and start using it.

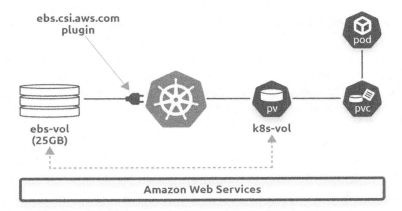

Figure 10.2

A few things worth noting:

1. This was a manual process involving the AWS administrator. StorageClasses automate things.

2. There are rules preventing multiple Pods accessing the same volume (more on this later).

3. You cannot map an external storage volume to multiple PVs. For example, you cannot provision a 50GB external volume that is used as two 25GB Kubernetes PVs.

Let's dig a bit deeper.

Storage Providers

As previously mentioned, Kubernetes uses storage from a wide range of 3rd-party systems including cloud storage and dedicated storage hardware devices.

Some obvious restrictions apply. For example, you can't use AWS storage services if your Kubernetes cluster is running in Microsoft Azure. However, each provider (a.k.a provisioner) needs a CSI plugin to expose their storage assets to Kubernetes. The plugin usually runs as a set of Pods in the kube-system Namespace.

The Container Storage Interface (CSI)

The CSI is a vital piece of the Kubernetes storage jigsaw and has been instrumental in bringing enterprise-grade storage from traditional vendors to Kubernetes. However, unless you're a developer writing storage plugins, you're unlikely to interact with it very often.

It's an open-source project that defines a standards-based interface so that storage can be leveraged in a uniform way across multiple container orchestrators. For example, a storage vendor *should* be able to write a single CSI plugin that works across multiple orchestrators such as Kubernetes and Docker Swarm. In practice, Kubernetes is the focus, but Docker is implementing support for the CSI.

From a day-to-day perspective, your main interaction with the CSI will be referencing the appropriate CSI plugin in your YAML manifest files and reading its documentation to find supported features and attributes.

Sometimes we call plugins *"provisioners"*, especially when we talk about Storage Classes later in the chapter.

The Kubernetes persistent volume subsystem

From a day-to-day perspective, this is where you'll spend most of your time configuring and interacting with storage.

You start out with raw storage on the left of Figure 10.3. This *plugs in* to Kubernetes via a CSI plugin. You then use persistent volume subsystem API resources to leverage and use the storage in your apps.

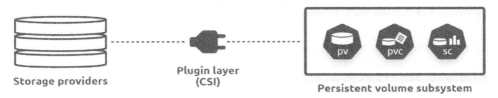

Storage providers   Plugin layer (CSI)   Persistent volume subsystem

Figure 10.3

The three core API resources in the persistent volume subsystem are:

- Persistent Volumes (PV)
- Persistent Volume Claims (PVC)
- Storage Classes (SC)

Others exist, and storage vendors can extend the Kubernetes API with their own resources to support advanced features.

At a high level, **PVs** are how external storage assets are represented in Kubernetes. **PVCs** are like tickets that grant a Pod access to a PV. **SCs** make it all dynamic.

Let's walk through another example.

Assume you have an external storage system with two tiers of storage:

- Flash/SSD fast storage
- Mechanical slow archive storage

You expect apps on your Kubernetes cluster to use both, so you create the following two *Storage Classes*.

External tier	Kubernetes Storage Class name
SSD	sc-fast
Mechanical	sc-slow

With the *StorageClass* objects in place, applications can create volumes on-the-fly by creating *Persistent Volume Claims (PVC)* that reference either of the storage classes. Each time this happens, the CSI plugin instructs the external storage system to create an appropriate storage asset. This is automatically mapped to a PV on Kubernetes and the app uses the PVC to claim it and mount it for use.

Don't worry if it seems confusing, it'll make sense when you go through the hands-on later.

Before doing that, you need to learn a bit more about PVCs and SCs.

Dynamic provisioning with Storage Classes

As the name suggests, storage classes allow you to define different classes/tiers of storage. How you define them is up to you and will depend on the types of storage you have available. For example, if your external storage systems support fast and slow storage, as well as remote replication, you might define these three classes:

- `fast-local`
- `fast-replicated`
- `slow-archive-local`

As far as Kubernetes goes, storage classes are resources in the `storage.k8s.io/v1` API group. The resource type is `StorageClass`, and you define them in regular YAML files that you post to the API server for deployment. You can use the `sc` shortname to refer to them when using `kubectl`.

> **Note:** You can use `kubectl api-resources` to see a full list of API resources and their shortnames. It also shows if the resource is namespaced, its API group, and what its equivalent `kind` is when writing YAML files.

A StorageClass YAML

The following SC defines a class of storage called "fast-local", based on AWS solid state drives (`io1`) in the Ireland Region (`eu-west-1a`). It also requests a performance level of 10 IOPs per gigabyte and encrypted volumes. Writing this file requires knowledge of AWS storage and reading the plugin documentation.

```
kind: StorageClass
apiVersion: storage.k8s.io/v1
metadata:
  name: fast-local
provisioner: ebs.csi.aws.com           <<==== AWS Elastic Block Store CSI plugin
parameters:
  type: io1                            <<==== AWS SSD drives
  iopsPerGB: "10"
  encrypted: true
allowedTopologies:
- matchLabelExpressions:
  - key: topology.ebs.csi.aws.com/zone
    values:
    - eu-west-1a
```

As with all Kubernetes YAML, `kind` tells the API server the type of object being defined and `apiVersion` tells it which version of the schema to use when creating it. `metadata.name` is an arbitrary string that lets you give the object a friendly name – this example is defining a class called "fast-local". The `provisioner` field tells Kubernetes which plugin to use, and the `parameters` block lets you finely tune the storage attributes. Finally, the `allowedTopologies` property lets you list where replicas should go.

A few quick things worth noting:

1. StorageClass objects are immutable – you can't modify them after they're deployed
2. `metadata.name` should be meaningful as it's how **you** and other objects refer to the class
3. The terms *provisioner* and *plugin* are used interchangeably
4. The `parameters` block is for plugin-specific values

Regarding point 4, each plugin is free to support its own set of values. Configuring this section requires knowledge of the storage plugin and the associated storage back-end. Each provisioner usually provides documentation to help with this.

Multiple StorageClasses

You can configure as many StorageClasses as you need. However, each one relates to a single type of storage on a single back-end. For example, if you have a Kubernetes cluster with OpenEBS and Portworx storage back-ends, you'll need at least one StorageClasses for each.

On the flip-side, each back-end storage system can offer multiple classes/tiers of storage, each of which needs its own StorageClass. A simple example we'll see later is the slower `standard persistent disk` and the faster `SSD persistent disk` tiers offered by the Google Cloud back-end. These are typically implemented with the following SCs on a GKE cluster:

1. `standard-rwo` for the slower standard disk
2. `premium-rwo` for the faster SSD

The following SC defines a block storage volume on a Commvault Distributed Storage System (formerly called Hedvig) that is replicated between datacenters in Sunderland and New York. It will only work if you have Commvault Distributed Storage Systems at both sites with appropriate replication configured.

```
kind: StorageClass
apiVersion: storage.k8s.io/v1
metadata:
  name: sc-hedvig-rep
provisioner: io.hedvig.csi
parameters:
  backendType: "hedvig-block"
  rp: "DataCenterAware"
  dcNames: "sunderland,new-york"
```

As you can see, the parameters block defines the interesting values and requires knowledge of the plugin and the storage back-end. Consult your storage plugin documentation for details.

Working with StorageClasses

The basic workflow for deploying *and using* a StorageClass is as follows:

1. Have a storage back-end (can be cloud or on premises)
2. Have a Kubernetes cluster connected to the back-end storage
3. Install and configure the CSI storage plugin
4. Create one or more StorageClasses on Kubernetes
5. Deploy Pods with PVCs that reference those StorageClasses

The following YAML snippet defines a StorageClass, a PersistentVolumeClaim, and a Pod. All three objects can be defined in a single YAML file by separating them with three dashes (---).

Pay close attention to how the Pod references the PVC by name, and in turn, the PVC references the SC by name.

```
kind: StorageClass
apiVersion: storage.k8s.io/v1
metadata:
  name: fast                      <<==== Referenced by the PVC
provisioner: pd.csi.storage.gke.io
parameters:
  type: pd-ssd
---
apiVersion: v1
kind: PersistentVolumeClaim
metadata:
  name: mypvc                     <<==== Referenced by the PodSpec
spec:
  accessModes:
```

```
    - ReadWriteOnce
  resources:
    requests:
      storage: 50Gi
  storageClassName: fast          <<==== Matches name of the SC
---
apiVersion: v1
kind: Pod
metadata:
  name: mypod
spec:
  volumes:
    - name: data
      persistentVolumeClaim:
        claimName: mypvc          <<==== Matches PVC name
  containers: ...
  <SNIP>
```

The previous YAML is truncated and doesn't include a full PodSpec.

So far, you've seen a few SC definitions. However, each one was slightly different as each one related to a different provisioner (storage plugin/back-end). You'll need to refer to your plugin documentation to know which options yours supports.

Additional volume settings

There are a few other important settings you can configure in a StorageClass. We'll cover:

- Access mode
- Reclaim policy

Access mode

Kubernetes supports three volume access modes:

- ReadWriteOnce (RWO)
- ReadWriteMany (RWM)
- ReadOnlyMany (ROM)

ReadWriteOnce defines a PV that can only be bound as R/W by a single PVC. Attempts to bind it from multiple PVCs will fail.

ReadWriteMany defines a PV that can be bound as R/W by multiple PVCs. This mode is usually only supported by file and object storage such as NFS. Block storage usually only supports RWO.

`ReadOnlyMany` defines a PV that can be bound as R/O by multiple PVCs.

It's important to understand that a PV can only be opened in one mode. For example, it's not possible for a single PV to be bound to a PVC in ROM mode and another PVC in RWM mode.

Reclaim policy

A volume's `ReclaimPolicy` tells Kubernetes how to deal with a PV when its PVC is released. Two policies currently exist:

- `Delete`
- `Retain`

`Delete` is the most dangerous and is the default for PVs created dynamically via *storage classes*. It deletes the PV **and associated storage resource on the external storage system** when the PVC is released. This means all data will be lost! Use with caution.

`Retain` will keep the associated PV object on the cluster as well as any data stored on the external system. However, other PVCs are prevented from using it in future. The obvious disadvantage is it requires manual clean-up.

Let's quickly summarize what you've learned about storage classes before walking through a demo.

StorageClasses (SC) let you dynamically create physical back-end storage resources that get automatically mapped to Persistent Volumes (PV) on Kubernetes. You define SCs in YAML files that reference a plugin and tie them to a particular tier of storage on a particular storage back-end. For example, *high-performance AWS SSD storage in the AWS Mumbai Region.* The SC needs a name, and you deploy it using `kubectl apply`. Once deployed, the SC watches the API server for new PVCs that reference it. When matching PVCs appear, the SC dynamically creates the required asset on the back-end storage system and maps it to a PV on Kubernetes. Apps can then claim it by referencing the PVC name.

There's always more detail, such as *mount options* and *volume binding modes*, but what you've learned so far is enough to get you started.

Let's bring everything together with a demo.

Hands-on

This section walks you through using StorageClasses to dynamically provision storage on an external storage system and map it to Kubernetes. We'll split the work as follows:

- Use an existing storage class
- Create and use a new storage class

The examples will only work on a *regional* Google Kubernetes Engine (GKE) cluster with the CSI plugin installed. If you created a GKE cluster as shown in Chapter 3, you're ready to go. If your Kubernetes cluster is somewhere else, the StorageClass YAML won't work, but the overall workflow will be the same.

Using an existing StorageClass

The following command lists all SCs defined on a typical GKE cluster. Yours may look different.

```
$ kubectl get sc
                                            RECLAIM                           ALLOWVOL
NAME                 PROVISIONER            POLICY   VOLUMEBINDINGMODE        EXPANSION
premium-rwo          pd.csi.storage.gke.io  Delete   WaitForFirstConsumer     true
standard             kubernetes.io/gce-pd   Delete   Immediate                true
standard-rwo (def)   pd.csi.storage.gke.io  Delete   WaitForFirstConsumer     true
```

There's quite a lot to learn from the output.

First up, all three SCs were automatically created when the cluster was built. This is common on hosted Kubernetes platforms.

The one on the second line is listed as the "default". This means it'll be used by PVCs that don't explicitly specify an SC. Default SCs are only useful in development environments and times when you don't have specific storage requirements. In production environments you should always specify an SC that meets application requirements.

The PROVISIONER column shows two of the SCs using the CSI plugin, the other is using the legacy in-tree plugin.

The RECLAIM POLICY is set to Delete for all three. This means PVs created by these SCs will be deleted when the PVC is released. The alternative is Retain.

Setting VOLUMEBINDINGMODE to "Immediate" will create the volume on the external storage system as soon as the PVC is created. This can be problematic if you have multiple datacenters or cloud regions, as the Pod that eventually consumes it might be in a different datacenter or region. Setting it to WaitForFirstConsumer will delay creation until a Pod using the PVC is created. This ensures the volume will always be created in the same datacenter or region as the Pod.

You can use kubectl describe to get more detailed information, and kubectl get sc <name> -o yaml will show the full configuration in YAML format.

```
$ kubectl describe sc premium-rwo
Name:                   premium-rwo
IsDefaultClass:         No
Annotations:            components.gke.io/component-name=pdcsi,components.gke...
Provisioner:            pd.csi.storage.gke.io
Parameters:             type=pd-ssd
AllowVolumeExpansion:   True
MountOptions:           <none>
ReclaimPolicy:          Delete
VolumeBindingMode:      WaitForFirstConsumer
Events:                 <none>
```

Let's create a new volume using the built-in premium-rwo SC.

List any existing PVs and PVCs so that it's easy to identify the ones you'll create in the next steps.

```
$ kubectl get pv
No resources found
$ kubectl get pvc
No resources found in default namespace.
```

The following PVC definition is from the pvc-gke-premium.yml file in the storage folder of the book's GitHub repo. It describes a PVC called pvc-prem that will provision a 10GB volume via the premium-rwo StorageClass. It will only work if your GKE cluster has a StorageClass called premium-rwo.

```
apiVersion: v1
kind: PersistentVolumeClaim
metadata:
  name: pvc-prem
spec:
  accessModes:
  - ReadWriteOnce
  storageClassName: premium-rwo
  resources:
    requests:
      storage: 10Gi
```

Create the PVC with the following command. Be sure to run it from the folder where the YAML file exists.

```
$ kubectl apply -f pvc-gke-premium.yml
persistentvolumeclaim/pvc-prem created
```

The following commands show the PVC has been created. However, it's in the pending state and no PV has been created. This is because the premium-rwo StorageClass volume binding mode is set to WaitForFirstConsumer meaning it won't provision a volume and PV until a Pod claims it.

```
$ kubectl get pv
No resources found

$ kubectl get pvc
NAME       STATUS    VOLUME    CAPACITY    ACCESS MODES    STORAGECLASS    AGE
pvc-prem   Pending                                         premium-rwo     39s
```

The following snipped YAML shows a Pod that will mount the volume via the `pvc-prem` PVC.

```
apiVersion: v1
kind: Pod
metadata:
  name: volpod
spec:
  volumes:
  - name: data                <<==== Create new volume called "data"
    persistentVolumeClaim:    <<==== based on the PVC
      claimName: pvc-prem.    <<==== with this name
  containers:
  - name: ubuntu-ctr
    ...
    volumeMounts:             <<==== Mount the volume
    - name: data              <<==== called data (see above)
      mountPath: /data        <<==== to this directory
```

Create the Pod with the following command.

```
$ kubectl apply -f prempod.yml
pod/volpod created
```

Give the Pod a minute to start, then re-check the status of any PVCs and PVs.

```
$ kubectl get pvc
NAME       STATUS    VOLUME          CAPACITY    ACCESS MODES    STORAGECLASS    AGE
pvc-prem   Bound     pvc-796afda3... 10Gi        RWO             premium-rwo     108s

$ kubectl get pv
NAME           CAPACITY    MODES    RECLAIM POLICY    STATUS    CLAIM              STORAGECLASS
pvc-796af...   10Gi        RWO      Delete            Bound     default/pvc-prem   premium-rwo
```

The PVC is now bound and an associated PV has been created. If you check the Google Cloud backend, you'll see a new persistent disk created with the same name (see Google Cloud Console > Kubernetes Engine > Storage). The PVC is also mounted into the running Pod and you can check this with a `kubectl get pods volpod` command.

Delete the Pod and the PVC.

```
$ kubectl delete pod volpod
pod "volpod" deleted

$ kubectl delete pvc pvc-prem
persistentvolumeclaim "pvc-prem" deleted
```

When the PVC is deleted, the PV and associated volume on the Google Cloud back-end will be automatically deleted. This is because the PVC was created through the premium-rwo SC which has the ReclaimPolicy set to Delete. Verify this.

```
$ kubectl get pv
No resources found
```

You can also check in the Google Cloud Console by going to Kubernetes Engine > Storage.

Creating and using a new storage class

In this section, you'll create your own new storage class and use it to create a new volume.

The SC you'll create is defined in the sc-gke-fast-repl.yml file in the storage folder of the book's GitHub repo and defines a class called "sc-fast-repl" with the following properties:

- Fast SSD storage (type: pd-ssd)
- Replicated (replication-type: regional-pd)
- Create on demand (volumeBindingMode: WaitForFirstConsumer)
- Keep data when the PVC is deleted (reclaimPolicy: Retain)

```
apiVersion: storage.k8s.io/v1
kind: StorageClass
metadata:
  name: sc-fast-repl
provisioner: pd.csi.storage.gke.io
parameters:
  type: pd-ssd
  replication-type: regional-pd
volumeBindingMode: WaitForFirstConsumer
reclaimPolicy: Retain
```

Deploy the SC and verify it exists. You must run the command from the folder containing the YAML file and it will only work on *regional* GKE clusters with the GKE CSI driver.

```
$ kubectl apply -f sc-gke-fast-repl.yml
storageclass.storage.k8s.io/sc-fast-repl created

$ kubectl get sc
                                         RECLAIM                          ALLOWVOLUME
NAME            PROVISIONER              POLICY    VOLUMEBINDINGMODE      EXPANSION
premium-rwo     pd.csi.storage.gke.io    Delete    WaitForFirstConsumer  true
sc-fast-repl    pd.csi.storage.gke.io    Retain    WaitForFirstConsumer  true
...
```

With the SC in place, deploy the app and PVC defined in the `vol-app.yml` file. It defines a 20G PVC called "pvc2" based on the newly created `sc-fast-repl` SC. It also defines a Pod that mounts a volume from it.

```
apiVersion: v1
kind: PersistentVolumeClaim            <<==== Create a new PVC
metadata:
  name: pvc2                           <<==== Call it pvc2
spec:
  accessModes:
  - ReadWriteOnce
  storageClassName: sc-fast-repl       <<==== Base it on this SC
  resources:
    requests:
      storage: 20Gi                    <<==== Make it 20Gi
---
apiVersion: v1                         <<==== This Pod claims it
kind: Pod
metadata:
  name: volpod
spec:
  volumes:
  - name: data
    persistentVolumeClaim:
      claimName: pvc2
      ...
```

When you deploy the app, a new PVC and PV will be created, as well as a replicated persistent disk on the Google Cloud back-end. It will also be mounted into the Pod called `volpod`.

```
$ kubectl apply -f vol-app.yml
persistentvolumeclaim/pvc2 created
pod/volpod created
```

Use `kubectl` to check the PVC and PV exist.

The mechanics behind the operation that created the PV are as follows:

1. You created the `sc-fast-repl` StorageClass
2. The SC controller started watching the API server for new PVCs referencing it
3. The app you deployed created the `pvc2` PVC requesting a 20GB volume from the `sc-fast-repl` *StorageClass*
4. The StorageClass controller noticed the PVC and dynamically created the back-end volume and PV

Congratulations. You've seen how to create a StorageClass and dynamically create volumes from it.

Clean-up

The Pod and PVC were both deployed from the `vol-app.yml` file. This means you can delete them both with the following command.

```
$ kubectl delete -f vol-app.yml
persistentvolumeclaim "pvc2" deleted
pod "volpod" deleted
```

Even though the Pod and PVC are deleted, a `kubectl get pv` will show the PV still exists. This is because the class it was created from is using the `Retain` reclaim policy. This keeps PVs, associated back-end volumes, **and data** even when PVCs are deleted. You can verify this in the Google Cloud back-end (`Compute Engine > Disks` and check for a 20G regional disk with the same name).

Manually delete the PV with a `kubectl delete pv` command and then be sure to delete the regional disk on the Google Cloud back-end. Failure to delete the regional disk on the back-end may result in unexpected charges.

Chapter Summary

In this chapter, you learned that Kubernetes has a powerful storage subsystem that allows it to dynamically provision and leverage storage from a wide variety of external storage systems.

Each back-end requires a CSI plugin to expose its assets to Kubernetes.

Once the plugin is installed, you create StorageClass objects that map to a type or tier of storage on the back-end. The StorageClass controller operates in the background watching the API server for new PVC objects referencing it. Each time it sees one, it creates the requested storage asset on the back-end and maps it to a new PV on the cluster. Pods can then reference the PVC to mount the PV for use.

11: ConfigMaps and Secrets

Most business applications comprise two main parts:

- The application
- The configuration

Simple examples include web servers such as NGINX or httpd (Apache). Neither is very useful without a configuration. However, when you combine them with a configuration, they become extremely useful.

In the past, we coupled the application and the configuration into a single easy-to-deploy unit. As we moved into the early days of cloud-native microservices we brought this model with us. However, it's an *anti-pattern* and modern applications should be decoupled from their configurations. Doing this brings the following benefits:

- Re-use
- Simpler development and testing
- Simpler and less-disruptive changes

We'll explain all of these, and more, as we go through the chapter.

> **Note:** An *anti-pattern* is something that seems like a good idea but turns out to be a bad idea.

The chapter is divided as follows:

- The big picture
- ConfigMap theory
- Hands-on with ConfigMaps
- Hands-on with Secrets

The big picture

As already mentioned, most applications comprise an application binary and a configuration. With Kubernetes, you build and store each one separately, and bring them together at run-time.

Quick example

Imagine you work for a company that deploys modern applications to Kubernetes, and you have three distinct environments:

- Dev
- Test
- Prod

Your developers write and update applications. Initial testing is performed in the *dev* environment. Further testing is done in the *test* environment where more stringent rules and policies are applied. Finally, stable components graduate to the *prod* environment.

However, each environment has subtle differences such as network policies, security policies, and different sets of credentials and certificates.

You currently package each application microservice with its configuration baked into the container. This forces you to perform all of the following for every business application:

- *Build* three distinct images (one for dev, one for test, one for prod)
- *Store* the images in three distinct repositories (one for dev, one for test, one for prod)
- *Run* different versions in specific environments (dev in dev, test in test, prod in prod)

Every time you change the config of the app, even small changes like fixing a typo, you'll need to build, test, store, and re-deploy three distinct images – one for dev, one for test, one for prod.

It's also harder to troubleshoot an issue if you push an update that includes both an application binary update as well as a configuration update. If the two are tightly coupled, it's harder to isolate the fault. Also, if you need to make a minor configuration change (such as fix a typo on a web page) you need to re-package, re-test, and re-deploy the entire application **and** configuration.

What it looks like in a de-coupled world

Now consider you work for the same company, but this time your application and its configuration are de-coupled. This time:

- You *build* and maintain a single application image that's shared across all environments

- You *store* and protect that single image in a single repository
- You *run* that single version of the image in all environments

To make this work, you build your application images as generically as possible with no embedded configuration. You then create and store distinct configurations for each environment in separate objects that you apply at runtime. For example, you have a single copy of a web server that you can use across all three environments. When you deploy it to *prod* you apply the *prod* configuration. When you run it in *dev*, you apply the *dev* configuration...

In this model, you create and test a single version of each application image that you store in a single repository. All staff can have access to the image repository as it contains no sensitive data. Finally, you can easily push changes to the application and its configuration independent of each other – updating a simple typo in a config no longer requires the entire application binary and image to be rebuilt, tested, and re-deployed (x3).

You can even re-use images across different apps. For example, a hardened stripped-down NGINX image can be used by lots of different apps – just apply different configs.

Let's see how Kubernetes makes this possible...

ConfigMap theory

Kubernetes provides an object called a ConfigMap (CM) that lets you store configuration data outside of a Pod and inject at runtime.

> **Note:** When we use the term *Pod* we often mean container. After all, it is ultimately a container that receives the configuration data and runs the app.

ConfigMaps are first-class objects in the *core* API group. They're also v1. This tells us a few things:

1. They're stable (v1)
2. They've been around for a while (new stuff never goes in the core API group)
3. You can operate on them with the usual kubectl commands
4. They can be defined and deployed via the usual YAML manifests

ConfigMaps are typically used to store non-sensitive configuration data such as:

- Environment variables

- Configuration files (things like web server configs and database configs)
- Hostnames
- Service ports
- Accounts names

You should **not** use ConfigMaps to store sensitive data such as certificates and passwords. Kubernetes provides *Secrets*, for storing sensitive data. Secrets and ConfigMaps are very similar in design and implementation, the major difference is that Kubernetes takes steps to obscure the data stored in Secrets. It makes no such efforts to obscure data in ConfigMaps.

You'll see Secrets at the end of the chapter.

How ConfigMaps work

At a high-level, a ConfigMap is a place to store configuration data that can be seamlessly injected into containers at runtime. As far as apps are concerned, there is no ConfigMap – the config data is simply where it's expected and the app has no idea it was put there by a ConfigMap.

Let's look a bit closer…

Behind the scenes, ConfigMaps are a map of key-value pairs and we call each pair an *entry*:

- **Keys** are an arbitrary name that can be created from alphanumerics, dashes, dots, and underscores
- **Values** can contain anything, including multiple lines with carriage returns
- Keys and values are separated by a colon – `key:value`

Some simple examples might be:

- db-port:13306
- hostname:msb-prd-db1

More complex examples include entire configuration files like this one:

```
key: conf
value:

directive in;
main block;
http {
  server {
    listen        80 default_server;
    server_name   *.nigelpoulton.com;
    root          /var/www/nigelpoulton.com;
    index         index.html

    location / {
      root  /usr/share/nginx/html;
      index index.html;
    }
  }
}
```

Once data is stored in a ConfigMap, it can be injected into containers at run-time via any of the following methods:

- Environment variables
- Arguments to the container's startup command
- Files in a volume

All of the methods work with existing applications and are transparent to the app – the application is unaware the data originally came from a ConfigMap.

Figure 11.1 shows how the pieces connect.

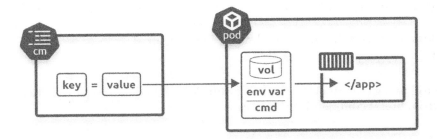

Figure 11.1

The most flexible of the three methods is the *volume* option, whereas the most limited is the *startup command*. You'll see each in turn, but before we do that let's quickly mention *Kubernetes-native* business applications.

ConfigMaps and Kubernetes-native apps

A *Kubernetes-native application* is one that knows it's running on Kubernetes and can talk to the Kubernetes API. This lets them access ConfigMap data directly via the API without needing things like environment variables or volumes. This can simplify things, but the application will only run on Kubernetes (Kubernetes lock-in). At the time of writing, Kubernetes-native applications are rare.

Hands-on with ConfigMaps

You'll need a Kubernetes cluster and the lab files from the book's GitHub repo if you want to follow along.

```
$ git clone https://github.com/nigelpoulton/TheK8sBook.git
Cloning into 'TheK8sBook'...
```

If you don't know how to use `git`, or can't install it, you can just go to the repo and copy the text from the relevant files into files with the same name on your local machine.

Be sure to run all of the following commands from within the `configmaps` folder.

As with most Kubernetes objects, you can create them imperatively and declaratively. We'll look at the imperative method first.

Creating ConfigMaps imperatively

The command to imperatively create a ConfigMap is `kubectl create configmap`, however, you can shorten `configmap` to `cm`. The command accepts two sources of data:

- Literal values on the command line (`--from-literal`)
- Files (`--from-file`)

Run the following command to create a ConfigMap called `testmap1` with two map entries from literal command-line values.

```
$ kubectl create configmap testmap1 \
  --from-literal shortname=AOS \
  --from-literal longname="Agents of Shield"
```

The following `kubectl describe` command shows how the two entries are stored in the map.

```
$ kubectl describe cm testmap1
Name:          testmap1
Namespace:     default
Labels:        <none>
Annotations:   <none>
Data
====
shortname:
----
AOS
longname:
----
Agents of Shield
BinaryData
====
Events:   <none>
```

You can see the object is essentially a map of key-value pairs dressed up as a Kubernetes object.

The next command creates a ConfigMap from a file called cmfile.txt. It assumes you have a local file called cmfile.txt in your working directory. The file contains the following single line of text and is available in the configmaps directory of the book's GitHub repo.

```
WebAssembly is coming!
```

Run this command to create the ConfigMap from the contents of the file. Notice that the command uses the --from-file argument instead of --from-literal.

```
$ kubectl create cm testmap2 --from-file cmfile.txt
configmap/testmap2 created
```

Inspecting ConfigMaps

ConfigMaps are first class API objects, meaning you can inspect and query them in the same way as any other API object.

List all ConfigMaps in the current Namespace.

```
$ kubectl get cm
AME         DATA    AGE
testmap1    2       11m
testmap2    1       2m23s
```

The following `kubectl describe` command shows some interesting info about the testmap2 map:

- A single map entry was created
- The name of the key is the name of the input file (`cmfile.txt`)
- The value is the contents of the file

```
$ kubectl describe cm testmap2
Name:          testmap2
Namespace:     default
Labels:        <none>
Annotations:   <none>
Data
====
cmfile.txt:              <<==== key
----
WebAssembly is coming!       <<==== value
BinaryData
====
Events:   <none>
```

You can also see the entire object by using the `-o yaml` flag with `kubectl get`.

```
$ kubectl get cm testmap1 -o yaml
apiVersion: v1
data:
  longname: Agents of Shield
  shortname: AOS
kind: ConfigMap
metadata:
  creationTimestamp: "2021-12-30T14:18:01Z"
  name: testmap1
  namespace: default
  resourceVersion: "20904"
  uid: 87b03869-e29d-4744-b43b-cb6178bc61fe
```

An interesting thing to note is that ConfigMap objects don't have the concept of state (desired state and actual state). This is why they have a data block instead of spec and status blocks.

Let's find out how to create a ConfigMap declaratively before you use one to inject data into a Pod.

Creating ConfigMaps declaratively

The following ConfigMap manifest defines two map entries: `given` and `family`. It's available in the book's GitHub repo under the `configmaps` folder called `multimap.yml`. Alternatively, you can create an empty file and practice writing your own manifests from scratch.

```
kind: ConfigMap
apiVersion: v1
metadata:
  name: multimap
data:
  given: Nigel
  family: Poulton
```

You can see that a ConfigMap manifest has the normal `kind` and `apiVersion` fields, as well as the usual `metadata` section. However, as previously mentioned, they don't have a `spec` section. Instead, they have a `data` section that defines the map of key-value pairs.

You can deploy it with the following command.

```
$ kubectl apply -f multimap.yml
configmap/multimap created
```

This next YAML looks slightly more complicated but it's actually not – it creates a ConfigMap with just a single map entry in the `data` block. It looks more complicated because the *value* portion of the map entry is a full configuration file.

```
kind: ConfigMap
apiVersion: v1
metadata:
  name: test-config
data:
  test.conf: |
    env = plex-test
    endpoint = 0.0.0.0:31001
    char = utf8
    vault = PLEX/test
    log-size = 512M
```

Notice the pipe character (|) after the name of the entry's *key* property. This tells Kubernetes that everything following the pipe is to be treated as a single literal value. Therefore, the ConfigMap object is called `test-config` and it has a single map entry as follows:

Object name	Key	Value
test-config	test.conf	env = plex-test
		endpoint = 0.0.0.0:31001
		char = utf8
		vault = PLEX/test
		log-size = 512M

You can deploy it with the following `kubectl` command. It assumes you have a local copy of the file called `singlemap.yml`.

```
$ kubectl apply -f singlemap.yml
configmap/test-config created
```

List and describe the `multimap` and `test-config` ConfigMaps you just created. The following shows the output of a `kubectl describe` against the `test-config` map.

```
$ kubectl describe cm test-config
Name:           test-config
Namespace:      default
Labels:         <none>
Annotations:    <none>
Data
====
test.conf:
----
env = plex-test
endpoint = 0.0.0.0:31001
char = utf8
vault = PLEX/test
log-size = 512M
BinaryData
====
Events:   <none>
```

Injecting ConfigMap data into Pods and containers

There are three main ways to get ConfigMap data into containers:

- As environment variables
- As arguments to container startup commands
- As files in a volume

Let's look at each.

ConfigMaps and environment variables

A common way to get ConfigMap data into a container is via environment variables. You create the ConfigMap, then you map its entries into environment variables in the container section of a Pod template. When the container starts, the environment variables appear in the container as standard Linux or Windows environment variables. This allows apps to consume them without any special magic.

Figure 11.2. shows this.

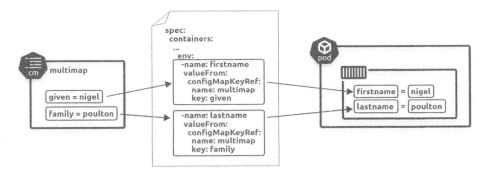

Figure 11.2

You already have a ConfigMap called `multimap` with two entries:

- given=Nigel
- family=Poulton

The following Pod manifest deploys a single container that creates two environment variables in the container:

- FIRSTNAME: Maps to the `given` entry
- LASTNAME: Maps to the `family` entry

```
apiVersion: v1
kind: Pod
<Snip>
spec:
  containers:
    - name: ctr1
      env:
        - name: FIRSTNAME
          valueFrom:
            configMapKeyRef:
              name: multimap
              key: given
        - name: LASTNAME
          valueFrom:
            configMapKeyRef:
              name: multimap
              key: family
<Snip>
```

When the Pod is scheduled and the container started, FIRSTNAME and LASTNAME will be created as standard Linux environment variables inside the container. Applications can use these like regular environment variables – because they are!

Run the following commands to deploy a Pod from the envpod.yml file and list environment variables that include the NAME string in their name. This will list the FIRSTNAME and LASTNAME variables and you'll see they're populated with the values from the multimap ConfigMap.

```
$ kubectl apply -f envpod.yml
pod/envpod created
```

Make sure the Pod is running before executing the following command.

```
$ kubectl exec envpod -- env | grep NAME
HOSTNAME=envpod
FIRSTNAME=Nigel
LASTNAME=Poulton
```

A drawback to using environment variables is that they're static. This means updates to the map don't get reflected in running containers. For example, if you update the values of the given and family entries in the ConfigMap, environment variables in existing containers won't see the updates. This is a major reason not to use environment variables.

ConfigMaps and container startup commands

The concept of using ConfigMaps with container startup commands is simple. You specify the startup command for a container in the Pod template and then customize it with variables.

The following Pod template is an extract from the startuppod.yml file and describes a single container called args1. It's based on the busybox image and runs the /bin/sh startup command on line 5.

```
spec:
  containers:
    - name: args1
      image: busybox
      command: [ "/bin/sh", "-c", "echo First name $(FIRSTNAME) last name $(LASTNAME)" ]
      env:
        - name: FIRSTNAME
          valueFrom:
            configMapKeyRef:
              name: multimap
              key: given
        - name: LASTNAME
          valueFrom:
            configMapKeyRef:
              name: multimap
              key: family
```

If you look closely at the YAML you'll notice the command is nested in the containers section, as is the env section that defines two environment variables: FIRSTNAME and LASTNAME. Each of these is pulled from the multimap ConfigMap. Take a close look at the YAML if that sounds confusing:

- FIRSTNAME is based on the given entry in the multimap ConfigMap
- LASTNAME is based on the family entry in the same ConfigMap

The relationship is shown in Figure 11.3.

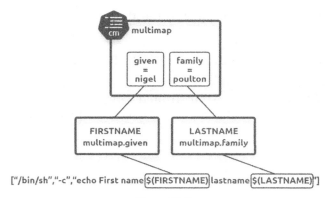

Figure 11.3

Start a new Pod based on the `startuppod.yml`. The Pod will start, print "First name Nigel last name Poulton" to the container's logs, then quit (succeed). It might take a few seconds for the Pod to start and execute.

```
$ kubectl apply -f startuppod.yml
pod/startup-pod created
```

Run the following command to inspect the logs from the `args1` container and verify it printed "First name Nigel last name Poulton".

```
$ kubectl logs startup-pod -c args1
First name Nigel last name Poulton
```

Describing the Pod will yield the following lines describing the environment of the Pod.

```
Environment:
  FIRSTNAME:   <set to the key 'given' of config map 'multimap'>
  LASTNAME:    <set to the key 'family' of config map 'multimap'>
```

Using ConfigMaps with container startup commands is an extension of environment variables. As such, it suffers from the same limitations – updates to map entries won't be reflected in running containers.

If you ran the `startup-pod` it should be in the completed state. This is because its startup command runs and completes, causing the Pod to succeed. Delete it with `kubectl delete pod startup-pod`.

ConfigMaps and volumes

Using ConfigMaps with volumes is the most flexible option. You can reference entire configuration files, as well as make updates to the ConfigMap that will be reflected in running containers. The updates may take a minute or so to be reflected in the running container.

The high-level process for exposing ConfigMap data via a volume looks like this:

1. Create the ConfigMap
2. Create a *ConfigMap volume* in the Pod template
3. Mount the *ConfigMap volume* into the container
4. Entries in the ConfigMap will appear in the container as individual files

This process is shown in Figure 11.4

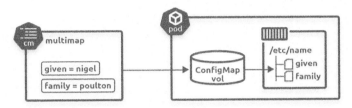

Figure 11.4

You still have the `multimap` ConfigMap with two values:

- given=Nigel
- family=Poulton

The following YAML creates a Pod called `cmvol` with the following configuration:

- `spec.volumes` creates a volume called **volmap** based on the **multimap** ConfigMap
- `spec.containers.volumeMounts` mounts the **volmap** volume to `/etc/name`

```
apiVersion: v1
kind: Pod
metadata:
  name: cmvol
spec:
  volumes:
    - name: volmap            <<==== Create a new volume called "volmap"
      configMap:              <<==== based on the ConfigMap
        name: multimap        <<==== called "multimap"
  containers:
    - name: ctr
      image: nginx
      volumeMounts:           <<==== These lines mount the
        - name: volmap        <<==== the "volmap" volume into the
          mountPath: /etc/name <<==== container at "/etc/name"
```

The following commands deploy the "cmvol" Pod, from the cmpod.yml manifest, and
run a kubectl exec command to list the files in the '/etc/name/' directory. Be sure the
Pod is running before executing the second command.

```
$ kubectl apply -f cmpod.yml
pod/cmvol created

$ kubectl exec cmvol -- ls /etc/name
family
given
```

Use kubectl edit to edit the ConfigMap and change any of the values in the data block,
you can even change them all. This method requires a basic understanding of the vi
editor, and when you save your changes they'll automatically be re-posted to Kubernetes.
If you're not comfortable with vi you can manually edit the YAML file in a different
editor and use kubectl apply to re-post it to the API server.

```
$ kubectl edit cm multimap

# Please edit the object below. Lines beginning with a '#' will be ignored,
# and an empty file will abort the edit. If an error occurs while saving
# this file will be reopened with the relevant failures.
#
apiVersion: v1
data:
  City: Macclesfield      <<==== changed
  Country: UK             <<==== changed
kind: ConfigMap
metadata:
<Snip>
```

Save your changes and re-run the previous kubectl exec command to list the contents
of the container's filesystem. It may take a minute for the changes to appear.

```
$ kubectl exec cmvol -- ls /etc/name
City
Country

$ kubectl exec cmvol -- cat /etc/name/Country
UK
```

Congratulations, the contents of the `multimap` ConfigMap have been exposed into the container's filesystem via a ConfigMap volume and you've tested making an update.

Hands-on with Secrets

Secrets are almost identical to ConfigMaps – they hold application configuration data that is injected into containers at run-time. However, Secrets are designed for sensitive data such as passwords, certificates, and OAuth tokens.

Are Kubernetes Secrets secure?

The quick answer to this question is "no". But here's the slightly longer answer…

Despite being designed for sensitive data, Kubernetes does not encrypt Secrets in the cluster store. It merely obscures them as base-64 encoded values that can easily be decoded. Fortunately, it's possible to configure encryption-at-rest with `Encryption-Configuration` objects, and most service meshes encrypt network traffic. Despite this, many people opt to use external 3rd-party tools, such as HashiCorp's Vault, for a more complete and secure secrets management solution.

We'll focus on the basic secrets management functionality provided natively by Kubernetes as it's still useful if augmented with 3rd-party tools.

A typical workflow for a Secret is as follows:

1. The Secret is created and persisted to the cluster store as an **un-encrypted** object
2. A Pod that uses it gets scheduled to a cluster node
3. The Secret is transferred over the network, **un-encrypted**, to the node
4. The kubelet on the node starts the Pod and its containers
5. The Secret is mounted into the container via an in-memory `tmpfs` filesystem and decoded from base64 to plain text
6. The application consumes it
7. When the Pod is deleted, the Secret is deleted from the node

While it's possible to encrypt the Secret in the cluster store and leverage a service mesh to encrypt it in-flight on the network, it's always mounted as plain-text in the Pod/container. This is so the app can consume it without having to perform decryption or base64 decoding operations.

Also, use of in-memory `tmpfs` filesystems mean they're never persisted to disk on a node.

So, to cut a long story short, no, Secrets aren't very secure. But, you can take extra steps to make them secure.

They're also limited to 1MiB (1,048,576 bytes) in size.

An obvious use-case for Secrets is a generic TLS termination proxy for use across your `dev`, `test`, and `prod` environments. You create a standard image and use a Secret to load the appropriate TLS keys at run-time for each environment. This is shown in Figure 11.5.

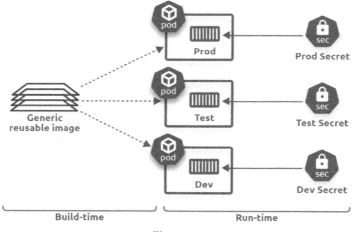

Figure 11.5

Creating Secrets

Before proceeding with this section, remember that Secrets are not encrypted in the cluster store, not encrypted in-flight on the network, and not encrypted when surfaced in a container. There are ways to encrypt them at-rest in the cluster store and to encrypt network traffic. However, they need to be surfaced in containers in plain text for applications to use them.

As with all API resources, Secrets can be created imperatively and declaratively.

Create a new Secret called **creds** with the following imperative command.

```
$ kubectl create secret generic creds --from-literal user=nigelpoulton \
  --from-literal pwd=Password123
```

Earlier you learned that Kubernetes obscures Secrets by encoding them as base64 values. Check this with the following command.

```
$ kubectl get secret creds -o yaml
apiVersion: v1
kind: Secret
data:
  pwd: UGFzc3dvcmQxMjM=
  user: bmlnZWxwb3VsdG9u
<Snip>
```

The username and password values are both base64-encoded. Run the following command to decode them. You'll need the base64 utility on your system for the decoding to work. If you don't have it, you can use an online decoder.

```
$ echo UGFzc3dvcmQxMjM= | base64 -d
Password123
```

The decoding completes without requiring a key, proving that base64 encoding is not secure.

The following YAML object is from the tkb-secret.yml file in the configmaps folder. It describes a Secret called "tkb-secret" with two base64-encoded entries. If you want to add plain text entries, rename the data object to stringData. Although this allows you to enter values in plain text, they'll still be stored as base64, and subsequent kubectl commands will retrieve them as base64.

```
apiVersion: v1
kind: Secret
metadata:
  name: tkb-secret
  labels:
    chapter: configmaps
type: Opaque
data:                           <<==== Change to stringData for plain text values
  username: bmlnZWxwb3VsdG9u
  password: UGFzc3dvcmQxMjM=
```

Deploy it to your cluster. Be sure to run the command from the configmaps folder.

```
$ kubectl apply -f tkb-secret.yml
secret/tkb-secret created
```

Run `kubectl get` and `kubectl describe` commands to inspect it.

Using Secrets in Pods

The most flexible way to inject a Secret into a Pod (container) is via a special type of volume called a *Secret volume*.

The following YAML describes a single-container Pod with a Secret volume called "secret-vol" based on the `tkb-secret` created in the previous step. It also mounts it into the container at `/etc/tkb`.

```
apiVersion: v1
kind: Pod
metadata:
  name: secret-pod
  labels:
    topic: secrets
spec:
  volumes:
  - name: secret-vol
    secret:
      secretName: tkb-secret
  containers:
  - name: secret-ctr
    image: nginx
    volumeMounts:
    - name: secret-vol
      mountPath: "/etc/tkb"
```

Secret volumes are automatically mounted as read-only to prevent containers and applications accidentally mutating them.

Deploy it with the following command. Doing this will transfer the unencrypted Secret over the network to the kubelet on the node running the Pod. From there, it will be mounted into the Pod via a tmpfs mount.

```
$ kubectl apply -f secretpod.yml
pod/secret-pod created
```

The following command shows the Secret is mounted as two files at `/etc/tkb` – one file for each entry in the Secret.

```
$ kubectl exec secret-pod -- ls /etc/tkb
password
username
```

Showing the contents of either file will show the entries have been exposed in the container in plain text for use by applications.

```
$ kubectl exec secret-pod -- cat /etc/tkb/password
Password123
```

There are more ways to use ConfigMaps and Secrets, but you know enough now to get started.

Clean-up

Use kubectl get to list the Pods, ConfigMaps and Secrets deployed in the chapter, and delete them with kubectl delete.

Chapter Summary

ConfigMaps and Secrets are the Kubernetes native way of decoupling applications and config data.

They're both first-class object in the Kubernetes API and can be created and manipulated with the usual kubectl apply, kubectl get, and kubectl describe commands. ConfigMaps are designed for application configuration parameters and even entire configuration files, whereas Secrets are designed for sensitive configuration data.

Both can be injected into containers at run-time via various constructs. Volumes are the preferred construct as they allow updates to eventually be reflected in running containers.

Kubernetes does not encrypt Secrets in the cluster store or when in transit on the network.

12: StatefulSets

In this chapter, you'll learn how to use *StatefulSets* to deploy and manage stateful applications on Kubernetes.

For the purposes of this chapter, we're defining a *stateful application* as one that creates and saves valuable data. An example might be an app that saves data about client sessions and uses it for future sessions. Other examples include data stores.

We'll divide the chapter as follows:

- StatefulSet theory
- Hands-on with StatefulSets

The theory section introduces you to the way StatefulSets work and what they bring to the game. But don't worry if you don't understand everything at first, you'll cover a lot of it again when you go through the hands-on section.

The theory of StatefulSets

It's often useful to compare StatefulSets with Deployments. Both are first-class API objects and follow the typical Kubernetes controller architecture. As such, both are implemented as controllers that operate reconciliation loops observing the state of the cluster, via the API server, and moving *observed state* into sync with *desired state*. Both also manage Pods and bring self-healing, scaling, rollouts, and more.

However, there are some vital differences. StatefulSets guarantee:

- Predictable and persistent Pod names
- Predictable and persistent DNS hostnames
- Predictable and persistent volume bindings

These three properties form the *state* of a Pod, sometimes referred to as its *sticky ID*. StatefulSets ensure this state/sticky ID is persisted across failures, scaling, and other scheduling operations, making them ideal for applications that require unique reliable Pods.

As a quick example, failed Pods managed by a StatefulSet will be replaced by new Pods with the exact same Pod name, the exact same DNS hostname, and the exact same volumes. This is true even if the replacement is started on a different cluster node. The same is not true of Pods managed by a Deployment.

The following YAML snippet shows *some* of the properties of a typical StatefulSet.

```
apiVersion: apps/v1
kind: StatefulSet
metadata:
  name: tkb-sts
spec:
  selector:
    matchLabels:
      app: mongo
  serviceName: "tkb-sts"
  replicas: 3
  template:
    metadata:
      labels:
        app: mongo
    spec:
      containers:
      - name: ctr-mongo
        image: mongo:latest
        ...
```

The name of the StatefulSet is `tkb-sts` and it defines three Pod replicas running the `mongo:latest` image. You post this to the API server, it's persisted to the cluster store, the replicas are assigned to worker nodes, and the StatefulSet controller monitors the state of the cluster ensuring *observed state* matches *desired state*.

That's the big picture. Let's take a closer look at some of the major characteristics of StatefulSets before walking through an example.

StatefulSet Pod naming

All Pods managed by a StatefulSet get *predictable* and *persistent* names. These names are vital and are at the core of how Pods are started, self-healed, scaled, deleted, and attached to volumes.

The format of StatefulSet Pod names is `<StatefulSetName>-<Integer>`. The integer is a *zero-based index ordinal*, which is just a fancy way of saying "number starting from 0". As such, the first Pod created by a StatefulSet always gets index ordinal "0", and each subsequent Pod gets the next highest. Assuming the previous YAML snippet, the first Pod created will be called `tkb-sts-0`, the second will be called `tkb-sts-1`, and the third `tkb-sts-2`.

Be aware that StatefulSet names need to be a valid DNS names, so no exotic characters.

Ordered creation and deletion

Another fundamental characteristic of StatefulSets is the controlled and ordered way they start and stop Pods.

StatefulSets create one Pod at a time, and always wait for previous Pods to be *running and ready* before creating the next. This is different from Deployments that use a ReplicaSet controller to start all Pods at the same time, causing potential race conditions.

As per the previous YAML snippet, `tkb-sts-0` will be started first and must be *running* and *ready* before the StatefulSet controller starts `tkb-sts-1`. The same applies to subsequent Pods – `tkb-sts-1` needs to be *running* and *ready* before `tkb-sts-2` starts etc. See Figure 12.1

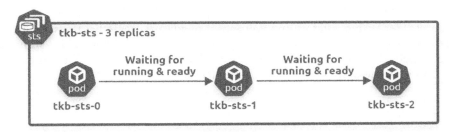

Figure 12.1

Note: *Running* and *ready* are terms used to indicate all containers in a Pod are *running* and the Pod is *ready* to service requests.

Scaling operations are also governed by the same ordered startup rules. For example, scaling from 3 to 5 replicas will start a new Pod called `tkb-sts-3` and wait for it to be *running and ready* before creating `tkb-sts-4`. Scaling down follows the same rules in reverse – the controller terminates the Pod with the highest index ordinal and waits for it to fully terminate before terminating the Pod with the next highest.

Knowing the order in which Pods will be scaled down, as well as knowing that Pods will not be terminated in parallel can be vital for many stateful apps. For example, clustered apps that store data can potentially lose data if multiple replicas are taken down at the same time. StatefulSets guarantee this will never happen. You can also inject other delays via things like `terminationGracePeriodSeconds` to further control the scaling down process.

Finally, it's worth noting that StatefulSet controllers do their own self-healing and scaling. This is architecturally different to Deployments which use a separate ReplicaSet controller for these operations.

Deleting StatefulSets

There are two major things to consider when deleting StatefulSets.

Firstly, deleting a StatefulSet object does **not** terminate Pods in order. With this in mind, you may want to scale a StatefulSet to 0 replicas before deleting it.

You can also use `terminationGracePeriodSeconds` to further control the way Pods are terminated. It's common to set this to at least 10 seconds to give applications running in Pods a chance to flush local buffers and safely commit any writes that are still "in-flight".

StatefulSets and Volumes

Volumes are an important part of a StatefulSet Pod's *sticky ID* (state).

When a StatefulSet Pod is created, any volumes it needs are created at the same time and named in a special way that connects them to the right Pod. Figure 12.2 shows a StatefulSet called "tkb-sts" requesting 3 replicas. You can see how each Pod and volume is created and how the names connect volumes to Pods.

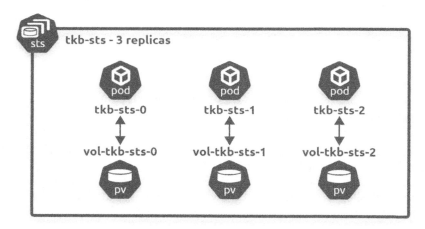

Figure 12.2

Volumes are appropriately decoupled from Pods via the normal Persistent Volume Claim system. This means volumes have separate lifecycles to Pods, allowing them to survive Pod failures and termination operations. For example, any time a StatefulSet Pod fails or is terminated, associated volumes are unaffected. This allows replacement Pods to attach to the exact same storage as the Pods they're replacing. This is true, even if replacement Pods are scheduled to different cluster nodes.

The same is true for scaling operations. If a StatefulSet Pod is deleted as part of a scale-down operation, subsequent scale-up operations will attach new Pods to the surviving volumes that match their names.

This behavior can be a life-saver if you accidentally delete a StatefulSet Pod, especially if it's the last replica!

Handling failures

The StatefulSet controller observes the state of the cluster and attempts to keep observed state in sync with desired state. The simplest example is a Pod failure. If you have a StatefulSet called `tkb-sts` with 5 replicas, and `tkb-sts-3` fails, the controller will start a replacement Pod with the same name and attach it to the same volumes.

However, if a failed Pod recovers after Kubernetes has replaced it, you'll have two identical Pods trying to write to the same volume. This can result in data corruption. As a result, **the StatefulSet controller is extremely careful how it handles failures.**

Possible node failures are very difficult to deal with. For example, if Kubernetes loses contact with a node, how does it know if the node is down and will never recover, or if it's a temporary glitch such as a network partition, a crashed kubelet, or the node is simply rebooting? To complicate matters further, the controller can't even force the affected Pod to terminate, as the local kubelet may never receive the instruction. With all of this in mind, manual intervention is needed before Kubernetes will replace Pods on nodes that it *thinks* have failed.

Network ID and headless Services

We've already said that StatefulSets are for applications that need Pods to be predictable and long-lived. As a result, other parts of the application, as well as other applications, may need to connect directly to individual Pods. To make this possible, StatefulSets use a ***headless Service*** to create predictable DNS hostnames for every Pod replica. Other apps can then query DNS for the full list of Pod replicas and use these details to connect directly to Pods.

The following YAML snippet shows a headless Service called "mongo-prod" that is listed in the StatefulSet YAML as the *governing Service*.

```
apiVersion: v1
kind: Service
metadata:
  name: mongo-prod
spec:
    clusterIP: None                  <<==== Headless Service
    selector:
      app: mongo
      env: prod
---
apiVersion: apps/v1
kind: StatefulSet
metadata:
  name: sts-mongo
spec:
    serviceName: mongo-prod          <<==== Governing Service
```

Let's explain the terms *headless Service* and *governing Service*.

A headless Service is just a regular Kubernetes Service object without an IP address (spec.clusterIP set to None). It becomes a StatefulSet's governing Service when you list it in the StatefulSet config under spec.serviceName.

When the two objects are combined like this, the Service will create DNS SRV records for every Pod matching the label selector of the headless Service. Other Pods and apps can then find members of the StatefulSet by performing DNS lookups against the name of the headless Service. You'll see this in action later, and obviously applications need coding with this intelligence.

That covers most of the theory, let's walk through an example and see how it all comes together.

Hands-on with StatefulSets

In this section, you'll deploy a working StatefulSet. The example is intended to demonstrate the way StatefulSets work and reinforce what you've already learned. It's not intended as a production-grade application configuration.

The examples we'll show are on Google Kubernetes Engine (GKE). StatefulSets and what you're about to see work just fine on other Kubernetes clusters, but the StorageClass YAML file used in the examples is designed for GKE.

All of the YAML files we'll refer to are in the statefulsets folder of the book's GitHub repo. You can clone the repo with the following command.

```
$ git clone https://github.com/nigelpoulton/TheK8sBook.git
```

If you're following along, you'll deploy the following three objects:

1. A StorageClass
2. A headless Service
3. A StatefulSet

To make things easier to follow, you'll inspect and deploy each object individually. However, all three can be grouped in a single YAML file separated by three dashes (see app.yml in the statefulsets folder of the repo).

Deploying the StorageClass

StatefulSets that use volumes need to be able to create them dynamically. You need two objects to do this:

- StorageClass (SC)
- PersistentVolumeClaim (PVC)

The following YAML is from the gcp-sc.yml file and defines a StorageClass object called flash that will dynamically provision SSD volumes (type=pd-ssd) from the Google Cloud using the GKE persistent disk CSI driver (pd.csi.storage.gke.io). It will only work on Kubernetes clusters running on GCP or GKE with the CSI driver enabled.

```
apiVersion: storage.k8s.io/v1
kind: StorageClass
metadata:
  name: flash
provisioner: pd.csi.storage.gke.io
volumeBindingMode: WaitForFirstConsumer
allowVolumeExpansion: true
parameters:
  type: pd-ssd
```

Deploy the Storage class.

```
$ kubectl apply -f gcp-sc.yml
storageclass.storage.k8s.io/flash created
```

List your cluster's StorageClasses to make sure it was created correctly.

```
$ kubectl get sc
                                          VOLUME            ALLOWVOLUME
NAME      PROVISIONER            RECLAIMPOLICY   BINDINGMODE       EXPANSION
flash     pd.csi.storage.gke.io  Delete          WaitForFirstConsumer   true
```

With the StorageClass in place, Persistent Volume Claims (PVC) can use it to dynamically create new volumes. We'll circle back to this in a later step.

Creating a governing headless Service

When learning about headless Services, it can be useful to visualize a Service object with a head and a tail. The head is the stable IP address, and the tail is the list of Pods it sends traffic to. Therefore, a headless Service is a Service object without an IP address.

The sole purpose of a headless Service is to create DNS SRV records for Pods that match its label selector. Clients can then use DNS to reach Pods directly instead of via a Service's ClusterIP. This is why a headless Service doesn't need a ClusterIP.

The following YAML is from the `headless-svc.yml` file and describes a headless Service called `dullahan` with no IP address (`spec.clusterIP: None`).

```
apiVersion: v1
kind: Service
metadata:
  name: dullahan
  labels:
    app: web
spec:
  ports:
  - port: 80
    name: web
  clusterIP: None
  selector:
    app: web
```

The only difference to a regular Service is that a headless Service must have its `clusterIP` set to None.

Deploy the headless Service to your cluster.

```
$ kubectl apply -f headless-svc.yml
service/tkb-sts created
```

Verify the operation.

```
$ kubectl get svc
NAME        TYPE        CLUSTER-IP    EXTERNAL-IP    PORT(S)    AGE
dullahan    ClusterIP   None          <none>         80/TCP     11s
```

Deploy the StatefulSet

With the StorageClass and headless Service in place, it's time to deploy the StatefulSet.

The following YAML is from the `sts.yml` file and defines the StatefulSet. Remember this is for learning purposes only, it's not intended as a production-grade deployment of an application.

```
apiVersion: apps/v1
kind: StatefulSet
metadata:
  name: tkb-sts
spec:
  replicas: 3
  selector:
    matchLabels:
      app: web
  serviceName: "dullahan"
  template:
    metadata:
      labels:
        app: web
    spec:
      terminationGracePeriodSeconds: 10
      containers:
      - name: ctr-web
        image: nginx:latest
        ports:
        - containerPort: 80
          name: web
        volumeMounts:
        - name: webroot
          mountPath: /usr/share/nginx/html
  volumeClaimTemplates:
  - metadata:
      name: webroot
    spec:
      accessModes: [ "ReadWriteOnce" ]
      storageClassName: "flash"
      resources:
        requests:
          storage: 1Gi
```

There's a lot to take in, so let's step through the important parts.

The name of the StatefulSet is `tkb-sts`. This is important as it forms part of the name of every Pod and volume the StatefulSet will create.

The `spec.replicas` field defines 3 replicas. These will be named `tkb-sts-0`, `tkb-sts-1`, and `tkb-sts-2`. They'll be created in numerical order, and the StatefulSet controller will wait for each replica to be running and ready before starting the next.

The `spec.serviceName` field designates the *governing Service*. This is the name of the headless Service created in the previous step and will create the DNS SRV records for each StatefulSet replica. It's called the *governing Service* because it's in charge of the DNS subdomain used by the StatefulSet.

The remainder of the `spec.template` section defines the Pod template that will be used to stamp out Pod replicas – things such as which container image to use and which ports to expose.

Last, but most certainly not least, is the `spec.volumeClaimTemplates` section...

Earlier in the chapter we said every StatefulSet that uses volumes needs to be able to create them dynamically. To do this you need a StorageClass and a PersistentVolumeClaim (PVC).

You've already created the StorageClass, so you're ready to go with that aspect. However, PVCs present an interesting challenge.

Each Pod in a StatefulSet needs its own unique storage. This means each one needs its own PVC. However, this isn't possible, as each Pod is created from the same template. Also, you'd have to pre-create a unique PVC for every potential StatefulSet Pod, which also isn't possible when you consider StatefulSets can scale up and down.

Clearly, a more intelligent *StatefulSet-aware* approach is needed. This is where *volume claim templates* come into play.

At a high-level, a volumeClaimTemplate dynamically creates a PVC each time the StatefulSet controller spawns a new Pod replica. It also has the intelligence to name the PVC so it connects to the right Pod. This way, the StatefulSet manifest contains a Pod template section for stamping out Pod replicas, and a volume claim template section for stamping out PVCs.

The following YAML snippet shows the volumeClaimTemplate from the example. It defines a claim template called `webroot` requesting a 10GB volume from the `flash` StorageClass created earlier.

```
volumeClaimTemplates:
- metadata:
    name: webroot
  spec:
    accessModes: [ "ReadWriteOnce" ]
    storageClassName: "flash"
    resources:
      requests:
        storage: 10Gi
```

When the StatefulSet object is deployed, it will create three Pod replicas and three PVCs. The names of the Pods and volumes will be based on the name of the StatefulSet and will be used to connect the Pods to the correct volumes.

Deploy the StatefulSet and watch the Pods and PVCs get created.

```
$ kubectl apply -f sts.yml
statefulset.apps/tkb-sts created
```

Watch the StatefulSet ramp up to 3 running replicas. It'll take a minute or so for the 3 Pods and associated PVCs to be created.

```
$ kubectl get sts --watch
NAME      READY   AGE
tkb-sts   0/3     14s
tkb-sts   1/3     30s
tkb-sts   2/3     60s
tkb-sts   3/3     90s
```

Notice how it took ~30 seconds to start the first replica. Once that was running and ready, it took another 30 seconds to start the second, and then another 30 for the third.

Now check the PVCs.

```
$ kubectl get pvc
NAME               STATUS   VOLUME          CAPACITY   MODES   STORAGECLASS   AGE
webroot-tkb-sts-0  Bound    pvc-1146...f274 10Gi       RWO     flash          100s
webroot-tkb-sts-1  Bound    pvc-3026...6bcb 10Gi       RWO     flash          70s
webroot-tkb-sts-2  Bound    pvc-2ce7...e56d 10Gi       RWO     flash          40s
```

There are 3 new PVCs, each created at the same time as one of the StatefulSet Pod replicas. See how the name of each PVC is based on the name of the StatefulSet and the Pod it's associated with.

```
Pod Name     |    PVC Name
tkb-sts-0   <->    webroot-tkb-sts-0
tkb-sts-0   <->    webroot-tkb-sts-1
tkb-sts-0   <->    webroot-tkb-sts-2
```

At this point, the StatefulSet is up and the app is running.

Testing peer discovery

You know that pairing a headless Service with a StatefulSet creates DNS SRV records for each Pod matching the Service's label selector. You already have a headless Service and 3 StatefulSet Pods running, so you should have three DNS SRV records – one for each Pod.

However, before testing this, it's worth taking a moment to understand how DNS hostnames and DNS subdomains work with StatefulSets.

By default, Kubernetes places all objects within the cluster.local DNS subdomain. You can choose something different, but most lab environments use this domain, so we'll assume it in this example. Within that domain, Kubernetes constructs DNS subdomains as follows:

```
<object-name>.<service-name>.<namespace>.svc.cluster.local
```

So far, you've got three Pods in the default Namespace called tkb-sts-0, tkb-sts-1, and tkb-sts-2 governed by the dullahan headless Service. This means the 3 Pods will have the following fully qualified DNS names:

- tkb-sts-0.dullahan.default.svc.cluster.local

- tkb-sts-1.dullahan.default.svc.cluster.local

- tkb-sts-2.dullahan.default.svc.cluster.local

To test this, you'll deploy a jump-pod that has the DNS dig utility pre-installed. You'll exec onto that Pod and use dig to query DNS for SRV records in the dullahan.default.svc.cluster.local subdomain.

Deploy the jump-pod from the jump-pod.yml file in the statefulsets folder of the book's GitHub repo.

```
$ kubectl apply -f jump-pod.yml
pod/jump-pod created
```

Exec onto the Pod.

```
$ kubectl exec -it jump-pod -- bash
root@jump-pod:/#
```

Your terminal is now connected to the jump-pod. Run the following `dig` command from within the jump-pod.

```
# dig SRV dullahan.default.svc.cluster.local
<Snip>
;; ADDITIONAL SECTION:
tkb-sts-0.dullahan.default.svc.cluster.local. 30 IN A 10.24.1.25
tkb-sts-2.dullahan.default.svc.cluster.local. 30 IN A 10.24.1.26
tkb-sts-1.dullahan.default.svc.cluster.local. 30 IN A 10.24.0.17
<Snip>
```

The query returns the fully qualified DNS names of each Pod, as well as each Pod's IP. Other applications, including the app itself, can use this method to discover an up-to-date list of Pods in the StatefulSet and connect to them.

For this method of discovery to be useful, applications need to know the name of the headless Service governing the StatefulSet and use this to query DNS.

Scaling StatefulSets

Each time a StatefulSet is scaled up, a Pod **and** a PVC is created. However, when scaling a StatefulSet down, the Pod is terminated but the PVC is not. This means future scale-up operations only need to create a new Pod, which is then connected to the surviving PVC. The StatefulSet controller includes the intelligence to track and manage all of this.

You currently have 3 StatefulSet Pod replicas and 3 PVCs. Edit the `sts.yml` file and change the replica count from 3 down to 2 and save your change. When you've done that, run the following command to re-post the YAML file to the cluster. You'll have to type `exit` first if you're still logged on to the jump Pod.

```
$ kubectl apply -f sts.yml
statefulset.apps/tkb-sts configured
```

Check the state of the StatefulSet and verify the Pod count has reduced to 2.

```
$ kubectl get sts tkb-sts
NAME       READY   AGE
tkb-sts    2/2     20m

$ kubectl get pods
NAME        READY   STATUS    RESTARTS   AGE
tkb-sts-0   1/1     Running   0          20m
tkb-sts-1   1/1     Running   0          20m
```

The number of Pod replicas has been successfully scaled down to 2, and the Pod with the highest index ordinal was deleted. However, you'll still have 3 PVCs – remember, scaling down and deleting Pod replicas does **not** delete associated PVCs.

Verify this.

```
$ kubectl get pvc
NAME               STATUS   VOLUME          CAPACITY   MODES   STORAGECLASS   AGE
webroot-tkb-sts-0  Bound    pvc-1146...f274 10Gi       RWO     flash          21m
webroot-tkb-sts-1  Bound    pvc-3026...6bcb 10Gi       RWO     flash          21m
webroot-tkb-sts-2  Bound    pvc-2ce7...e56d 10Gi       RWO     flash          21m
```

The status for all three still shows as Bound despite the fact the tkb-sts-2 Pod no longer exists. If you run a kubectl describe against the webroot-tkb-sts-2 PVC you'll see the Used by field shows as <none>.

The fact all three PVCs still exist means that scaling back up to three replicas only requires a new Pod to be created. As the name of the surviving PVC is webroot-tkb-sts-2, the StatefulSet controller knows to automatically connect it to the new Pod.

Edit the sts.yml file and increment the number of replicas back to 3 and save your change. When you've done that, re-post the YAML file to the API server with the following command.

```
$ kubectl apply -f sts.yml
statefulset.apps/tkb-sts configured
```

Give it a few seconds to deploy the new Pod and then verify with the following command.

```
$ kubectl get sts tkb-sts
NAME       READY   AGE
tkb-sts    3/3     25m
```

You have 3 Pods again. Describe the new tkb-sts-2 Pod to verify it's mounted the webroot-tkb-sts-2 volume.

```
$ kubectl describe pod tkb-sts-2 | grep ClaimName
ClaimName:  webroot-tkb-sts-2
```

The output confirms the replacement Pod connected to the correct storage volume.

It's worth noting that scale down operations will be put on hold if any of the Pods are in a failed state. This is to protect the resiliency of the app and integrity of any data.

Finally, it's possible to tweak the controlled and ordered starting and stopping of Pods via the StatefulSet's spec.podManagementPolicy property.

The default setting is OrderedReady and implements the strict methodical ordering previously explained. Setting the value to Parallel will cause the StatefulSet to act more like a Deployment where Pods are created and deleted in parallel. For example, scaling from 2 > 5 Pods will create all three new Pods instantaneously, and scaling down from 5 > 2 will delete three Pods in parallel. StatefulSet naming rules are still implemented, and the setting only applies to scaling operations and does not impact rollouts and rollbacks.

Performing rollouts

StatefulSets support rolling updates (a.k.a. rollouts). You update the image version in the YAML and re-post it to the API server. Once authenticated and authorized, the controller replaces old Pods with new ones. However, the process always starts with the highest numbered Pod and works down through the set, one-at-a-time, until all Pods are on the new version. The controller also waits for each new Pod to be running and ready before replacing the one with the next lowest index ordinal.

For more information, run kubectl explain sts.spec.updateStrategy.

Test a Pod failure

A simple way to test a failure is to manually delete a Pod. This will delete the Pod but not the associated PVC. The StatefulSet controller will notice observed state vary from desired state, realise a Pod is missing, and start a new identical one in its place. This new Pod will have the same name and will be connected to the same PVC volume.

Let's test it.

Confirm you have three healthy Pods in your StatefulSet.

```
$ kubectl get pods
NAME        READY   STATUS    AGE
tkb-sts-0   1/1     Running   37m
tkb-sts-1   1/1     Running   37m
tkb-sts-2   1/1     Running   15m
```

You're about to delete the `tkb-sts-0` Pod. But before you do that, run a quick `kubectl` `describe` to confirm the PVC it's currently using. You don't *need* to do this, as you can deduce the name of the PVC from the name of the volumeClaimTemplate and the StatefulSet. However, it's good to confirm.

```
$ kubectl describe pod tkb-sts-0
Name:        tkb-sts-0
Namespace:   default
<Snip>
Status:      Running
IP:          10.24.1.13
<Snip>
Volumes:
  webroot:
    Type:        PersistentVolumeClaim (a reference to a PersistentVolumeClaim...)
    ClaimName:   webroot-tkb-sts-0
<Snip>
```

Based on the output (your lab will be different) the values are as follows:

- Name: `tkb-sts-0`
- PVC: `webroot-tkb-sts-0`

Let's delete the `tkb-sts-0` Pod and see if the StatefulSet controller recreates it.

```
$ kubectl delete pod tkb-sts-0
pod "tkb-sts-0" deleted

$ kubectl get pods --watch
NAME        READY   STATUS             RESTARTS   AGE
tkb-sts-1   1/1     Running            0          43m
tkb-sts-2   1/1     Running            0          24m
tkb-sts-0   0/1     Terminating        0          43m
tkb-sts-0   0/1     Pending            0          0s
tkb-sts-0   0/1     ContainerCreating  0          0s
tkb-sts-0   1/1     Running            0          34s
```

Placing a `--watch` on the `kubectl get` command shows the StatefulSet controller noticing the terminated Pod and creating a replacement – desired state is 3 replicas but observed state dropped to 2. As the failure was clean and easy to verify, the controller immediately kicked off the process to create the replacement Pod.

You can see the new Pod has the same name as the failed one, but does it have the same PVC?

The following command confirms it does.

```
$ kubectl describe pod tkb-sts-0 | grep ClaimName
    ClaimName:  webroot-tkb-sts-0
```

As previously mentioned, recovering from potential node failures is a lot more complex and requires manual intervention. This is because there's always a risk the failure is transient. If the StatefulSet controller assumes a node has failed and replaces any StatefulSet Pods, but the node subsequently recovers, there's a chance of duplicate Pods on the network contending for the same storage. This can cause all kinds of bad things to happen, including data corruption.

Deleting StatefulSets

Earlier in the chapter, you learned that deleting a StatefulSet does not guarantee to terminate its Pods in order. Therefore, if your application is sensitive to ordered shutdown, you should scale the StatefulSet to 0 replicas before initiating the delete operation.

Scale your StatefulSet to 0 replicas and confirm the operation. It may take a few seconds for the set to scale all the way down to 0.

```
$ kubectl scale sts tkb-sts --replicas=0
statefulset.apps/tkb-sts scaled

$ kubectl get sts tkb-sts
NAME      READY   AGE
tkb-sts   0/0     86m
```

Once the StatefulSet has no replicas you can delete it.

```
$ kubectl delete sts tkb-sts
statefulset.apps "tkb-sts" deleted
```

You can also delete the StatefulSet by referencing its YAML file with $ kubectl delete -f sts.yml.

Feel free to exec onto the jump-pod and run another dig to prove the SRV records have been removed from DNS.

At this point, the StatefulSet object is deleted, but the headless Service, volumes, StorageClass, and jump-pod still exist and should be deleted manually. Failure to delete the volumes may incur unexpected cloud costs.

Chapter Summary

In this chapter, you learned how StatefulSets can be used to deploy and manage applications that need to persist state.

They can self-heal, scale up and down, and perform rollouts. Rollbacks require manual attention.

Each Pod replica spawned by a StatefulSet gets a predictable and persistent name, DNS hostname, and unique set of volumes. These stay with the Pod for its entire lifecycle, including failures, restarts, scaling, and other scheduling operations. In fact, StatefulSet Pod names are integral to scaling operations and connecting to storage volumes.

Finally, StatefulSets are only a framework. Applications need to be written in ways to take advantage of the way StatefulSets behave.

13: API security and RBAC

Kubernetes is *API-centric* and the API is served through the *API server*. In this chapter, you'll follow a typical API request as it passes through various security-related checks.

The chapter is divided as follows:

- API security big picture
- Authentication
- Authorization (RBAC)
- Admission control

See chapter 14 for an in-depth look at the API.

API security big picture

All of the following make CRUD-style requests to the API server (create, read, update, delete):

- Operators and developers using kubectl
- Pods
- Kubelets
- Control plane services
- More...

Figure 13.1 shows the flow of a typical API request passing through all the standard checks. The flow is the same no matter where the request originates.

Figure 13.1

Consider a quick example where a user called "grant-ward" is trying to create a Deployment called "hive" in the "terran" Namespace.

User **grant-ward** issues a `kubectl apply` command to create the Deployment. This generates a request to the API server with the user's credentials embedded. Thanks to the magic of TLS, the connection between the client and the API server is secure. The *authentication* module determines whether it's **grant-ward** or an imposter. After that, the *authorization* module (RBAC) determines whether **grant-ward** is allowed to create Deployments in the `terran` Namespace. If the request passes authentication and authorization, *admission control* checks and applies policies, and the request is finally accepted and executed.

It's a lot like flying on a plane. You travel to the airport and *authenticate* yourself with a photo ID, usually your passport. You then present a ticket *authorizing* you to board the plane and occupy a seat. If you pass authentication and are authorized to board, admission controls may then check and apply airline policies such as not taking hot food onboard, restricting your hand luggage, and prohibiting alcohol in the cabin. After all of that, you're finally allowed to take your seat and fly to your destination.

Let's take a closer look at authentication.

Authentication

Authentication is about proving your identity. You might see or hear it shortened to *authN*, pronounced "auth en".

At the heart of authentication are credentials. **All requests to the API server have to include credentials,** and the authentication layer is responsible for verifying them. If verification fails, the API server returns an HTTP 401 and the request is denied. If it succeeds, the request moves on to authorization.

The authentication layer in Kubernetes is pluggable, and popular modules include *client certs, webhooks,* and integration with external identity management systems such as *Active Directory (AD)* and cloud-based *Identity Access Management (IAM)*. In fact, Kubernetes does **not** have its own built-in identity database, instead, it forces you to use an external system. This avoids creating yet another identity management silo.

Out-of-the-box, most Kubernetes clusters support *client certificates*, but in the real-world you'll want to integrate with your chosen cloud or corporate identity management system. Many of the hosted Kubernetes services make it easy to integrate with their native identity management systems.

Checking your current authentication setup

Your cluster details and credentials are stored in a kubeconfig file. Tools like kubectl read this file to know which cluster to send commands to, as well as which credentials to use. It's usually stored in the following locations:

- Windows: C:\Users<user>\.kube\config
- Linux/Mac: /home/<user>/.kube/config

Here's what a kubeconfig file looks like. As you can see, it defines a *cluster* and a *user*, combines them into a *context*, and sets the default context for kubectl commands. It's been snipped to fit the page.

```
apiVersion: v1
kind: Config
clusters:
- cluster:                <<==== Cluster block defining clusters and certs
  name: prod-shield
    server: https://<url-or-ip-address-of-api-server>:443
    certificate-authority-data: LS0tLS1CRUdJTiBDRVJUSUZJQ0FURS0tLS0…LS0tCg==
users:                    <<==== Users block defining users and creds
- name: njfury
  user:
    as-user-extra: {}
    token: eyJhbGciOiJSUzI1NiIsImtpZCI6IlZwMzl…SZY3uUQ
contexts:                 <<==== Context block
- context:
  name: shield-admin      <<==== Context friendly name
    cluster: prod-shield  <<==== Cluster
    user: njfury          <<==== User
    namespace: default
current-context: shield-admin
```

You can see it's divided into 4 top-level sections:

- Clusters
- Users
- Contexts
- Current-context

The clusters section defines one or more Kubernetes clusters. Each one has a friendly name, an API server endpoint, and the public key of its certificate authority (CA). The cluster in the example is exposing the secure API endpoint on port 443 (HTTPS), but it's also common to see it exposed on 6443.

The users section defines one or more users. Each user requires a name and token. The token is often an X.509 certificate that is the user's ID. If it is, it has to be signed by the cluster's CA or a CA trusted by the cluster.

The contexts section combines users and clusters, and the current-context is the cluster and user kubectl will use for all commands.

Assuming the previous kubeconfig, all kubectl commands will go to the "prod-shield" cluster and authenticate as the "njfury" user. The authentication module is responsible for determining if the user really is njfury, and if using client certificates, it'll determine if the certificate is signed by a trusted CA.

If your cluster integrates with an external IAM system, it'll hand-off authentication to that system.

Assuming authentication is successful, the request progresses to the authorization phase.

Authorization (RBAC)

Authorization happens immediately after successful authentication, and you'll sometimes see it shortened to *authZ* (pronounced "auth zee").

Kubernetes authorization is pluggable and you can run multiple authZ modules on a single cluster. However, as soon as any of the modules authorizes a request, it moves immediately to *admissions control*.

This section covers the following:

- RBAC big picture
- Users and permissions
- Cluster-level users and permissions
- Pre-configured users and permissions

RBAC big picture

The most common authorization module is RBAC (Role-Based Access Control). At the highest level, it's about three things:

1. Users
2. Actions
3. Resources

Which *users* can perform which *actions* against which *resources*.

The following table shows a few examples.

User (subject)	Action	Resource
Bao	create	Pods
Kalila	list	Deployments
Josh	delete	ServiceAccounts

RBAC is enabled on most Kubernetes clusters and has been stable/GA since Kubernetes 1.8. It's a least-privilege deny-by-default system, meaning you enable specific actions by creating *allow rules*. In fact, Kubernetes doesn't support *deny rules*, it only supports *allow rules*. This might seem like a small thing, but it makes Kubernetes RBAC much simpler to implement and troubleshoot.

Users and Permissions

Two concepts are vital to understanding Kubernetes RBAC:

- Roles
- RoleBindings

Roles define a set of permissions, and RoleBindings bind them to users.

The following resource manifest defines a Role object. It's called "read-deployments", and grants permission to get, watch, and list Deployment objects in the "shield" Namespace.

```
apiVersion: rbac.authorization.k8s.io/v1
kind: Role
metadata:
  namespace: shield
  name: read-deployments
rules:
- apiGroups: ["apps"]
  resources: ["deployments"]
  verbs: ["get", "watch", "list"]
```

On their own, Roles don't do anything. They need binding to a user.

The following RoleBinding grants the previous "read-deployments" Role to a user called "sky".

```
apiVersion: rbac.authorization.k8s.io/v1
kind: RoleBinding
metadata:
  name: read-deployments
  namespace: shield
subjects:
- kind: User
  name: sky                    <<==== This is the authenticated user
  apiGroup: rbac.authorization.k8s.io
roleRef:
  kind: Role
  name: read-deployments       <<==== This is the Role to bind to the user
  apiGroup: rbac.authorization.k8s.io
```

If both of these are deployed to a cluster, an authenticated user called "sky" will be able to run commands such as kubectl get deployments -n shield.

It's important to understand that the username listed in the RoleBinding has to be a string and has to match the username that was successfully authenticated.

Looking closer at rules

The previous Role object has three properties:

- apiGroups
- resources
- verbs

Together, they define which actions are allowed against which objects. apiGroups and resources define the object, and verbs define the actions. The example allows read access (get, watch and list) against Deployment objects.

The following table shows some apiGroup and resources combinations.

apiGroup	resource	Kubernetes API path
""	pods	/api/v1/namespaces/{namespace}/pods
""	secrets	/api/v1/namespaces/{namespace}/secrets
"storage.k8s.io"	storageclass	/apis/storage.k8s.io/v1/storageclasses
"apps"	deployments	/apis/apps/v1/namespaces/{namespace}/deployments

An empty set of double quotes ("") in the apiGroups field indicates the core API group. All other API sub-groups need specifying as a string enclosed in double quotes.

Kubernetes uses a standard set of *verbs* to describe the actions a subject can perform on a resource. Verb names are self-explanatory and case-sensitive. The following table lists them and demonstrates the REST-based nature of the API by showing how they map to

HTTP methods. It also lists some common HTTP response codes.

HTTP method	Kubernetes verbs	Common responses
POST	create	201 created, 403 Access Denied
GET	get, list and watch	200 OK, 403 Access Denied
PUT	update	200 OK, 403 Access Denied
PATCH	patch	200 OK, 403 Access Denied
DELETE	delete	200 OK, 403 Access Denied

The **Kubernetes verbs** column lists the verbs you use in the rules section of a Role object.

Running the following command shows all API resources supported on your cluster. It also shows API group and supported verbs and is a great resource for helping build rule definitions. The example has been trimmed to fit the page

```
$ kubectl api-resources --sort-by name -o wide
NAME          APIGROUP          KIND          VERBS
deployments   apps              Deployment    [create delete ... get list patch update watch]
ingresses     networking.k8s.io Ingress       [create delete ... get list patch update watch]
pods                            Pod           [create delete ... get list patch update watch]
secrets                         Secret        [create delete ... get list patch update watch]
services                        Service       [create delete get list patch update watch]
```

If you compare the output columns with the `rules` block of the previous Role object, you see how things map.

```
rules:
- apiGroups: ["apps"]
  resources: ["deployments"]
  verbs: ["get", "watch", "list"]
```

You can use the asterisk (*) to refer to all API groups, all resources, and all verbs. For example, the following rule block grants all actions on all resources in every API group (basically cluster admin). It's just for demonstration purposes and you probably shouldn't create rules like this.

```
rules:
- apiGroups: ["*"]
  resources: ["*"]
  verbs: ["*"]
```

Cluster-level users and permissions

So far, you've seen Roles and RoleBindings. However, Kubernetes actually has 4 RBAC objects:

- Roles
- ClusterRoles
- RoleBindings
- ClusterRoleBindings

Roles and *RoleBindings* are namespaced objects. This means they can only be applied to a single Namespace. *ClusterRoles* and *ClusterRoleBindings* are cluster-wide objects and apply to all Namespaces. All 4 are defined in the same API sub-group and their YAML structures are almost identical.

A powerful pattern is to use ClusterRoles to define roles at the cluster level, and then bind them to specific Namespaces via RoleBindings. This lets you define common roles once, and re-use them in specific Namespaces. For example, the following YAML defines the same "read-deployments" role, but this time at the cluster level. This can be re-used in selected Namespaces via RoleBindings – one RoleBinding per Namespace.

```
apiVersion: rbac.authorization.k8s.io/v1
kind: ClusterRole                    <<==== Cluster-scoped role
metadata:
  name: read-deployments
rules:
- apiGroups: ["apps"]
  resources: ["deployments"]
  verbs: ["get", "watch", "list"]
```

Look closely at the previous YAML. The only differences with the earlier one is that this one has its kind set to ClusterRole instead of Role and it doesn't have a metadata.namespace property.

Figure 13.2 shows a role defined at the cluster level being applied to two Namespaces via two RoleBindings. It can easily be applied to the other Namespaces via two more RoleBindings. The role was defined once and re-used across multiple Namespaces.

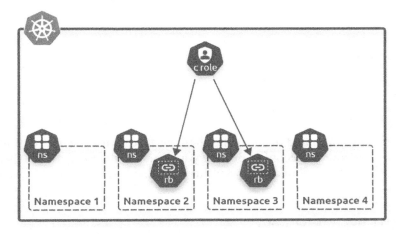

Figure 13.2

Pre-created users and permissions

To help with initial configuration and getting started, most clusters have a set of pre-created roles and bindings that grant permissions to an all-powerful user. Most will also configure kubectl to operate under the context of that all-powerful user.

The following example walks you through how Docker Desktop uses ClusterRoles and ClusterRoleBindings to configure kubectl with admin rights to the Docker Desktop Kubernetes cluster. Other clusters may do things differently, but the principles will be similar and you'll get a general idea of how things work.

Docker Desktop Kubernetes clusters run the API server in a Pod called "kube-apiserver-docker-desktop" in the kube-system Namespace. It has an --authorization flag that tells Kubernetes which authorization modules to use. The following command shows the *Node* and *RBAC* modules are both enabled.

```
$ kubectl describe pod kube-apiserver-docker-desktop \
  --namespace kube-system | grep authorization

    --authorization-mode=Node,RBAC
```

You won't be able to interrogate the API server like this on hosted clusters as the control plane is hidden from you.

Docker Desktop also configures your kubeconfig file with a user called docker-desktop that uses a client certificate to authenticate with Kubernetes.

```
$ kubectl config view
<Snip>
users:
- name: docker-desktop
  user:
    client-certificate-data: REDACTED
    client-key-data: REDACTED
<Snip>
```

The following long command decodes the client certificate for the user defined in the current context of your kubeconfig. Be sure your docker-desktop user is specified in your current context. You'll need the jq utility installed and it will only work on Linux-style systems.

```
$ kubectl config view --raw -o json \
    | jq ".users[] | select(.name==\"$(kubectl config current-context)\")" \
    | jq -r '.user["client-certificate-data"]' \
    | base64 -d | openssl x509 -text | grep "Subject:"

  Subject: O=system:masters, CN=docker-for-desktop
```

The output of the command shows the client certificate authenticates as a user called "docker-for-desktop" that is a member of the "system:masters" group. The certificate is signed by the cluster's CA.

> **Note:** Kubernetes lists users in the CN property of a client certificate and groups in the "O" property.

So far, Docker Desktop has configured the kubeconfig file to authenticate with the cluster as a user called "docker-for-desktop" that is a member of the "system:masters" group. Now let's see how ClusterRoles and ClusterRoleBindings are used to grant permissions to the cluster.

The following command shows a ClusterRole called cluster-admin. The PolicyRule section shows this role has access to all *verbs* on all *resources* in all Namespaces. This is the equivalent of root and is a very powerful and very dangerous set of permissions.

```
kubectl describe clusterrole cluster-admin
Name:          cluster-admin
Labels:        kubernetes.io/bootstrapping=rbac-defaults
Annotations:   rbac.authorization.kubernetes.io/autoupdate: true
PolicyRule:
  Resources   Non-Resource URLs   Resource Names   Verbs
  ---------   -----------------   --------------   -----
  *.*         []                  []               [*]
              [*]                 []               [*]
```

We've already learned that ClusterRoles need binding to users. The following command shows the cluster-admin role is bound to a ClusterRoleBinding with the same name.

```
$ kubectl get clusterrolebindings | grep cluster-admin
NAME                    ROLE
cluster-admin           ClusterRole/cluster-admin
```

If you describe the cluster-admin ClusterRoleBinding, you'll see it maps to all users that are members of the system:masters group.

```
$ kubectl describe clusterrolebindings cluster-admin
Name:          cluster-admin
Labels:        kubernetes.io/bootstrapping=rbac-defaults
Annotations:   rbac.authorization.kubernetes.io/autoupdate: true
Role:
  Kind:  ClusterRole
  Name:  cluster-admin
Subjects:
  Kind    Name            Namespace
  ----    ----            ---------
  Group   system:masters                <<==== Bind to authenticated members of this group
```

That's a lot to take in, so this summary might help.

Docker Desktop configures your kubeconfig file with a client certificate signed by the cluster's certificate authority (CA). This means the certificate is trusted by the cluster. It contains credentials for a user called "docker-for-desktop" that is a member of a group called "system:masters". A cluster-admin ClusterRole exists on the cluster that has admin rights to all objects in all Namespaces. This is bound to members of the system:masters group via a ClusterRoleBinding that is also called cluster-admin.

Summarising authorization

Authorization ensures authenticated users are allowed to execute the actions they're attempting. RBAC is a popular Kubernetes authorization module and implements least privilege access based on a deny-by-default model where all actions are assumed to be denied unless a rule exists that allows them.

Kubernetes RBAC uses Roles and ClusterRoles to create permissions, and it uses RoleBindings and ClusterRoleBindings to grant those permissions to users.

Once a request passes authentication and authorization, it moves on to admission control.

Admission control

Admission control runs immediately after successful authentication and authorization, and it's all about *policies.*

There are two types of admission controllers:

- Mutating
- Validating

The names are self-explanatory. *Mutating* controllers check for compliance and can modify requests, whereas *validating* controllers check for policy compliance but cannot modify requests. Mutating controllers always run first, and both types only apply to requests that will modify state. Requests to read state are not subjected to admission control.

Assume a quick example where you have a policy that all new and updated objects must have the env=prod label. A mutating controller can check for the presence of the label and add it if it doesn't exist. On the flip side, a validating controller can only reject the request if the label doesn't exist.

The following command on a Docker Desktop cluster shows the API server is configured to use the NodeRestriction admission controller.

```
$ kubectl describe pod/kube-apiserver-docker-desktop \
  --namespace kube-system | grep admission

--enable-admission-plugins=NodeRestriction
```

Most real-world clusters will have a lot more admission controllers enabled.

There are lots of admission controllers, but the AlwaysPullImages controller is a great example. It's a mutating controller that sets the spec.containers.imagePullPolicy of all new Pods to "Always". This forces container images to always be pulled from the registry. It accomplishes quite a few things, including the following:

- Preventing the use of local images that could be malicious
- Only nodes with valid credentials can pull images and run containers

If any admission controller rejects a request, it's immediately rejected without checking other admission controllers. However, if all admission controllers approve the request, it gets persisted to the cluster store and instantiated on the cluster.

As previously mentioned, there are lots of admission controllers, and they're becoming more and more important in real-world production clusters.

Chapter summary

In this chapter, you learned that all requests to the API server include credentials and pass-through authentication, authorization, and admission control. The connection between the client and the API server is also secured with TLS.

The authentication layer is responsible for validating the identity of requests. Client certificates are commonly used, and integration with AD and other IAM services is recommended for production clusters. Kubernetes does not have its own identity database, meaning it doesn't store or manage user accounts.

The authorization layer checks whether the authenticated user is allowed to carry out the action in the request. This layer is also pluggable, and the most common module is RBAC. RBAC comprises 4 objects that define permissions and assign them to users.

Admission control kicks in after authorization and is responsible for enforcing policies. Validating admission controllers reject requests if they don't conform to policy, whereas mutating admission controllers can modify requests to enforce policies.

14: The Kubernetes API

Understanding the Kubernetes API, and how it works, is vital to true mastery of Kubernetes. However, it can be extremely confusing if you're new to APIs and not comfortable with terms like *RESTful*. If that's you, this chapter will blow away the confusion and get you up-to-speed with the fundamentals of the Kubernetes API.

The chapter is divided as follows:

- Kubernetes API big picture
- The API server
- The API

A couple of quick things before we get cracking with the chapter.

First up. I've made no attempt to make this chapter jargon-free. In fact, I've intentionally included a lot of jargon, so you get comfortable with it. I've also included an extended chapter summary, full of jargon, that you should be able to understand if you've read the whole chapter.

Last up. I've included some hands-on commands and exercises. I've made them as simple as possible, and I highly recommend you complete them as they'll help reinforce the theory.

Kubernetes API big picture

Let's start out with the super high level.

Kubernetes is *API centric*. This means everything in Kubernetes is about the API, and everything goes through the API and API server.

Clients send requests to Kubernetes to create, read, update, and delete objects such as Pods and Services. For the most part, you'll use kubectl to send these requests, however, you can craft them in code or use API testing and development tools to generate them. The point is, no matter how you generate requests, they go to the *API server* where they're authenticated and authorized. Assuming they pass the auth tests, they're executed on the cluster. If it's a create request, the object is deployed to the cluster and the serialized state of it is persisted to the cluster store.

The overall process is depicted in Figure 14.1 and shows the central nature of the API and API server.

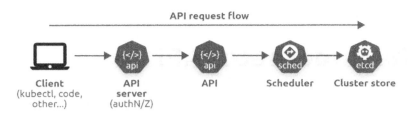

Figure 14.1

JSON serialization

We've already introduced a fair bit of jargon, so let's start busting some of it.

What is meant by "serialized state of an object".

Serialization is the process of converting an object into a string, or stream of bytes, so it can be sent over a network and persisted to a data store. The reverse process of converting a string or stream of bytes into an object is *deserialization*.

Kubernetes serializes objects, such as Pods and Services, as JSON strings to be sent over HTTP. The process happens in both directions, with clients like kubectl serializing objects when posting to the API server, and the API server serializing responses back to clients. In the case of Kubernetes, the serialised state of objects is also persisted to the cluster store which is usually based on the etcd database.

So, in Kubernetes, serialization is the process of converting an object into a JSON string to be sent over an HTTP connection and persisted to the cluster store.

However, as well as JSON, Kubernetes also supports Protobuf as a serialization schema. This is faster, more efficient, and scales better than JSON. But it's not as user-friendly when it comes to introspection and troubleshooting. At the time of writing, Protobuf is mainly used for internal cluster traffic, whereas JSON is used when communicating with external clients.

One final thing on serialization. When clients send requests to the API server, they use the Content-Type header to list the serialization schemas they support. For example, a client that only supports JSON will specify Content-Type: application/json in the HTTP header of the request. Kubernetes will honour this with a serialized response in JSON.

You'll see this in some of the examples later.

API analogy

Let's consider a quick analogy that might help you conceptualise the Kubernetes API.

Amazon sells lots of stuff. That *stuff* is stored in warehouses and listed online on the Amazon website. You use a browser to search the website and buy stuff. 3rd-parties even sell their own stuff through Amazon and you use the same browser and website. When you buy stuff through the website, it gets delivered to you and you can start using it. The Amazon website even lets you track your stuff while it's being prepared and delivered. Once it's delivered, it's yours and Amazon is only involved if you want to do things like order more or send stuff back.

Well, it's pretty much the same with the Kubernetes API.

Kubernetes offers lots of objects such as Pods, Services, and Ingresses. They're defined in the API and exposed through the API server. You use tools like kubectl to request them. 3rd-parties even define their own objects in Kubernetes and you use the same kubectl and API server to request them. When you request an object through the API server, it gets created on your cluster and you can start using it. The API server even lets you watch it while it's being created. Once it's created, Kubernetes continues to observe it and you can query its state through the API server. Actions like creating more and deleting objects are also done through the API server.

The comparison is shown in Figure 14.2, and a feature-for-feature comparison is shown in the following table. Keep in mind, however, it's just an analogy and not everything is a perfect match.

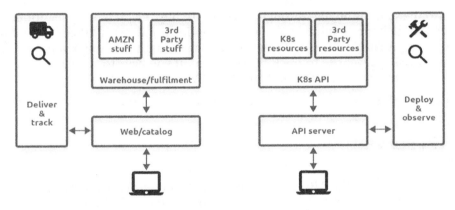

Figure 14.2

Amazon	Kubernetes
Stuff	Objects
Warehouse	API
Browser	kubectl
Amazon website	API server

To recap. All deployable objects, such as Pods, Services, Ingresses and more, are defined as resources in the API. If an object isn't defined in the API, you can't deploy it. This is the same with Amazon – you can only buy stuff that's listed on the website.

API Resources have properties you can view and configure. For example, Pod objects are defined in the API with all of the following properties (they have more properties than shown):

- metadata (name, labels, Namespace, annotations...)
- restart policy
- service account name
- runtime class
- containers
- volumes

This is the same as buying things on Amazon. For example, when buying a USB cable, you can configure choices such as USB type, cable length, and even cable color.

To deploy a Pod, you send a Pod YAML file to the API server. Assuming it's valid and you're authorized to create Pods, it gets deployed to the cluster. After that, you can query the API server to get its current status. When it's time to delete it, you send the delete request to the API server.

This is also the same as buying through Amazon. To buy the previously mentioned USB cable, you input all the colour, length, and type options, and submit them to the Amazon website. Assuming it's in stock and you provide the funds, it gets shipped to you. After that, you can use the website to track the shipment. If you have to return the item or make a complaint, you do all of that through the Amazon website.

OK, that's enough with analogies. Let's take a closer look at the *API server*.

The API server

The API server exposes the API over a secure RESTful interface using HTTPS. It acts as the front-end to the API and is a bit like Grand Central for Kubernetes – everything talks to everything else via REST API calls to the API server. For example:

- All kubectl commands go to the API server (creating, retrieving, updating, deleting objects)
- All node Kubelets watch the API server for new tasks and report status to the API server
- All control plane services communicate with each other via the API server (they don't talk directly to each other)

Let's demystify a bit more jargon.

The *API server* is a Kubernetes control plane service. This usually means it runs as a set of Pods in the kube-system Namespace on the control plane nodes of your cluster. If you build and manage your own Kubernetes clusters, you need to make sure the control plane is highly-available and has enough performance to keep the API server up-and-running and responding quickly to requests. If you're using a *hosted Kubernetes* cluster, the way the API server is implemented, including performance and availability, is hidden from you.

The main job of the API server is to make the API available to clients inside and outside the cluster. It uses TLS to encrypt the client connection, and it leverages a bunch of authentication and authorization mechanisms to ensure only valid requests are accepted and actioned. Requests from internal and external sources all have to pass through the same authentication and authorization.

The API is *RESTful*. This is jargon for a modern web API that accepts CRUD-style requests via standard HTTP methods. *CRUD-style operations* are simple *create, read, update, delete* operations, and the common *HTTP methods* include POST, GET, PUT, PATCH, and DELETE.

The following table shows how HTTP methods, CRUD operations, and kubectl commands match-up. If you've read the chapter on API security, you'll know we use the term *verb* to refer to CRUD operations.

HTTP method	K8s CRUD verb	kubectl example
POST	create	$ kubectl create -f <filename>
GET	get list, watch	$ kubectl get pods
PUT/PATCH	update	$ kubectl edit deployment <deployment-name>
DELETE	delete	$ kubectl delete ingress <ig-name>

As you can see, method names, CRUD verb names, and kubectl command names don't always match. For example, a kubectl **edit** command requires a user be authorized to use the **update** verb and will send an HTTP **PATCH** request to the API server.

It's common for the API server to be exposed on port 443 or 6443, but it's possible to configure it to operate on whatever port you require. Running the following command shows the address and port your Kubernetes cluster is exposed on.

```
$ kubectl cluster-info

Kubernetes control plane is running at https://34.105.153.166
GLBCDefaultBackend is running at https://34.105.153.166/api/v1/namespaces/...
KubeDNS is running at https://34.105.153.166/api/v1/namespaces/kube-system...
Metrics-server is running at https://34.105.153.166/api/v1/namespaces/...
```

A word on REST and RESTful

You'll hear the terms REST and RESTful a lot. REST is short for REpresentational State Transfer and is the de facto standard for communicating with web-based APIs. Systems, such as Kubernetes, that use REST are often referred to as *RESTful*.

REST requests comprise a *verb* and a *path* to a resource. Verbs relate to actions and are the standard HTTP methods you saw in the previous table. Paths are a URI path to the resource in the API.

> **Disambiguation:** We often use the term *verb* to refer to CRUD operations as well as HTTP methods. CRUD operations include *create, read, update* and *delete*, whereas the HTTP methods are *GET, POST, PUT, PATCH* and *DELETE*. If it's confusing, the term "verb" is used to refer to an *action*.

The following example shows a kubectl command and associated REST request and path that will list all Pods in the shield Namespace.

```
$ kubectl get pods --namespace shield
```

```
GET /api/v1/namespaces/shield/pods
```

To visualise this, start a kubectl proxy and use curl to generate the request. The kubectl proxy command exposes the API on your localhost adapter and takes care of authentication. You can use a different port.

```
$ kubectl proxy --port 9000 &
[1] 14774
Starting to serve on 127.0.0.1:9000
```

With the proxy running, use a tool like curl to form a request to the API server.

```
$ curl http://localhost:9000/api/v1/namespaces/shield/pods
{
  "kind": "PodList",
  "apiVersion": "v1",
  "metadata": {
    "resourceVersion": "34148"
  },
  "items": []
}
```

The example returned an empty list because there are no Pods running in the shield Namespace. Try another request to list all Namespaces.

```
$ curl http://localhost:9000/api/v1/namespaces
<Snip>
```

Responses from the API server include common HTTP response codes, content type, and the actual payload. As you learned earlier in the chapter, Kubernetes uses JSON as its preferred content type. As a result, the previous kubectl get command will result in an HTTP 200 (OK) response code, content type will be application/json and the payload will be a serialized JSON list of all Pods in the shield Namespace.

Run one of the previous curl commands again but add the -v flag to see the send and receive headers. The response has been trimmed to fit the book and draw your attention to the most important parts.

```
$ curl -v http://localhost:9000/api/v1/namespaces/shield/pods

> GET /api/v1/namespaces/shield/pods HTTP/1.1    <<==== HTTP GET method to REST path of Pods
> Accept: */*                                    <<==== Accept all serialization schemas
>
< HTTP/1.1 200 OK                                <<==== Accepted and starting response
< Content-Type: application/json                 <<==== Responding using JSON serialization
< X-Kubernetes-Pf-Flowschema-Uid: 499...
< X-Kubernetes-Pf-Prioritylevel-Uid: aeb...
<
{                                                <<==== Start of response (serialized object)
  "kind": "PodList",
  "apiVersion": "v1",
  "metadata": {
    "resourceVersion": "34217"
  },
  "items": []
}
```

Lines starting with a > are header data *sent* by curl, whereas lines starting with a < are header data returned by the API server.

The > lines show curl sending a GET request to the /api/v1/namespaces/shield/pods REST path and telling the API server it can accept any valid serialization schema – Accept: */*. The lines starting with < show the API server returning an HTTP response code and using JSON as the serialization schema. The X-Kubernetes lines are additional priority and fairness settings specific to Kubernetes.

A word on CRUD

CRUD is an acronym for the four basic functions web APIs use to manipulate and persist objects – create, read, update, delete. As previously mentioned, the Kubernetes API exposes and implements CRUD-style operations via the common HTTP methods.

Let's consider an example.

The following JSON is from the "ns.json" file in the api folder of the book's GitHub repo. It defines a new Namespace object called "shield".

```
{
  "kind": "Namespace",
  "apiVersion": "v1",
  "metadata": {
    "name": "shield",
    "labels": {
      "chapter": "api"
    }
  }
}
```

You can create it with the kubectl apply -f ns.json command. Behind the scenes, kubectl forms a request to the API server using the HTTP POST method. This is why you'll occasionally see some documentation refer to "POSTing" to the API server. The POST method creates a new object of the specified resource type. In this example, it'll create a new Namespace object called "shield".

The following is a simplified example of the request header. The body will be the contents of the JSON file.

Request header:

```
POST https://<api-server>/api/v1/namespaces
Content-Type: application/json
Accept: application/json
```

If the request is successful, the response will include a standard HTTP response code, content type, and actual payload.

```
HTTP/1.1 200 (OK)
Content-Type: application/json
{
    ...
}
```

Talk is cheap though... try posting it to the API server with the following curl command. You'll need a kubectl proxy process exposing the API server on port 9000 (kubectl proxy --port 9000 &) and you'll need to run the command from the directory containing the ns.json file. If you already created it with the kubectl apply -f ns.json command you'll need to delete the Namespace first.

```
$ curl -X POST -H "Content-Type: application/json" \
  --data-binary @ns.json http://localhost:9000/api/v1/namespaces

<Snip>
```

The -X POST argument forces curl to use the HTTP POST method. The -H "Content-Type..." tells the API server the request contains serialized JSON. The --data-binary @ns.json specifies the manifest file, and the URI is the address the API server is exposed on by kubectl proxy and includes the REST path.

You can verify the new Namespace was created with the kubectl get namespaces command.

Feel free to delete the newly created Namespace by specifying the DELETE HTTP method.

```
$ curl -X DELETE \
  -H "Content-Type: application/json" http://localhost:9000/api/v1/namespaces/shield
{
  "kind": "Namespace",
  "apiVersion": "v1",
  "metadata": {
    "name": "shield",
    <Snip>
  },
  "spec": {
    "finalizers": [
      "kubernetes"
    ]
  },
  "status": {
    "phase": "Terminating"
  }
}
```

In summary, the API server exposes the API over a secure RESTful interface that lets you manipulate and query the state of objects on the cluster. It runs on the control plane, which needs to be highly available and have enough performance to service requests quickly.

The API

The API is where all Kubernetes resources are defined. It's large, modular, and RESTful.

When Kubernetes was originally created, the API was monolithic in design with all resources existing in a single global namespace. However, as Kubernetes grew, it became necessary to divide it into smaller and more manageable groups. Figure 14.3 shows a simplified view of what it currently looks like.

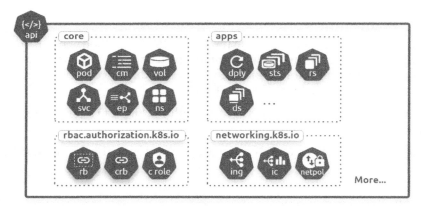

Figure 14.3

As you can see, the image shows the API with 4 groups. There are a lot more than 4, but the image only shows 4 for simplicity.

At the highest level, there are two types of API group:

- The **core** group
- The **named** groups

The core API group

Resources in the core group are mature objects that were created in the early days of Kubernetes before the API was divided into groups. They tend to be fundamental objects such as Pods, nodes, Services, Secrets, and ServiceAccounts. They're located in the API below /api/v1. The following table lists some example paths for resources in the core group. You'll sometimes see and hear these paths referred to as *REST paths*.

Resource	REST Path
Pods	/api/v1/namespaces/{namespace}/pods/
Services	/api/v1/namespaces/{namespace}/services/
Nodes	/api/v1/nodes/
Namespaces	/api/v1/namespaces/

Notice that some objects are namespaced and some aren't. Namespaced objects have longer REST paths as you have to include two additional segments – ../namespaces/{namespace}/... For example, listing all Pods in the "shield" Namespace requires the following path.

```
GET /api/v1/namespaces/shield/pods/
```

Expected HTTP response codes for read requests are either 200: OK or 401: Unauthorized.

On the topic of REST paths, GVR stands for group, version, resource, and can be a good way to remember the structure of REST paths in the Kubernetes API. A simple example is shown in Figure 14.4, but paths for namespaced objects include longer resource segments.

Figure 14.4

You shouldn't expect any new resources to be added to the core group. Anything new will be added to a *named group*.

Named API groups

The named API groups are the future of the API, and all new resources get added to named groups. Sometimes we refer to them as "sub-groups"

Each of the named groups is a collection of related resources. For example, the "apps" group is where all resources that manage application workloads such as Deployments, ReplicaSets, DaemonSets, and StatefulSets are defined. Likewise, the "networking.k8s.io" group is where Ingresses, Ingress Classes, Network Policies, and other network-related resources exist. Notable exceptions to this pattern are older resources in the core group that came along before the named groups existed. For example, Pods and Services are both in the core group. However, if they were invented today, Pods would probably go in the "apps" group, and Services in the "networking.k8s.io" group.

Resources in the named groups live below the /apis/{group-name}/{version}/ path. The following table lists some examples.

Resource	Path
Ingress	/apis/networking.k8s.io/v1/namespaces/{namespace}/ingresses/
RoleBinding	/apis/rbac.authorization.k8s.io/v1/namespaces/{namespace}/rolebindings/
ClusterRole	/apis/rbac.authorization.k8s.io/v1/clusterroles/
StorageClass	/apis/storage.k8s.io/v1/storageclasses/

Notice how the URI paths for named groups start with /apis and include the name
of the group. This is different to the core group that starts with /api in the singular
and doesn't include a group name. In fact, in some places you'll see the core API group
referred to by empty double quotes (""). This is because when the API was first designed,
no thought was given to groups – everything was "just in the API".

Dividing the API into smaller groups makes it more scalable and easier to navigate. It
also makes it easier to extend.

The following commands are good for seeing API related info for your clusters.

kubectl api-resources is great for seeing which resources are available on your cluster, as well as which API groups they're served from. It also shows resource shortnames
and whether objects are namespaced or cluster-scoped. The output has been tweaked to
fit the book as well as show a mix of resources from different groups.

```
$ kubectl api-resources
NAME              SHORTNAMES    APIGROUP              NAMESPACED    KIND
namespaces        ns                                  false         Namespace
nodes             no                                  false         Node
pods              po                                  true          Pod
deployments       deploy        apps                  true          Deployment
replicasets       rs            apps                  true          ReplicaSet
statefulsets      sts           apps                  true          StatefulSet
cronjobs          cj            batch                 true          CronJob
jobs                            batch                 true          Job
ingresses         ing           networking.k8s.io     true          Ingress
networkpolicies   netpol        networking.k8s.io     true          NetworkPolicy
storageclasses    sc            storage.k8s.io        false         StorageClass
```

The next command shows which API versions are supported on your cluster. It doesn't
list which resources belong to which APIs, but it's good for finding out whether you
have things such as alpha APIs enabled or not. Notice how some API groups have
multiple versions enabled such as beta and a stable.

```
$ kubectl api-versions
admissionregistration.k8s.io/v1
apiextensions.k8s.io/v1
apps/v1
<Snip>
autoscaling/v1
autoscaling/v2
autoscaling/v2beta1
autoscaling/v2beta2
v1
```

The next one is a more complicated command that lists just the kind and version fields
for resources supported on your cluster. The output is trimmed so that it gives you an
idea of what you get. It doesn't work on Windows.

```
$ for kind in `kubectl api-resources | tail +2 | awk '{ print $1 }'`; \
 do kubectl explain $kind; done | grep -e "KIND:" -e "VERSION:"

KIND:       Binding
VERSION:    v1
KIND:       ComponentStatus
VERSION:    v1
<Snip>
KIND:       HorizontalPodAutoscaler
VERSION:    autoscaling/v2
KIND:       CronJob
VERSION:    batch/v1
KIND:       Job
VERSION:    batch/v1
<Snip>
```

A quick word on accessing the API

While kubectl can be useful for getting API info, it's often better to explore the API more directly using one of the following options:

- API development tools
- Commands like curl, wget, and Invoke-WebRequest
- Web browser

The simplest way to do this, is to run a kubectl proxy command that exposes the API on your localhost adapter and handles all security and authentication.

The following command exposes the API on port 9000 on your localhost adapter. The proxy remains up until you terminate the process (process ID 14781 in the example). If you run the command without the "&" on the end, you'll need to open a new terminal window to run commands.

You don't need to run this if you already have a kubectl proxy running.

```
$ kubectl proxy --port 9000 &
[1] 14781
Starting to serve on 127.0.0.1:9000
```

Kubectl is now proxying the API server on localhost:9000. Run some curl commands to explore the API.

The following two commands list all API versions available below the core API group, and the same for the named API groups. The outputs are trimmed to save space.

```
$ curl http://localhost:9000/api
{
  "kind": "APIVersions",
  "versions": [
    "v1"
  ],
  "serverAddressByClientCIDRs": [
    {
      "clientCIDR": "0.0.0.0/0",
      "serverAddress": "172.21.0.4:6443"
    }
  ]
}

$ curl http://localhost:9000/apis
{
  "kind": "APIGroupList",
  "apiVersion": "v1",
  "groups": [
    <Snip>
    {
      "name": "apps",
      "versions": [
        {
          "groupVersion": "apps/v1",
          "version": "v1"
        }
      ],
      "preferredVersion": {
        "groupVersion": "apps/v1",
        "version": "v1"
      }
    },
    <Snip>
```

You can list specific object instances or lists of objects on your cluster. The following shows a list of all Namespaces on a cluster.

```
$ curl http://localhost:9000/api/v1/namespaces
{
  "kind": "NamespaceList",
  "apiVersion": "v1",
  "metadata": {
    "resourceVersion": "35234"
  },
  "items": [
    {
      "metadata": {
        "name": "kube-system",
        "uid": "05fefa13-cbec-458b-aece-d65eb1972dfb",
```

```
        "resourceVersion": "4",
        "creationTimestamp": "2021-12-29T12:32:48Z",
        "labels": {
          "kubernetes.io/metadata.name": "kube-system"
        },
        "managedFields": [
          {
            "manager": "Go-http-client",
            "operation": "Update",
            "apiVersion": "v1",
<Snip>
```

Feel free to poke around. You can put the same URI paths into a browser and API tools like Postman.

Leave the `kubectl proxy` process running as you'll use it again later in the chapter.

Alpha beta and stable

Kubernetes has a strict process for adding new resources to the API. They come in as *alpha*, progress through *beta*, and eventually reach *stable*.

Resources in **alpha** are experimental and should be considered *hairy and scary*. Expect bugs, expect features to be dropped without warning, and expect lots of change as they graduate through beta to stable. A lot of clusters disable alpha APIs by default, and you should use them with extreme caution.

A resource that progresses through two alpha versions will go through the following APIs:

- /apis/some-api/v1alpha1/...
- /apis/some-api/v1alpha2/...

The phase after alpha is beta.

Resources in **beta** are considered "pre-release" and are starting to look and feel a lot like they will when they graduate to stable. Features that are part of beta resources will rarely be dropped when the resource graduates to stable. However, small changes should be expected. Most clusters enable beta APIs by default, and many people use beta objects in production environments. However, that's not a recommendation, you need to make those decisions yourself.

A resource that progresses through two beta versions will be served through the following APIs:

- /apis/some-api/vbeta1/...

- /apis/some-api/vbeta2/...

The final phase after beta is *stable*, sometimes referred to as *generally available (GA)*. Stable resources are considered production-ready and Kubernetes has a strong long-term commitment to them.

Examples of paths to stable resources include the following:

- /apis/some-api/v1/...
- /apis/some-api/v2/...

Most stable resources are currently at v1, but some continue being developed and change so much that a v2 is required. For an object to become v2, it progresses through alpha and beta again as follows:

- /apis/some-api/v2alpaX/... ->>
- /apis/some-api/v2betaX/... ->>
- /apis/some-api/v2

It's usually possible to deploy beta objects and continue to work with them through later stable API versions. For example, you can deploy an object via a v1beta1 API but update and manage it at a later date through the stable v1 API.

Resource deprecation

As mentioned in the previous section, alpha and beta objects are subject to changes before graduating to stable. However, once an object is stable, Kubernetes has a strong commitment to maintaining long-term usability and support. Basically, once an object is stable (v1, v2 etc.) it has a long life.

Kubernetes commits to support beta and stable objects as follows:

- Stable/GA: Objects are expected to be long-lived. When deprecated, stable objects will be supported for a further 12 months, or 3 releases, whichever's longest.
- Beta: Objects in beta have a 9-month window to either graduate to stable or release a newer beta version. This is to avoid beta features going stale or staying in beta for too long. For example, the Ingress resource remained in beta for more than 15 releases of Kubernetes!

Recent versions of Kubernetes return deprecation warning messages any time you use a deprecated resource. For example, deploying an Ingress from the old extensions/v1beta1 API resulted in the following deprecation warning while the v1beta1 API was being deprecated.

```
$ kubectl apply -f deprecate.yml
Warning: extensions/v1beta1 Ingress is deprecated in v1.14+, unavailable in v1.22+;
Use networking.k8s.io/v1 Ingress
```

Resources, objects, and primitives

You'll often see the terms *resources, objects,* and even *primitives* used interchangeably. And that's fine, most people do it and everyone understands what you mean.

However, technically speaking, the Kubernetes API is *resource-based.* This means everything in the API is a resource. It just so happens that most API resources, such as Pods, Services, and Ingresses are *objects.* However, some resources are *lists,* and an even smaller number are *operations.* However, most resources are objects, so we often use the terms "resource" and "object" to mean the same thing.

Resources can be either namespaced or cluster-scoped. Namespaced objects have to be deployed to a particular Namespace, whereas cluster-scoped objects can either be bound to multiple Namespaces or exist entirely outside the realm of Namespaces. Node objects are an example of a cluster-scoped resource that exists entirely outside of Namespaces and cannot ever be deployed to one. On the flip side, ClusterRoles are an example of a cluster-scoped object that can be bound to specific Namespaces via RoleBindings.

Remember, `kubectl api-resources` lists all resources and whether they're namespaced or cluster-scoped.

Extending the API

Kubernetes runs a set of controllers that read an object's `spec`, deploy and maintain it on the cluster, and keep its `status` section up-to-date. However, you can extend Kubernetes by adding your own resources and controllers.

A common example of 3rd-parties extending the Kubernetes API can be seen in the storage world where vendors expose advanced features, such as snapshot schedules, via custom resources in the Kubernetes API. In this model, storage is surfaced inside of Kubernetes via CSI drivers, Pods consume it via built-in Kubernetes resources such as StorageClasses and PersistentVoumeClaims, but advanced features such as snapshot scheduling is consumed via custom resources in the API.

The high-level pattern for extending the API involves two main things:

- Writing your custom *controller*
- Creating the custom *resource*

Kubernetes has a CustomResourceDefinition (CRD) object that lets you create new resources in the API that look, smell, and feel like native Kubernetes resources. This means you can create a custom resource, and then use kubectl to create and inspect it just like it's a native resource. They also get their own REST paths in the API.

The following YAML is from the crd.yml file in the api folder of the book's GitHub repo. It defines a new namespaced custom resource called "books" in the "nigelpoulton.com" named group that is served via the "v1" path.

```
apiVersion: apiextensions.k8s.io/v1
kind: CustomResourceDefinition
metadata:
  name: books.nigelpoulton.com
spec:
  group: nigelpoulton.com        <<==== Named API group
  scope: Cluster                 <<==== Can be "Namespaced" or "Cluster"
  names:
    plural: books                <<==== All resources need a plural and singular name
    singular: book               <<==== Singular names are used on CLI and command outputs
    kind: Book                   <<==== kind property used in YAML files
    shortNames:
    - bk                         <<==== Short name used by kubectl
  versions:                      <<==== Resources can be served by multiple API versions
    - name: v1
      served: true               <<==== If set to false, "v1" will not be served
      storage: true              <<==== Store instances of the object as this version
      schema:                    <<==== This block defines properties of custom resource
        openAPIV3Schema:
          type: object
          properties:
            spec:
              type: object
              properties:
                <Snip>
```

Use the following command to make a local copy of the GitHub repo and the lab files. You'll need to have git installed for this to work.

```
$ git clone https://github.com/nigelpoulton/TheK8sBook.git
```

Change into the api directory.

```
$ cd TheK8sBook/api
```

If you're following along, deploy the custom resource with the following command. Be sure to run it from the api folder containing the crd.yml file.

```
$ kubectl apply -f crd.yml
customresourcedefinition.apiextensions.k8s.io/books.nigelpoulton.com created
```

Once deployed, the new resource exists in the API and you can deploy objects from it. This particular one will be served on the following REST path.

```
apis/nigelpoulton.com/v1/books/
```

Verify it exists in the API.

```
$ kubectl api-resources | grep books
NAME       SHORTNAMES      APIGROUP             NAMESPACED    KIND
books      bk              nigelpoulton.com     false         Book

$ kubectl explain book
KIND:      Book
VERSION:   nigelpoulton.com/v1
DESCRIPTION:
     <empty>
FIELDS:
     <Snip>
```

The following YAML is from the kcna.yml file in the api folder of the book's GitHub repo. It defines a new Book object called "kcna". Notice how the fields in the spec section match the names and types defined in the custom resource YAML definition (crd.yml).

```
apiVersion: nigelpoulton.com/v1
kind: Book
metadata:
  name: kcna
spec:
  bookTitle: "The KCNA Book"
  topic: Certifications
  edition: 1
```

Deploy it with the following command.

```
$ kubectl apply -f kcna.yml
book.nigelpoulton.com/kcna created
```

You can now list and describe it with the usual commands. The following GET command uses the resource's "bk" shortname.

```
$ kubectl get bk
NAME    TITLE            EDITION
kcna    The KCNA Book.   1
```

Finally, you can use tools like `curl` to query the new API group and resource. The simplest way to do this is to run a kubectl proxy.

The following commands start a kubectl proxy and list all resources under the new `nigelpoulton.com` named group. You may already have a `kubectl proxy` process running.

```
$ kubectl proxy --port 9000 &
[1] 14784
Starting to serve on 127.0.0.1:9000

$ curl http://localhost:9000/apis/nigelpoulton.com/v1/
{
  "kind": "APIResourceList",
  "apiVersion": "v1",
  "groupVersion": "nigelpoulton.com/v1",
  "resources": [
    {
      "name": "books",
      "singularName": "book",
      "namespaced": false,
      "kind": "Book",
      "verbs": [
        "delete",
        "deletecollection",
        "get",
        "list",
        "patch",
        "create",
        "update",
        "watch"
      ],
      "shortNames": [
        "bk"
      ],
      "storageVersionHash": "F2QdXaP5vh4="
    }
  ]
}
```

This is all good and interesting. But a custom resource doesn't do anything until you create a custom controller to go with it. Doing this is beyond the scope of this chapter, but you've learned a lot about the Kubernetes API and how it works.

Chapter summary

Now that you've read the chapter, all of the following should make sense. But don't worry if some bits are still vague or confusing. APIs can be hard to understand, and the Kubernetes API is large and complex. Anyway, here goes…

Kubernetes is API centric, and the API is exposed internally and externally via the API server.

The API server runs as a control plane service, and all internal and external clients interact with each other and the API, via the API server. This means your control plane needs to be highly available and high performance. If it's not, you risk slow API response times or entirely losing access to the API. Also, all requests to the API server are authenticated, authorized, and protected by TLS.

The API itself is a modern resource-based RESTful API that accepts CRUD-style operations via uniform HTTP methods such as POST, GET, PUT, PATCH, and DELETE. It's divided into named groups for convenience and extensibility. Older resources created in the early days of Kubernetes exist in the original core group which is accessed via the /api/v1 REST path. All newer objects go into named groups. For example, newer network resources are defined in the networking.k8s.io sub-group available at the /apis/networking.k8s.io/v1/ REST path.

Resources in the Kubernetes API are usually objects. However, they can also be lists or operations. The vast majority are objects, so we sometimes use the terms "resources" and "objects" to mean the same thing. It's common to refer to their API definitions as resources, or resource definitions, whereas running instances on a cluster are often referred to as objects. For example, *the Pod "resource" exists in the core API group, and there are 5 Pod "objects" running in the default Namespace.*

All new resources come into the API as alpha, progress through beta, and eventually graduate to stable. Alpha resources are subject to change and are disabled in many clusters due to their unstable nature. Beta resources are more stable and consist of features expected to be carried through to the stable version. Most clusters enable beta resources by default, but you should be cautious using them in production. Stable resources are considered *production-grade* and Kubernetes has a strong commitment to them that is backed by a clear deprecation policy that guarantees they'll be supported for at least 12 months, or three versions, after the deprecation announcement.

Finally, the Kubernetes API is becoming the de facto cloud API with many 3rd-party technologies extending it so they can be exposed through it. Kubernetes makes it easy to extend the API with your own custom resources through CustomResourceDefinitions that make your custom resources look like native Kubernetes resources.

OK, hopefully that made sense. But don't worry if you're still a bit unsure about some of the points. I highly recommend you play around with as many of the examples as possible. Also consider reading the chapter again in a day or so, as it often takes time and more than one reading of something before you grasp it.

If you liked this chapter, or any other chapter in the book, jump over to Amazon and show the book some love with a quick review. The cloud-native gods will smile on you ;-)

15: Threat modeling Kubernetes

Security is more important than ever and Kubernetes is no exception. Fortunately, there's a lot you can do to secure Kubernetes and you'll see some ways in the next chapter. However, before doing that, it's a good idea to model some of the common threats.

Threat modeling

Threat modeling is the process of identifying vulnerabilities so you can put measures in place to prevent and mitigate them. This chapter introduces the popular **STRIDE** model and shows how it can be applied to Kubernetes.

STRIDE defines six categories of potential threat:

- Spoofing
- Tampering
- Repudiation
- Information disclosure
- Denial of service
- Elevation of privilege

While the model is good, it's important to keep in mind that it's just a model, and no model guarantees to cover all possible threats. However, they are good at providing a structured way to asses things.

For the rest of this chapter we'll look at each of the six threat categories in turn. For each one, we'll give a quick description and then look at some of the ways it applies to Kubernetes and how we can prevent and mitigate.

The chapter doesn't try to cover everything. It's just giving you ideas and getting you started.

Spoofing

Spoofing is pretending to be somebody else with the aim of gaining extra privileges on a system.

Let's look at some of the ways Kubernetes prevents different types of spoofing.

Securing communications with the API server

Kubernetes comprises of lots of small components that work together. These include the API server, controller manager, scheduler, cluster store, and others. It also includes Node components such as the kubelet and container runtime. Each one has its own set of privileges that allow it to interact with, and even modify the cluster. Even though Kubernetes implements a least-privilege model, spoofing the identity of any of these can cause problems.

If you read the RBAC and API security chapter, you'll know that Kubernetes requires all components to authenticate via cryptographically signed certificates (mTLS). This is good, and Kubernetes makes it easy by auto-rotating certificates. However, it's vital you consider the following:

1. A typical Kubernetes installation auto-generates a self-signed certificate authority (CA) that issues certificates to all cluster components. While this is better than nothing, on its own it's not enough for production environments.
2. Mutual TLS (mTLS) is only as secure as the CA issuing the certificates. Compromising the CA can render the entire mTLS layer ineffective. With this in mind, it's vital to keep the CA secure!

A good practice is to ensure that certificates issued by the internal Kubernetes CA are only used and trusted *within* the Kubernetes cluster. This requires careful approval of certificate signing requests, as well as ensuring the Kubernetes CA doesn't get added as a trusted CA for any systems outside the cluster.

As mentioned in previous chapters, all internal and external requests to the API server are subject to authentication and authorization checks. As a result, the API server needs a way to authenticate (trust) internal and external sources. A good way to do this is having two trusted key pairs:

- One for authenticating internal systems
- A second for authenticating external systems

In this model, you'd use the clusters self-signed CA to issue keys to internal systems, and configure Kubernetes to trust one or more trusted 3rd-party CAs for external systems.

Securing Pod communications

As well as spoofing access to the *cluster*, there's also the threat of spoofing app-to-app communications. In Kubernetes, this can be when one Pod spoofs another. Fortunately, you can mount certificates into Pods that are used to authenticate Pod identity.

Every Pod has an associated `ServiceAccount` that is used to provide an identity for the Pod within the cluster. This is achieved by automatically mounting a service account token into every Pod as a *Secret*. Two points to note:

1. The service account token allows access to the API server
2. Most Pods probably don't need to access the API server

With these two points in mind, it's often recommended to set `automountServiceAccountToken` to false for Pods that you know don't need to communicate with the API server. The following Pod manifest shows how to do this.

```
apiVersion: v1
kind: Pod
metadata:
  name: service-account-example-pod
spec:
  serviceAccountName: some-service-account
  automountServiceAccountToken: false
  <Snip>
```

If the Pod does need to talk to the API server, the following non-default configurations are worth exploring:

- expirationSeconds
- audience

These let you force a time when the token will expire, as well as restrict the entities it works with. The following example, inspired from official Kubernetes docs, sets an expiry period of one hour and restricts it to the `vault` audience in a projected volume.

```
apiVersion: v1
kind: Pod
metadata:
  name: nginx
spec:
  containers:
  - image: nginx
    name: nginx
    volumeMounts:
    - mountPath: /var/run/secrets/tokens
      name: vault-token
  serviceAccountName: my-pod
  volumes:
  - name: vault-token
    projected:
      sources:
```

```
- serviceAccountToken:
    path: vault-token
    expirationSeconds: 3600      <<==== This line
    audience: vault              <<==== And this one
```

Tampering

Tampering is the act of changing something, in a malicious way, to cause one of the following:

- Denial of service. Tampering with the resource to make it unusable.
- Elevation of privilege. Tampering with a resource to gain additional privileges.

Tampering can be hard to avoid, so a common counter-measure is to make it obvious when something has been tampered with. A common non-Kubernetes example is packaging medication. Most over-the-counter drugs are packaged with tamper-proof seals that make it obvious if the product has been tampered with.

Tampering with Kubernetes components

Tampering with any of the following Kubernetes components can cause problems:

- etcd
- Configuration files for the API server, controller-manager, scheduler, etcd, and kubelet
- Container runtime binaries
- Container images
- Kubernetes binaries

Generally speaking, tampering happens either *in transit* or *at rest*. In transit refers to data while it is being transmitted over the network, whereas at rest refers to data stored in memory or on disk.

TLS is a great tool for protecting against *in transit* tampering as it provides built-in integrity guarantees – you'll be warned if the data has been tampered with.

The following recommendations can also help prevent tampering with data when it is *at rest* in Kubernetes:

- Restrict access to the servers that are running Kubernetes components – especially control plane components.

- Restrict access to repositories that store Kubernetes configuration files.
- Only perform remote bootstrapping over SSH (remember to safely guard your SSH keys).
- Always perform SHA-2 checksums on downloads.
- Restrict access to your image registry and associated repositories.

This isn't an exhaustive list. However, implementing it will greatly reduce the chances of your data being tampered with while at rest.

As well as the items listed, it's good production hygiene to configure auditing and alerting for important binaries and configuration files. If configured and monitored correctly, these can help detect potential tampering attacks.

The following example uses a common Linux audit daemon to audit access to the `docker` binary. It also audits attempts to the change the binary's file attributes.

```
$ auditctl -w /usr/bin/docker -p wxa -k audit-docker
```

We'll refer to this example later in the chapter.

Tampering with applications running on Kubernetes

As well as infrastructure components, application components are also potential tampering targets.

A good way to prevent a live Pod from being tampered with is setting its filesystems to read-only. This guarantees filesystem immutability and can be accomplished via the securityContext section of a Pod manifest file.

You can make a container's root filesystem read-only by setting the `readOnlyRoot-Filesystem` property to `true`. The same can be done for other filesystems that are mounted into containers via the `allowedHostPaths` property.

The following YAML shows how to use both settings in a Pod manifest. The `allowed-HostPaths` section makes sure anything mounted beneath `/test` will be read-only.

```
apiVersion: v1
kind: Pod
metadata:
  name: readonly-test
spec:
  securityContext:
    readOnlyRootFilesystem: true      <<==== R/O root filesystem
    allowedHostPaths:                 <<==== Make anything below
    - pathPrefix: "/test"             <<==== this mount point
      readOnly: true                  <<==== read-only (R/O)
<Snip>
```

Repudiation

At a very high level, *repudiation* is creating doubt about something. *Non-repudiation* is providing proof about something. In the context of information security, non-repudiation is **proving** certain actions were carried out by certain individuals.

Digging a little deeper, non-repudiation includes the ability to prove:

- What happened
- When it happened
- Who made it happen
- Where it happened
- Why it happened
- How it happened

Answering the last two usually requires the correlation of several events over a period of time.

Fortunately, auditing Kubernetes API server events can usually help answer these questions. The following is an example of an API server audit event (you may need to manually enable auditing on your API server).

```
{
  "kind":"Event",
  "apiVersion":"audit.k8s.io/v1",
  "metadata":{ "creationTimestamp":"2022-11-11T10:10:00Z" },
  "level":"Metadata",
  "timestamp":"2022-11-11T10:10:00Z",
  "auditID":"7e0cbccf-8d8a-4f5f-aefb-60b8af2d2ad5",
  "stage":"RequestReceived",
  "requestURI":"/api/v1/namespaces/default/persistentvolumeclaims",
  "verb":"list",
  "user": {
    "username":"fname.lname@example.com",
    "groups":[ "system:authenticated" ]
  },
  "sourceIPs":[ "123.45.67.123" ],
  "objectRef": {
    "resource":"persistentvolumeclaims",
    "namespace":"default",
    "apiVersion":"v1"
  },
  "requestReceivedTimestamp":"2022-11-11T10:10:00.123456Z",
  "stageTimestamp":"2022-11-11T10:10:00.123456Z"
}
```

The API server isn't the only component you should audit for non-repudiation. At a minimum, you should collect audit logs from container runtimes, kubelets, and the applications running on your cluster. You should also audit non-Kubernetes infrastructure such as network firewalls and the likes.

As soon as you start auditing multiple components, you'll need a centralised location to store and correlate events. A common way to do this is deploying an agent to all nodes via a DaemonSet. The agent collects logs (runtime, kubelet, application…) and ships them to a secure central location.

If you do this, it's vital the centralised log store is secure. If it's not, you won't be able to trust the logs and their contents can be *repudiated*.

To provide non-repudiation relative to tampering with binaries and configuration files, it might be useful to use an audit daemon that watches for write actions on certain files and directories on your Kubernetes control plane nodes and worker nodes. For example, earlier in the chapter you saw a way to enable auditing of changes to the docker binary. With this enabled, starting a new container with the docker run command will generate an event like this:

```
type=SYSCALL msg=audit(1234567890.123:12345): arch=abc123 syscall=59 success=yes \
exit=0 a0=12345678abca1=0 a2=abc12345678 a3=a items=1 ppid=1234 pid=12345 auid=0 \
uid=0 gid=0 euid=0 suid=0 fsuid=0 egid=0 sgid=0 fsgid=0 tty=pts0 ses=1 comm="docker" \
exe="/usr/bin/docker" subj=system_u:object_r:container_runtime_exec_t:s0 \
key="audit-docker" type=CWD msg=audit(1234567890.123:12345):  cwd="/home/firstname"\
type=PATH msg=audit(1234567890.123:12345): item=0 name="/usr/bin/docker"\
 inode=123456 dev=fd:00 mode=0100600 ouid=0 ogid=0 rdev=00:00...
```

Audit logs like this, when combined and correlated with Kubernetes' audit features, create a comprehensive and trustworthy picture that cannot be repudiated.

Information Disclosure

Information disclosure is when sensitive data is leaked. Common examples include hacked data stores and APIs that unintentionally expose sensitive data.

Protecting cluster data

The entire configuration of a Kubernetes cluster is stored in the cluster store (usually etcd). This includes network and storage configuration, passwords, the cluster CA and more. This makes the cluster store a prime target for information disclosure attacks.

As a minimum, you should limit *and* audit access to the nodes hosting the cluster store. As will be seen in the next paragraph, gaining access to a cluster node can allow the logged-on user to bypass some of the security layers.

Kubernetes 1.7 introduced encryption of Secrets but doesn't enable it by default. Even when this becomes default, the data encryption key (DEK) is stored on the same node as the Secret! This means gaining access to a node lets you to bypass encryption. This is especially worrying on nodes that host the cluster store (etcd nodes).

Fortunately, Kubernetes 1.11 enabled a beta feature that lets you store *key encryption keys (KEK)* outside of your Kubernetes cluster. These types of keys are used to encrypt and decrypt data encryption keys and should be safely guarded. You should seriously consider Hardware Security Modules (HSM) or cloud-based Key Management Stores (KMS) for storing your key encryption keys.

Keep an eye on upcoming versions of Kubernetes for further improvements to encryption of Secrets.

Protecting data in Pods

As previously mentioned, Kubernetes has an API resource called a Secret that is the preferred way to store and share sensitive data such as passwords. For example, a front-end container accessing an encrypted back-end database can have the key to decrypt the database mounted as a Secret. This is a far better solution than storing the decryption key in a plain-text file or environment variable.

It is also common to store data and configuration information outside of Pods and containers in Persistent Volumes and ConfigMaps. If the data on these is encrypted, keys for decrypting them should also be stored in Secrets.

Despite all of this, it's vital that you consider the caveats outlined in the previous section relative to Secrets and how their encryption keys are stored. You don't want to do the hard work of locking the house but leaving the keys in the door.

Denial of Service

Denial of Service (DoS) is about making something unavailable.

There are many types of DoS attack, but a well-known variation is overloading a system to the point it can no longer service requests. In the Kubernetes world, a potential attack might be to overload the API server so that cluster operations grind to a halt (even essential system services have to communicate via the API server).

Let's take a look at some potential Kubernetes systems that might be targets of DoS attacks, as well as some ways to protect and mitigate.

Protecting cluster resources against DoS attacks

It's a time-honored best practice to replicate essential control plane services on multiple nodes for high availability (HA). Kubernetes is no different, and you should run multiple control plane nodes in an HA configuration for your production environments. Doing this prevents a single control plane node from becoming a single point of failure. In relation to certain types of DoS attacks, an attacker may need to attack more than one control plane node to have a meaningful impact.

You should also consider replicating control plane nodes across availability zones. This may prevent a DoS attack on the *network* of a particular availability zone from taking down your entire control plane.

The same principle applies to worker nodes. Having multiple worker nodes not only allows the scheduler to spread your applications over multiple availability zones, it may also render DoS attacks on any single node or zone ineffective (or less effective).

You should also configure appropriate limits for the following:

- Memory

- CPU
- Storage
- Kubernetes objects

Limits like these can help prevent important system resources from being starved, therefore preventing potential DoS.

Limiting Kubernetes objects can also be a good practice. This includes limiting things such as; the number of ReplicaSets, Pods, Services, Secrets, and ConfigMaps in a particular Namespace.

Here's an example manifest that limits the number of Pod objects in the `skippy` namespace to 100.

```
apiVersion: v1
kind: ResourceQuota
metadata:
  name: pod-quota
  namespace: skippy
spec:
  hard:
    pods: "100"
```

One more feature – *podPidsLimit* – restricts the number of processes a Pod can create.

Assume a scenario where a Pod is the target of a fork bomb attack. This is a specialised attack where a rogue process creates as many new processes as possible in an attempt to consume all resources on a system with the intent of grinding it to a halt. Placing a limit on the number of processes a Pod can create will prevent the Pod from exhausting the node's resources and confine the impact of the attack to the Pod. Once the *podPidsLimit* is exhausted, a Pod will typically be restarted.

This also ensures a single Pod doesn't exhaust the PID range for all the other Pods on the node, including the Kubelet. One thing to note though… setting the correct value requires a good estimate of how many Pods will run simultaneously on each Node. Without a ballpark estimate, you can easily over or under allocate PIDs to each pod.

Protecting the API Server against DoS attacks

The API server exposes a RESTful interface over a TCP socket. This makes it a target for botnet-based DoS attacks.

The following may be helpful in either preventing or mitigating such attacks:

- Highly available control plane nodes. Having multiple API server replicas running on multiple nodes across multiple availability zones.

- Monitoring and alerting API server requests based on sane thresholds
- Using things like firewalls to limit API server exposure to the internet

As well as botnet DoS attacks, an attacker may also attempt to spoof a user or other control plane service in an attempt to cause an overload. Fortunately, Kubernetes has robust authentication and authorization controls to prevent spoofing. However, even with a robust RBAC model, it's vital that you safeguard access to accounts with high privileges.

Protecting the cluster store against DoS attacks

Cluster configuration is stored in etcd, making it vital that etcd be available and secure. The following recommendations help accomplish this:

- Configure an HA etcd cluster with either 3 or 5 nodes
- Configure monitoring and alerting of requests to etcd
- Isolate etcd at the network level so that only members of the control plane can interact with it

A default installation of Kubernetes installs etcd on the same servers as the rest of the control plane. This is usually fine for development and testing, however, large production clusters should seriously consider a dedicated etcd cluster. This will provide better performance and greater resilience.

On the performance front, etcd is probably the most common choking point for large Kubernetes clusters. With this in mind, you should perform testing to ensure the infrastructure it runs on is capable of sustaining performance at scale – a poorly performing etcd can be as bad as an etcd cluster under a sustained DoS attack. Operating a dedicated etcd cluster also provides additional resilience by protecting it from other parts of the control plane that might be compromised.

Monitoring and alerting of etcd should be based on sane thresholds and a good place to start is by monitoring etcd log entries.

Protecting application components against DoS attacks

Most Pods expose their main service on the network, and, without additional controls in place, anyone with access to the network can perform a DoS attack on the Pod. Fortunately, Kubernetes provides Pod resource request limits to prevent such attacks from exhausting Pod and Node resources. As well as these, the following will be helpful:

- Define Kubernetes Network Policies to restrict Pod-to-Pod and Pod-to-external communications

- Utilize mutual TLS and API token-based authentication for application-level authentication (reject any unauthenticated requests)

For defence in depth, you should also implement application-layer authorization policies that implement least privilege.

Figure 15.1 shows how all of these can be combined to make it hard for an attacker to successfully DoS an application.

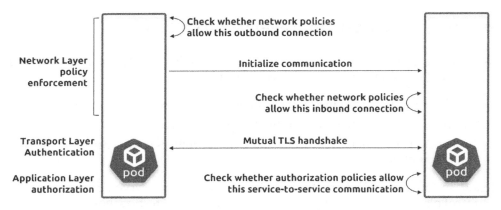

Figure 15.1

Elevation of privilege

Privilege escalation is gaining higher access than what is granted. The aim is to cause damage or gain unauthorized access.

Let's look at a few ways to prevent this in a Kubernetes environment.

Protecting the API server

Kubernetes offers several authorization modes that help safeguard access to the API server. These include:

- Role-based Access Control (RBAC)
- Webhook
- Node

You should run multiple authorizers at the same time. For example, a common best practice is to always have *RBAC* and *node* enabled.

RBAC mode lets you restrict API operations to sub-sets of users. These *users* can be regular user accounts as well as system services. The idea is that all requests to the API server must be authenticated **and** authorized. Authentication ensures that requests are coming from a validated user, whereas authorization ensures the validated user is allowed to perform the requested operation. For example, can *Mia create Pods?* In this example, *Mia* is the user, *create* is the operation, and *Pods* is the resource. Authentication makes sure that it really is Mia making the request, and authorization determines if she's allowed to create Pods.

Webhook mode lets you offload authorization to an external REST-based policy engine. However, it requires additional effort to build and maintain the external engine. It also makes the external engine a potential single-point-of-failure for every request to the API server. For example, if the external webhook system becomes unavailable, you may not be able to make any requests to the API server. With this in mind, you should be rigorous in vetting and implementing any webhook authorization service.

Node authorization is all about authorizing API requests made by kubelets (Nodes). The types of requests made to the API server by Nodes is obviously different to those generally made by regular users, and the node authorizer is designed to help with this.

Protecting Pods

The next few sections will look at a few technologies that help reduce the risk of elevation of privilege attacks against Pods and containers. We'll look at the following:

- Preventing processes from running as `root`
- Dropping capabilities
- Filtering syscalls
- Preventing privilege escalation

As you proceed through these sections, it's important to remember that a Pod is just an execution environment for one or more containers – application code runs in containers, which in turn, run inside of Pods. Some of the terminology used will refer to Pods and containers interchangeably, but usually we will mean container.

Do not run processes as root

The `root` user is the most powerful user on a Linux system and is always User ID 0 (UID 0). This means running application processes as `root` is almost always a bad idea as it grants the application process full access to the container. This is made even worse by the fact that the `root` user of a container often has unrestricted `root` access on the host system as well. If that doesn't make you afraid, nothing will!

Fortunately, Kubernetes lets you force container processes to run as unprivileged non-root users.

The following Pod manifest configures all containers that are part of this Pod to run processes as UID 1000. If the Pod has multiple containers, all processes in all containers will run as UID 1000.

```
apiVersion: v1
kind: Pod
metadata:
  name: demo
spec:
  securityContext:        <<==== Applies to all containers in this Pod
    runAsUser: 1000       <<==== Non-root user
  containers:
  - name: demo
    image: example.io/simple:1.0
```

`runAsUser` is one of many settings that can be configured as part of what we refer to as a PodSecurityContext (`.spec.securityContext`).

It's possible for two or more Pods to be configured with the same `runAsUser` UID. When this happens, the containers from both Pods will run with the same security context and potentially have access to the same resources. This *might* be fine if they are replicas of the same Pod or container. However, there's a high chance this will cause problems if they're different containers. For example, two different containers with R/W access to the same host directory or volume can cause data corruption (both writing to the same dataset without co-ordinating write operations). Shared security contexts also increase the possibility of a compromised container tampering with a dataset it shouldn't have access to.

With this in mind, it is possible to use the `securityContext.runAsUser` property at the container level instead of at the Pod level:

```
apiVersion: v1
kind: Pod
metadata:
  name: demo
spec:
  securityContext:        <<==== Applies to all containers in this Pod
    runAsUser: 1000       <<==== Non-root user
  containers:
  - name: demo
    image: example.io/simple:1.0
    securityContext:
      runAsUser: 2000     <<==== Overrides the Pod-level setting
```

This example sets the UID to 1000 at the Pod level, but overrides it at the container level so that processes in the "demo" container run as UID 2000. Unless otherwise specified, all other containers in the Pod will use UID 1000.

A couple of other things that might help get around the issue of multiple Pods and containers using the same UID include:

- *User namespaces*
- Maintaining a map of UID usage

User namespaces is a Linux kernel technology that allows a process to run as root within a container but run as a different user outside of the container. For example, a process can run as UID 0 (the root user) in the container but get mapped to UID 1000 on the host. This can be a good solution for processes that *need* to run as root inside the container. However, you should check if it is fully-supported by your version of Kubernetes and your container runtime.

Maintaining a map of UID usage is a clunky way to prevent multiple different Pods and containers using overlapping UIDs. It's a bit of a hack and requires strict adherence to a gated release process for releasing Pods into production.

> **Note:** A strict gated release process is a good thing for production environments. The *hacky* part of the previous section is the UID map itself, as well as the fact that you're introducing an external dependency and complicating releases and troubleshooting.

Capability dropping

While most applications don't need the full set of root capabilities, they often require more capabilities than a typical non-root user.

What is needed, is a way to grant the exact set of privileges a process requires in order to run. Enter *capabilities*.

Time for a quick bit of background...

We've already said the root user is the most powerful user on a Linux system. However, its power is a combination of lots of small privileges that we call *"capabilities"*. For example, the SYS_TIME capability allows a user to set the system clock, whereas the NET_ADMIN capability allows a user to perform network-related operations such as modifying the local routing table and configuring local interfaces. The root user holds every *capability* and is therefore extremely powerful.

Having a modular set of *capabilities* like this allows you to be extremely granular when granting permissions. Instead of an all or nothing (root –vs– non-root) approach, you can grant a process the exact set of capabilities it requires to run.

There are currently over 30 capabilities, and choosing the right ones can be daunting. With this in mind, many container runtimes implement a set of *sensible-defaults* that are designed to allow most processes to run without *leaving all the doors open*. While sensible defaults like these are better than nothing, they're often not good enough for a lot of production environments.

A common way to find the absolute minimum set of capabilities an application requires, is to run it in a test environment with all capabilities dropped. This causes the application to fail and log messages about the missing permissions. You map those permissions to *capabilities,* add them to the application's Pod spec, and run the application again. You rinse and repeat this process until the application runs properly with the minimum set of capabilities.

As good as this is, there are a few things to consider.

Firstly, you **must** perform extensive testing of each application. The last thing you want is a production *edge case* that you hadn't accounted for in your test environment. Such occurrences can crash your application in production!

Secondly, every revision of your application requires the exact same extensive testing against the capability set.

With these considerations in mind, it is vital that you have testing procedures and production release processes that can handle all of this.

By default, Kubernetes implements the default set of *capabilities* implemented by your chosen container runtime (E.g. containerd). However, you can override this as part of a container's `securityContext` field.

The following Pod manifest shows how to add the NET_ADMIN and CHOWN capabilities to a container.

```
apiVersion: v1
kind: Pod
metadata:
  name: capability-test
spec:
  containers:
  - name: demo
    image: example.io/simple:1.0
    securityContext:
      capabilities:
        add: ["NET_ADMIN", "CHOWN"]
```

Filter syscalls

seccomp, short for secure computing, is similar in concept to *capabilities* but works by filtering syscalls rather than capabilities.

The way an application asks the Linux kernel to perform an operation is by issuing a *syscall*. seccomp lets you control which syscalls a particular container can make to the host kernel. As with capabilities, you should implement a least privilege model where the only syscalls a container is allowed to make are the ones it needs to in order to run.

seccomp went GA in Kubernetes 1.19 and can be used in different ways based on the following seccomp profiles:

1. **Non-blocking**: Allows a Pod to run, and records every syscall to an audit log you can use to create a custom profile. The idea is to run your application Pod in a dev/test environment and make it do everything it's designed to do. When you're done, you'll have a log file listing every syscall the Pod needs in order to run. You then use this to create a custom profile that only allows those syscalls (least privilege).
2. **Blocking**: Blocks all syscalls. It's extremely secure, but prevents a Pod from doing anything useful.
3. **Runtime Default**: Forces a Pod to use the seccomp profile defined by its container runtime. This is a common place to start if you haven't created a custom profile yet. Profiles that ship with container runtimes are designed to be balance of *usable* and *secure*. They're also thoroughly tested.
4. **Custom**: A profile that only allows the syscalls your application needs in order to run. Everything else is blocked. It's common to extensively test your application in dev/test with a non-blocking profile that records all syscalls to an audit log. You then use this log to identify the syscalls your app makes and build the customized profile. The danger with this approach is that your app has some edge-cases that you miss during testing. If this happens, your application can fail in production when it hits an edge-cases and uses a syscall not captured during testing.

Obviously, custom profiles operate the *least privilege* model and are the preferred approach from a security perspective.

Prevent privilege escalation by containers

The only way to create a new process in Linux is for one process to clone itself and then load new instructions on to the new process. We're over-simplifying, but the original process is called the *parent* process and the copy is called the *child*.

By default, Linux allows a *child* process to claim more privileges than its *parent*. This is usually a bad idea. In fact, you'll often want a child process to have the same, or less privileges than its parent. This is especially true for containers as their security configurations are defined against their initial configuration and not against potentially escalated privileges.

Fortunately, it's possible to prevent privilege escalation through the securityContext property of an individual container as shown.

```
apiVersion: v1
kind: Pod
metadata:
  name: demo
spec:
  containers:
  - name: demo
    image: example.io/simple:1.0
    securityContext:
      allowPrivilegeEscalation: false
```

Standardizing Pod Security with PSS and PSA

Modern Kubernetes clusters implement two technologies to help enforce Pod security settings:

- **Pod Security Standards (PSS)** are policies that specify required Pod security settings.
- **Pod Security Admission (PSA)** enforces one or more PSS policies when Pods are created.

Both work together for effective centralised enforcement of Pod security – you choose which PSS policies to apply and PSA enforces them.

They came in as alpha features in Kubernetes v1.22, progressed to beta in v1.23, and graduated to stable in v1.25. As most Kubernetes clusters automatically enable beta features, most Kubernetes clusters running v1.23 or higher will have PSS and PSA enabled.

> **What happened to Pod Security Policies?** *Pod Security Policies* were the old way of centrally managing Pod security but were hard to understand and complicated to implement. As a result, they were deprecated in Kubernetes v1.21 and removed in v1.25.

Let's look at Pod Security Standards and Pod Security Admission in more detail.

Pod Security Standards (PSS)

Every Kubernetes cluster gets the following three PSS *policies* that are maintained and kept up-to-date by the community:

- Privileged

- Baseline
- Restricted

Privileged is a wide-open allow-all policy.

*Baseline implements "sensible defaults". It's more secure than *privileged* but less secure than *restricted*.

Restricted is the gold-standard that implements all of the current Pod security best practices. Be warned though, it's highly restricted and a lot of Pods will fail to meet its strict requirements.

At the time of writing, you cannot tweak or modify any of these polices and you cannot import others or create your own.

Pod Security Admission

Pod Security Admission (PSA) is responsible enforcing your desired PSS policies. It works at the Namespace level and is implemented as a validating admission controller.

PSA offers three enforcement modes:

- **Warn.** Allows violating Pods to be created but issues a user-facing warning.
- **Audit.** Allows violating Pods to be created but logs an audit event.
- **Enforce.** Rejects Pods if they violate the policy.

It's a good practice to configure every Namespace with at least the *baseline* policy configured to either *warn* or *audit*. This allows you to start gathering data on which Pods are failing the policy and why. The next step is to enforce the *baseline* policy and start warning and auditing on the *restricted* policy.

Any Namespaces without a Pod Security configuration are a gap in your security configuration and you should attach a policy as soon as possible – even if it's only logging and auditing.

Applying the following label to a Namespace will apply the *baseline* policy to it. Violating Pods will be allowed but a user-facing warning will be issued.

```
pod-security.kubernetes.io/warn: baseline
```

The format of the label is `<prefix>/<mode>: <policy>` with the following options:

- Prefix is always `pod-security.kubernetes.io`
- Mode is one of `warn`, `audit`, or `enforce`
- Policy is always one of `privileged`, `baseline` or `restricted`

As PSA is implemented as a *validating* admission controller, it cannot modify Pods and it has no impact on Pods that are already running.

PSA examples

Let's walk through some examples to show you PSA in action. You'll complete the following steps:

1. Create a Namespace called **psa-test**
2. Apply a label to *enforce* the **baseline** PSS policy
3. Attempt to deploy a Pod that runs a privileged container (will fail)
4. Modify the Pod to conform to the PSS policy and re-deploy it (will work)
5. Test the potential impact of switching to the **restricted** policy
6. Switch to the **restricted** policy
7. Test any impact on existing Pods

You'll need kubectl, a Kubernetes cluster, and a local clone of the book's GitHub repo if you want to follow along. See chapter 3 if you don't have these.

The book's GitHub repo can be found here.

```
https://github.com/nigelpoulton/TheK8sBook
```

Be sure to run the following commands from the **psa** directory.

Create a new Namespace called psa-test.

```
$ kubectl create ns psa-test
```

Add the pod-security.kubernetes.io/enforce=baseline label to the new Namespace. This will prevent the creation of any new Pods violating the **baseline** PSS policy.

```
$ kubectl label --overwrite ns psa-test \
    pod-security.kubernetes.io/enforce=baseline
```

Verify the label was correctly applied.

```
$ kubectl describe ns psa-test

Name:         psa-test
Labels:       kubernetes.io/metadata.name=psa-test
              pod-security.kubernetes.io/enforce=baseline   <<==== label correctly applied
Annotations:  <none>
Status:       Active
```

With the Namespace created and the *baseline* policy being enforced, attempt to deploy the following Pod. It's defined in the psa-pod.yml file and is targeted to the psa-pod Namespace. It runs a privileged container which violates the *baseline* policy.

```
apiVersion: v1
kind: Pod
metadata:
  name: psa-pod
  namespace: psa-test      <<==== Deploy it to the new psa-test Namespace
spec:
  containers:
  - name: psa-ctr
    image: nginx
    securityContext:
      privileged: true      <<==== Violates the baseline policy
```

Deploy it with the following command.

```
$ kubectl apply -f psa-pod.yml

Error from server (Forbidden): error when creating "psa-pod.yml": pods "psa-pod" is
forbidden: violates PodSecurity "baseline:latest": privileged (container "psa-ctr"
must not set securityContext.privileged=true)
```

The output shows the Pod creation was forbidden and lists the reason why.

Edit the psa-pod.yml file so the container's securityContext.privileged field is set to **false** and save your changes.

```
apiVersion: v1
kind: Pod
<Snip>
spec:
  containers:
  - name: psa-ctr
    image: nginx
    securityContext:
      privileged: false         <<==== Change from true to false
```

Attempt to deploy the updated Pod.

```
$ kubectl apply -f psa-pod.yml
pod/psa-pod created
```

The Pod passes the requirements for the *baseline* security policy and is successfully deployed.

You can use the `--dry-run=server` flag to **test the impact of applying a PSS policy to a Namespace**. Using this flag **will not** apply the policy.

```
$ kubectl label --dry-run=server --overwrite ns psa-test \
    pod-security.kubernetes.io/enforce=restricted

Warning: existing pods in namespace "psa-test" violate the new PodSecurity enforce
level "restricted:latest"
Warning: psa-pod: allowPrivilegeEscalation != false, unrestricted capabilities,
runAsNonRoot != true, seccompProfile
```

The output shows the **psa-pod** Pod fails to meet 4 policy requirements:

- The `allowPrivilegeEscalation` is not set to false
- It's running unrestricted `capabilities`
- The `runAsNonRoot` field is not set to true
- It fails the `seccompProfile` test

Go ahead and apply the policy to the Namespace and see if it has any impact on the psa-pod that is already running.

```
$ kubectl label --overwrite ns psa-test \
    pod-security.kubernetes.io/enforce=restricted

Warning: existing pods in namespace "psa-test" violate the new PodSecurity enforce level
"restricted:latest"
Warning: psa-pod: allowPrivilegeEscalation != false, unrestricted capabilities,
runAsNonRoot != true, seccompProfile
namespace/psa-test labeled

$ kubectl get pods --namespace psa-test

NAME      READY   STATUS    RESTARTS   AGE
psa-pod   1/1     Running   0          11m
```

You get the same warning message, but existing Pods are not terminated. This is because PSA runs as an admission controller which only acts on the creation and modification of Pods.

Finally, it's possible to configure multiple polices and modes against a single Namespace. In fact, it's a common practice to do this.

The following example applies three labels to the psa-test Namespace *enforcing* the **baseline** policy and *warning* and *auditing* against the **restricted** policy. This is a good way of implementing the **baseline** policy while preparing for **restricted**.

```
$ kubectl label --overwrite ns psa-test \
    pod-security.kubernetes.io/enforce=baseline \
    pod-security.kubernetes.io/warn=restricted \
    pod-security.kubernetes.io/audit=restricted

$ kubectl describe ns psa-test

Name:         psa-test
Labels:       kubernetes.io/metadata.name=psa-test
              pod-security.kubernetes.io/audit=restricted
              pod-security.kubernetes.io/enforce=baseline
              pod-security.kubernetes.io/warn=restricted
Annotations:  <none>
Status:       Active
```

Alternatives to Pod Security Admission

As previously mentioned, PSS and PSA have limitations. These include being implemented as a validating admission controller and the inability to modify, import, or roll your own policies. If you need more than PSS and PSA can offer, you may want to consider the following 3rd-party solutions:

- Kyverno

- OPA Gatekeeper

Others also exist.

Towards a more secure Kubernetes

As demonstrated by the following examples, Kubernetes is on a continual journey towards better security:

- Starting with Kubernetes v1.26, all binary artifacts and container images used to build Kubernetes clusters are cryptographically signed.
- The Kubernetes community maintains an official feed for all publicly announced Kubernetes vulnerabilities (CVEs).
- Default seccomp profiles implementing strong security defaults.

As well as these, an up-to-date third-party security audit of Kubernetes is expected later in 2023. This is the second report of its kind and follows-on from the original in 2019. These are great tools for identifying potential threats to your Kubernetes environments, as well as potential ways to mitigate them.

The *Cloud Native Security Whitepaper* is worth reading as a way to level-up and gain a more holistic perspective on securing cloud native environments such as Kubernetes. v2.0 of this report can be found here: https://tinyurl.com/bdfeaca2

Chapter summary

In this chapter, you learned how the STRIDE model can be used to threat-model Kubernetes. You stepped through the six categories of threat and looked at some ways to prevent and mitigate them.

You saw that one threat can often lead to another, and that there are multiple ways to mitigate a single threat. As always, defence in depth is a key tactic.

The chapter finished by discussing how Pod Security Admission is the preferred way to implement Pod security defaults.

In the next chapter, you'll see some best practices and lessons learned from running Kubernetes in production.

16: Real-world Kubernetes security

The previous chapter showed you how to threat-model Kubernetes using STRIDE. In this chapter, you'll cover some common security-related challenges that you're likely to encounter when implementing Kubernetes in the real world.

While every Kubernetes environment is different, there are many similarities. As a result, the examples you'll see will apply to most Kubernetes environments, large and small.

Now then, we're not offering *cookbook style* solutions. Instead, we're looking at things from the kind of high-level view a *security architect* has.

The chapter's divided into the following four sections:

- CI/CD pipeline
- Infrastructure and networking
- Identity and access management
- Security monitoring and auditing

CI/CD pipeline

Containers are a revolutionary application *packaging* and *runtime* technology.

On the packaging front, they bundle application code and dependencies into a single artefact called an *image*. As well as code and dependencies, images have metadata listing things like the command required to start the application. This model has enabled containers to hugely simplify the process of building, sharing, and running applications. It's also overcome the infamous *"it worked on my laptop"* issue.

However, containers make running dangerous code easier than ever.

With this in mind, let's look at some ways you can secure the flow of application code from a developer's laptop to production servers.

Image Repositories

You store images in registries that are either public or private, and each registry is divided into one or more repositories. In fact, you actually store images in repositories.

Public registries are on the internet and are the easiest way to download images and run containers. However, not all the images they host can be trusted. Some registries have the concept of *official images* and *community images*. Official images are usually provided by product vendors and have undergone a vetting process to ensure certain levels of quality. Typically, they implement good practices, are regularly scanned for known vulnerabilities, contain up-to-date code, and may be supported by the product vendor or the company hosting the registry. *Community images* are none of that. Yes, there are some excellent community images, but you should practice extreme caution when using them.

With all of this in mind, it's important you implement a standard way for developers to obtain and consume images. It's also vital that any such process be as frictionless as possible – if there's too much friction, your developers will look for ways to bypass the process.

Let's discuss a few things that might help.

Use approved base images

Images often have multiple layers that build on top of each other to form a useful image. However, all images start with a base layer.

Figure 16.1 shows an over-simplified example of an image with three layers. The base layer contains the core OS and filesystem components applications need in order to run. The middle layer contains the libraries and dependencies. The top layer contains the code that your developers have written. The combination of the three is the *image* and it contains everything needed to run the application.

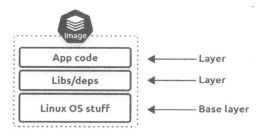

Figure 16.1

It's a common practice to have a small number of *approved base images*. It's also common, but not essential, for these base images to be derived from *official images*. For example, if you write Linux applications, your base images *may* be based on the official Alpine Linux image – you take the official Alpine Linux base image and tweak it for your requirements.

In this model, all of your applications will build on top of a common approved base image like shown in Figure 16.2.

Figure 16.2

While there's up-front effort required to create and implement an approved set of base images, the long-term security benefits are worth it. For example, it allows developers to focus on applications without worrying about maintaining OS stuff such as patching, drivers, audit settings, and more.

From an operations perspective, base images reduce software sprawl which makes testing easier. This is because you'll always be testing on a known base image. It makes pushing updates easier as you only need to update a small number of approved base images that can be easily made available to all developers. It also makes troubleshooting easier as you have a small number of well-known base images to use as building blocks. It may also reduce the number of base image configurations that need tying into support contracts.

Non-standard base images

As good as it is to have a small number of approved base images, there may still be applications that need something more bespoke. This means you will need processes in place to:

- Identify why an existing approved base image cannot be used
- Determine whether an existing approved base image can be updated to meet requirements (including if it's worth the effort)
- Determine the support implications of bringing an entirely new image into the environment

Generally speaking, updating an existing base image – such as adding a device driver for GPU computing – should be preferred over introducing an entirely new image.

Control access to images

There are several ways to protect your organization's container images. The most secure practical option is to host your own private registry inside your own firewalls. This allows you to manage how the registry is deployed, how it's replicated, and how it is patched. It may also enable you to integrate permissions with existing identity management providers, such as Active Directory, as well as allow you to create repositories that fit your organizational structure.

If you don't have the means for a dedicated private registry, you can host your images in private repositories on public registries such as Docker Hub or your cloud provider's public registry. However, this is not as secure as hosting your own private registry within your own firewalled network.

Whichever solution you choose, you should only host images that are approved to be used within your organization. Normally, these will be from a *trusted* source and vetted by your information security team. You should place access controls on repositories so that only approved users can push and pull them.

Away from the registry itself, you should also:

- Restrict which cluster nodes have internet access, keeping in mind that your image registry may be on the internet
- Configure access controls that only allow authorized users or Nodes can push to repositories

Expanding on the list above...

If you're using a public registry, you'll probably need to grant your Nodes access to the internet so they can pull images. In this situation, a best practice is to limit internet access to the addresses and ports of any registries you use. You should also implement strong RBAC rules to maintain control over who is pushing and pulling images from which repositories. For example, you might restrict developers so they can only push and pull from dev and test repositories, whereas your operations teams should probably be able to push and pull to production repos.

Finally, you may only want a sub-set of Nodes (*build nodes*) to be able to push images. You may even want to lock things down so that only your automated build systems can push to certain repositories.

Moving images from non-production to production

Many organizations have separate environments for development, testing, and production.

Generally speaking, development environments have less rules and are commonly used as places where developers can experiment. This can often involve non-standard images that your developers eventually want to use in production.

The following sections outline some measures you can take to ensure only safe images get approved into production.

Vulnerability scanning

Top of the list for vetting images before allowing them into production should be *vulnerability scanning*. This is a process where your images are scanned at a binary level and their contents checked against databases of known security vulnerabilities (CVEs).

If you have an automated CI/CD build pipeline, you should definitely integrate vulnerability scanning. As part of this, you should consider implementing policies that automatically fail builds and quarantine images if they're found to have certain categories of vulnerabilities. For example, you might implement a build phase that scans images and automatically fails anything using images with known *critical* vulnerabilities.

Two things to keep in mind if you do this...

Firstly, scanning engines are only as good as the vulnerability databases they use.

Secondly, scanning engines might not implement intelligence. For example, a *method* in Python that performs TLS verification might be vulnerable to Denial of Service attacks when the Common Name contains a lot of wildcards. However, if you never use Python in this way, the vulnerability *might not* be relevant and you *might* want to consider it a false positive. With this in mind, you may want to implement a solution that provides the ability to mark certain vulnerabilities as *not applicable*.

Configuration as code

Scanning app code for vulnerabilities is widely accepted as good production hygiene. However, reviewing application configurations, such as Dockerfiles and Kubernetes YAML files, is less widely adopted.

The *build once, run anywhere* mantra of containers means a single container or Pod configuration can have hundreds or thousands of running instances. If any one of these configurations pulls in vulnerable code, you can easily end up running hundreds or thousands of instances of vulnerable code. With this in mind, if you are not already reviewing your Dockerfiles and Kubernetes YAML files for security issues, you should start now!

A well-publicised example of not reviewing configurations was when an IBM data science experiment embedded private TLS keys in its container images. This made it possible for an attacker to pull the image and gain root access to the Nodes that were hosting the containers. This wouldn't have happened if a security review had been performed against the application's Dockerfiles.

There continue to be advancements in automating these types of checks with tools that implement *policy as code* rules.

Sign container images

Trust is a big deal in today's world, and cryptographically signing content at every stage in the software delivery pipeline is becoming a *must have*. Fortunately, Kubernetes, and many container runtimes, support the ability to cryptographically sign and verify images.

In this model, developers cryptographically sign their images and consumers cryptographically verify them when they pull and run them. This process gives the consumer confidence they're working with the correct image and that it hasn't been tampered with.

Figure 16.3 shows the high-level process for signing and verifying images.

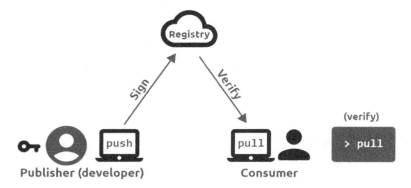

Figure 16.3

Image signing, and the verification of signatures, is usually implemented by the container runtime and Kubernetes doesn't get actively involved.

As well as signing images, higher-level tools often allow you to implement enterprise-wide policies that require certain teams to sign images before allowing them to be used.

Image promotion workflow

With everything that we've covered so far, a CI/CD pipeline for promoting an image to production should include as many of the following security-related steps as possible:

1. Configure environment to only `pull` and `run` signed images
2. Configure network rules to restrict which Nodes can `push` and `pull` images
3. Configure repositories with RBAC rules
4. Developers build on top of approved base images
5. Developers sign images and push to approved repos
6. Images are scanned for known vulnerabilities and policies dictate whether images are promoted or quarantined based on scan results
7. Security team:
   - Reviews source code and scan results
   - Updates vulnerability rating as appropriate
   - Reviews container and Pod configuration files
8. Security team signs the image
9. All *pull* and *run* operations verify image signatures

These steps are examples and not intended to represent an exact workflow.

Let's switch our focus away from images and CI/CD pipelines.

Infrastructure and networking

In this section, you'll see a few ways you can isolate workloads.

We'll start at the cluster level, switch to the runtime level, and then look outside of the cluster at supporting infrastructure such as network firewalls.

Cluster-level workload isolation

Cutting straight to the chase, **Kubernetes doesn't support secure multi-tenant clusters. The only way to isolate two workloads is to run them on their own clusters.**

Let's look a bit closer…

The only way to divide a Kubernetes cluster is by creating *Namespaces*. A Kubernetes Namespace is not the same as a Linux kernel namespace, it's a logical partition of a single Kubernetes cluster. In fact, it's little more than a way of grouping resources and applying things such as:

- Limits
- Quotas
- RBAC rules

The take-home point is that Kubernetes Namespaces do not guarantee Pods in one Namespace will not impact Pods in other Namespaces. As a result, you should not run potentially hostile production workloads on the same Kubernetes cluster. The only way to run potentially hostile workloads, and guarantee true isolation, is to run them on separate clusters.

Despite this, Kubernetes Namespaces are useful and you *should* use them. Just don't use them as security boundaries.

Let's look at how Namespaces relate to *soft multi-tenancy* and *hard multi-tenancy*.

Namespaces and soft multi-tenancy

For our purposes, *soft multi-tenancy* is hosting multiple trusted workloads on shared infrastructure. By *trusted*, we mean workloads that don't require absolute guarantees that one Pod or container cannot impact another.

An example of trusted workloads might be an e-commerce application comprising a web front-end service and a back-end recommendation service. Both are part of the same application, so are not hostile. However, they might benefit from:

- Isolating the teams responsible for each service
- Having different resource limits and quotas

In this situation, a single cluster with a Namespace for the front-end service and another for the back-end service might be a good solution. However, exploiting a vulnerability in one service might give the attacker access to Pods in the other service.

Namespaces and hard multi-tenancy

Let's define *hard multi-tenancy* as hosting untrusted and potentially hostile workloads on shared infrastructure. Only... as we said before, this isn't *currently* possible with Kubernetes.

This means that truly hostile workloads – workloads that require a strong security boundary – need to run on separate Kubernetes clusters! Examples include:

- Isolating production and non-production workloads
- Isolating different customers

- Isolating sensitive projects and business functions

Other examples exist, but you get the picture – workloads requiring strong separation need their own clusters.

> **Note:** The Kubernetes project has a dedicated *Multitenancy Working Group* that's actively working on the multitenancy models Kubernetes supports. This means that future releases of Kubernetes might support hard multitenancy.

Node isolation

There are times when individual applications require non-standard privileges such as running as root or executing non-standard syscalls. Isolating these on their own clusters might be overkill but running them on a ring-fenced subset of worker Nodes might be justified. In this case, if one Pod is compromised it can only impact other Pods on the same Node.

You should also apply *defence in depth* principles by enabling stricter audit logging and tighter runtime defence options on Nodes running workloads with non-standard privileges.

Kubernetes offers several technologies, such as labels, affinity and anti-affinity rules, and taints, to help target workloads to specific Nodes.

Runtime isolation

Containers versus virtual machines can be a polarizing topic. However, when it comes to workload isolation there is only one winner... the virtual machine.

The most popular container model has multiple containers sharing a single kernel, with isolation provided by kernel constructs that were never designed as *strong* security boundaries. The technical term for these types of containers is *namespaced containers*. The most popular container runtimes, such as containerd, create namespaced containers.

In the hypervisor model, every virtual machine gets its own dedicated kernel and is strongly isolated from other virtual machines using hardware enforcement.

From a workload isolation perspective, virtual machines win.

However, it's becoming easier and more common to augment containers with additional security technologies such as apparmor and SELinux, seccomp, capabilities, and user namespaces. Unfortunately, these can add significant complexity and may still be less secure than a virtual machine.

Another thing to consider is different classes of container runtime. Two examples are **gVisor** and **Kata Containers**, both of which have re-written the rules and are providing stronger levels of workload isolation. Integrating runtimes like these with Kubernetes is made simple thanks to the Container Runtime Interface (CRI) and Runtime Classes.

There are also projects that enable Kubernetes to orchestrate other workload types such as virtual machines and serverless functions.

While all of this might feel overwhelming, everything discussed here needs to be considered when determining the levels of isolation your workloads require.

To summarize, the following workload isolation options exist:

1. **Virtual Machines:** Every workload gets its own virtual machine and kernel. It provides excellent isolation but is slow and resource intensive.

2. **Traditional namespaced containers:** Every workload gets its own container but shares a common kernel. Not the best isolation, but fast and light-weight.

3. **Run every container in its own virtual machine:** This option attempts to combine the versatility of containers with the security of VMs by running every container in its own dedicated VM. Despite using specialized lightweight VMs, this loses some of the appeal of containers and is not a popular solution.

4. **Use appropriate runtime classes:** This allows you to run all workloads as containers, but target those requiring stronger isolation to an appropriate container runtime.

Finally, running a mix of containers and virtual machines can increase network complexity.

Network isolation

Firewalls are an integral part of any layered security system. They implement rules that *allow* or *deny* system-to-system communication.

As the names suggest, *allow rules* permit traffic to flow, whereas *deny rules* prevent traffic flow. The overall intent is to only allow authorized communications.

In Kubernetes, Pods communicate with each other over a special internal network called the *pod network*. However, Kubernetes doesn't implement the *pod network*, instead, it implements a plugin model called the Container Network Interface (CNI). Vendors and the community are responsible for writing CNI plugins that actually implement the *pod network*. There are lots of CNI plugins available, but they fall into two broad types:

• Overlay
• BGP

Each of these is different, and each has a different impact on firewall implementation and network security. Let's take a quick look at each.

Kubernetes and overlay networking

The most common way to build the *pod network* is as a simple flat overlay network that hides any complexity that might exist between cluster nodes. For example, your cluster nodes might be deployed across two different subnets with routers in between, however, all Pods connect to the flat pod network. In this scenario, the Pods only know about the flat overlay Pod network and have no knowledge of the networks the Nodes are on. Figure 16.4 shows four Nodes on two different networks with Pods connected to a single overlay Pod network.

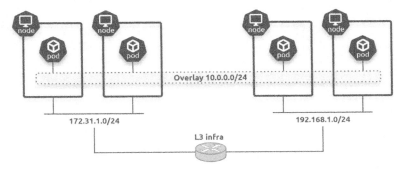

Figure 16.4

Overlay networks encapsulate packets for transmission over VXLAN tunnels. In this model, the overlay network is a virtual Layer 2 network operating on top of existing Layer 3 infrastructure. Traffic is encapsulated in order to pass between Pods on different Nodes. This simplifies implementation, but encapsulation poses challenges for some firewalls. See Figure 16.5

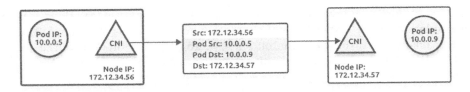

Figure 16.5

Kubernetes and BGP

BGP is the protocol that powers the internet. However, at its core it's a simple and scalable protocol that creates peer relationships that are used to share routes and perform routing.

The following analogy might help. Imagine you want to send a birthday card to a friend who you lost contact with and no longer have their address. However, your child has a friend at school whose parents are still in touch with your old friend. In this situation, you give the card to your child and ask them to give it to their friend at school. This friend gives it to their parents who deliver it to your friend.

BGP routing is similar and happens through a network of *peers* that help each other find a route for packets to get from one Pod to another.

BGP doesn't encapsulate packets, making life easier for firewalls. See Figure 16.6.

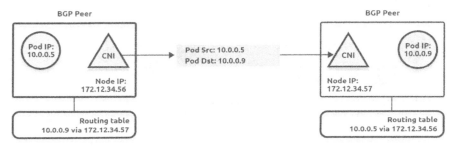

Figure 16.6

How this impacts firewalls

We've already said that firewalls allow or disallow traffic-flow based on source and destination addresses. For example:

- Allow traffic from the 10.0.0.0/24 network
- Disallow traffic from the 192.168.0.0/24 network

If your Pod network is an overlay network, source and destination Pod IP addresses are encapsulated so they can traverse the underlay network. This means only firewalls that open packets and inspect the contents will be able to filter on Pod source and Pod destination IPs. You need to consider this when choosing your Pod network and firewall solutions.

With this in mind, if your Pod-to-Pod traffic has to traverse existing firewalls that don't perform deep packet inspection, it might be a better idea to choose a BGP pod network as they don't obscure Pod source and destination addresses.

You should also consider whether to deploy *physical firewalls*, *host-based firewalls*, or a combination of both.

Physical firewalls are dedicated network hardware devices that are usually managed by a central team. Host-based firewalls are operating system (OS) features and are usually managed by the team that deploys and manages your OSes.

Both solutions have their pros and cons, and a combination of the two is often the most secure. However, you should consider things such as whether your organization has a long and complex procedure for implementing changes to physical firewalls. If it does, it might not suit the nature of your Kubernetes environment.

Packet capture

On the topic of networking and IP addresses, not only are Pod/container IP addresses sometimes obscured by encapsulation, they are also dynamic and can be recycled and re-used by different Pods and containers. This is called *IP churn* and reduces how useful IP addresses are in identifying systems and workloads. With this in mind, the ability to associate IP addresses with Kubernetes-specific identifiers such as Pod IDs, Service aliases, and container IDs when performing things like packet capturing is extremely useful.

Let's switch tack and look at some ways of controlling user access to Kubernetes.

Identity and access management (IAM)

Controlling user access to Kubernetes is important in any production environment. Fortunately, Kubernetes has a robust RBAC subsystem that integrates with existing IAM providers such as Active Directory and other LDAP systems.

Most organizations already have a centralized IAM provider that's integrated with company HR systems to simplify employee lifecycle management.

Fortunately, Kubernetes leverages existing IAM providers instead of implementing its own. For example, a new employee joining the company will automatically get an identity in Active Directory, which integrates with Kubernetes RBAC and can grant that user certain permissions in Kubernetes. Likewise, an employee leaving the company will automatically have his or her Active Directory identity removed or disabled resulting in their access to Kubernetes being revoked.

RBAC has been a stable Kubernetes feature since v1.8 and it's highly recommended you leverage its full capabilities.

Managing Remote SSH access to cluster nodes

Almost all Kubernetes administration is done via the API server, meaning it should be rare for a user to require remote SSH access to Kubernetes cluster nodes. In fact, remote

SSH access to cluster nodes should only be for the following types of activity:

- *Node management* activities that cannot be performed via the Kubernetes API
- *Break the Glass* activities such as when the API server is down
- Deep troubleshooting

You should have tighter controls over who has remote access to control plane nodes.

Multi-factor authentication (MFA)

With great power comes great responsibility...

Accounts with administrator access to the API server and root access to cluster nodes are extremely powerful and are prime targets for attackers and disgruntled employees. As such, their use should be protected by multi-factor authentication (MFA) where possible. This is where a user has to input a username and password followed by a second stage of authentication. For example:

- Stage 1: Tests *knowledge* of a username and password
- Stage 2: Tests *possession* of something like a one-time password

You should also secure access to workstations and user profiles that have kubectl installed.

Auditing and security monitoring

No system is 100% secure, and you should plan for the eventuality that you'll be breached. When breaches happen, it's vital you can do at least two things:

1. Recognize that a breach has occurred
2. Build a detailed timeline of events that cannot be repudiated

Auditing is key to both of these, and the ability to build a reliable timeline helps answer the following post-event questions; *what happened, how did it happen, when did it happen* and *who did it...* In extreme circumstances, information like this can even be called upon in court.

Good auditing and monitoring solutions also help identify vulnerabilities in your security systems.

With these points in mind, you should ensure reliable auditing and monitoring is high on your list of priorities and you shouldn't go live in production without them.

Secure Configuration

There are various tools and checks that can be useful in ensuring your Kubernetes environment is provisioned according to best practices and in-line with company policies.

The Center for Information Security (CIS) has published an industry standard benchmark for Kubernetes security, and Aqua Security (aquasec.com) has written an easy-to-use tool called kube-bench to implement the CIS tests. In its most basic form, you run kube-bench against each node in your cluster and get a report outlining which tests passed and which failed.

Many organizations consider it a best practice to run kube-bench on all production nodes as part of node provisioning and pass or fail provisioning based on the results.

Reports from kube-bench can also serve as a valuable baseline in the aftermath of an incident. In situations like this, you run an additional kube-bench after a breach and compare the results with the initial baseline to determine *if* and *where* the configuration has changed.

Container and Pod lifecycle Events

Pods and containers are ephemeral in nature, meaning they don't live for long compared to VMs and physical servers. This means you'll see a lot of events announcing new Pods and containers, as well as a lot of events announcing terminated Pods and containers. As a result, you may need a solution that stores logs and keeps them around after Pods and containers have terminated. If you don't, you *may* find it frustrating that you don't have logs for old terminated containers available for inspection.

Logs entries relating to container lifecycle events may also be available from your container runtime logs.

Application logs

It's important to capture and analyse application logs as a way to identify potential security-related issues.

Fortunately, most containerized applications send log messages to standard out (stdout) or standard error (stderr) where they can be picked up with container logs. However, some applications send log messages to proprietary log files in bespoke locations. Be sure to check your application's documentation.

Actions performed by users

Most of your Kubernetes configuration will be done via the API server where all requests should be logged. However, it's also possible to gain remote SSH access to control plane nodes and directly manipulate Kubernetes objects. This may also include access to etcd and etcd nodes.

We've already spoken about limiting SSH access to control plane and worker nodes, as well as bolstering security via things like multi-factor authentication. However, logging all activities performed via SSH sessions, and shipping them to a secure log aggregator, is highly recommended. As is the practice of always having a second pair of eyes involved in remote access sessions.

Managing log data

A key advantage of containers is application density – you can run a lot more applications on your servers and in your datacenters. While this is great, it has the side-effect of generating massive amounts of logging and audit data that require specialised tools and specialised tools such as machine.

On the negative side, such vast amounts of log-related data makes proactive analysis difficult – too much data to analyse. However, on the positive side, you have a lot of valuable data that can be used by security first-responders, as well as for post-event reactive analysis.

Migrating existing apps to Kubernetes

Every business has a mix of apps – some more business critical than others. With this in mind, it's important to adopt a careful and planned approach to migrating apps to Kubernetes.

One approach may be a crawl, walk then run strategy as follows:

1. *Crawl*: Threat modeling your existing apps will help you understand the current security posture. For example, which of your existing apps do and don't communicate over TLS.
2. *Walk*: When moving to Kubernetes, ensure the security posture of these apps remains unchanged. For example, if an app doesn't communicate over TLS, do **not** change this as part of the migration.
3. *Run*: Start improving the security of applications after the migration. Start with simple non-critical apps and carefully work your way up to mission critical apps. You may also want to methodically deploy deeper levels of security such as initially

configuring apps to communicate over one-way TLS and then eventually over two-way TLS.

Real world example

An example of a container-related vulnerability that can be prevented by implementing some of the best practices we've discussed occurred back in February 2019. CVE-2019-5736 allowed a container process running as `root` to gain root access on the worker node **and** all containers running on the host.

As dangerous as the vulnerability is, the following things already covered in this chapter would've prevented the issue:

- Vulnerability scanning
- Not running processes as root
- Enabling SELinux

As the vulnerability has a CVE number, security scanning tools would've found it and alerted on it. Common best-practices such as not allowing root containers, and common SELinux policies would have prevented the issue.

All in all, a great real-world example demonstrating the benefits of defence-in-depth and other security-related best practices.

Chapter summary

The purpose of this chapter was to introduce some of the real-world security considerations affecting many Kubernetes clusters.

We started by looking at ways to secure the software delivery pipeline and discussing some image-related best practices. These included how to secure your image registries, scanning images for vulnerabilities, and cryptographically signing and verifying images. Then we looked at some of the workload isolation options that exist at different layers of the infrastructure stack. In particular, we looked at cluster-level isolation, node-level isolation, and some of the different runtime isolation options. We talked about identity and access management, including places where additional security measures might be useful. We then talked about auditing and finished up with a real-world issue that could have been avoided by implementing some of the best practices already covered.

Hopefully you have enough to go away and start securing your own Kubernetes clusters.

Terminology

This glossary defines some of the most common Kubernetes-related terms used throughout the book. Ping me if you think I've missed anything important:

- tkb@nigelpoulton.com
- https://nigelpoulton.com/contact-us
- https://twitter.com/nigelpoulton
- https://www.linkedin.com/in/nigelpoulton/

Now then… I know that some of you are passionate about the definitions of technical terms. I'm OK with that, and I'm not saying my definitions are the best – they're designed to be helpful for readers.

OK, here goes.

Term	Definition (according to Nigel)
Admission controller	Code that validates or mutates resources to enforce policy. Runs as part of the API admission chain immediately after authentication and authorization.
Annotation	Object metadata often used to expose alpha or beta capabilities, or integrate with 3rd-party systems.
API	Application Programming Interface. In the case of Kubernetes, all resources are defined in the API, which is RESTful and exposed via the *API server*.
API group	A set of related API resources. For example, networking resources are usually located in the networking.k8s.io API group.
API resource	All Kubernetes objects, such as Pods, Deployments and Services, are defined in the API as resources.
API Server	Exposes the API on a secure port over HTTPS. Runs on the control plane.
Cloud controller manager	Control plane service that integrates with underlying cloud platform. For example, when creating a LoadBalancer Service, the cloud controller manager implements the logic to provision one of the underlying cloud's internet-facing load-balancers.

Term	Definition (according to Nigel)
Cloud native	A loaded term and means different things to different people. Cloud native is a way of designing, building, and working with modern applications and infrastructure. I personally consider an application to be *cloud native* if it can self-heal, scale on-demand, perform rolling updates, and possibly rollbacks.
ConfigMap	Kubernetes object used to hold non-sensitive configuration data. A great way to add custom configuration data to a generic container, at runtime, without editing the image.
Container	Lightweight environment for running modern apps. Each container is a virtual operating system with its own process tree, filesystem, shared memory, and more. One container runs one application process.
Container Network Interface (CNI)	Pluggable interface enabling different network topologies and architectures. 3rd-parties provide CNI plugins that enable overlay networks, BGP networks, and various implementations of each.
Container runtime	Low-level software running on every cluster Node responsible for pulling container images, starting containers, stopping containers, and other low-level container operations. Typically containerd, Docker, or cri-o. Docker was deprecated in Kubernetes 1.20 and support will be removed in a future version.
Container Runtime Interface (CRI)	Low-level Kubernetes feature that allows container runtimes to be pluggable. With the CRI you can choose the best container runtime for your requirements (Docker, containerd, cri-o, kata, etc.)
Container Storage Interface (CSI)	Interface enabling external 3rd-party storage systems to integrate with Kubernetes. Storage vendors write a CSI driver/plugin that runs as a set of Pods on a cluster and exposes the storage system's enhanced features to the cluster and applications.
Controller	Control plane process running as a reconciliation loop monitoring the cluster and making the necessary changes so the observed state of the cluster matches desired state.

Term	Definition (according to Nigel)
Control plane	The brains of every Kubernetes cluster. Comprises the API, API server, scheduler, all controllers, and more. These components run on all *control plane nodes* of every cluster.
control plane node	A cluster node hosting control plane services. Usually doesn't run user applications. You should deploy 3 or 5 for high availability.
Cluster	A set of worker and control plane nodes that work together to run user applications.
Cluster store	Control plane feature that holds the state of the cluster and apps. Typically based on the `etcd` distributed data store and runs on the control plane. Can be deployed to its own cluster for higher performance and higher availability.
containerd	Container runtime. Default on many modern clusters. Donated to the CNCF by Docker, Inc.
cri-o	Container runtime. Commonly used in OpenShift based Kubernetes clusters.
CRUD	The four basic Create, Read, Update, and Delete operations used by many storage systems.
Custom Resource Definition (CRD)	API resource used for adding your own resources to the Kubernetes API.
Data plane	The worker Nodes of a cluster that host user applications.
Deployment	Controller that deploys and manages a set of stateless Pods. Performs rollouts and rollbacks, and can self-heal. Uses a ReplicaSet controller to perform scaling and self-healing operations.
Desired state	What the cluster and apps should be like. For example, the *desired state* of an application microservice might be 5 replicas of xyz container listening on port 8080/tcp. Vital to reconciliation.
Endpoints object	Up-to-date list of healthy Pods matching a Service's label selector. Basically, it's the list of Pods a Service will send traffic to. Might eventually be replaced by EndpointSlices.

Term	Definition (according to Nigel)
etcd	The open-source distributed database used as the cluster store on most Kubernetes clusters.
Ingress	API resource that exposes multiple internal Services over a single external-facing LoadBalancer Service. Operates at layer 7 and implements path-based and host-based HTTP routing.
Ingress class	API resource that allows you to specify multiple different Ingress controllers on your cluster.
Init container	A specialised container that runs and completes before the main app container starts. Commonly used to check/initialize the environment for the main app container.
JSON	JavaScript Object Notation. The preferred format for sending and storing data used by Kubernetes.
K8s	Shorthand way to write Kubernetes. The "8" replaces the eight characters between the "K" and the "s" of Kubernetes. Pronounced "Kates". The reason why people say Kubernetes' girlfriend is called Kate.
kubectl	Kubernetes command line tool. Sends commands to the API server and queries state via the API server.
Kubelet	The main Kubernetes agent running on every cluster Node. It watches the API Server for new work assignments and maintains a reporting channel back.
Kube-proxy	Runs on every cluster node and implements low-level rules that handle routing of traffic from Services to Pods. You send traffic to stable Service names and kube-proxy makes sure the traffic reaches Pods.
Label	Metadata applied to objects for grouping. Works with label selectors to match Pods with higher level controllers. For example, Services send traffic to Pods based on sets of matching labels.
Label selector	Used to identify Pods to perform actions on. For example, when a Deployment performs a rolling update, it knows which Pods to update based on its label selector – only Pods with the labels matching the Deployment's label selector will be replaced and updated.

Term	Definition (according to Nigel)
Manifest file	YAML file that holds the configuration of one or more Kubernetes objects. For example, a Service manifest file is typically a YAML file that holds the configuration of a Service object. When you post a manifest file to the API Server, its configuration is deployed to the cluster.
Microservices	A design pattern for modern applications. Application features are broken into their own small applications (microservices/containers) and communicate via APIs. They work together to form a useful application.
Namespace	A way to partition a single Kubernetes cluster into multiple virtual clusters. Good for applying different quotas and access control policies on a single cluster. Not suitable for strong workload isolation.
Node	Also known as worker node. The nodes in a cluster that run user applications. Runs the kubelet process, a container runtime, and kube-proxy.
Observed state	Also known as *current state* or *actual state*. The most up-to-date view of the cluster and running applications. Controllers are always working to make observed state match desired state.
Orchestrator	A piece of software that deploys and manages apps. Modern apps are made from lots of small microservices that work together to form a useful application. Kubernetes orchestrates/manages these and keeps them healthy, scales them up and down, and more... Kubernetes is the de facto orchestrator of microservices apps based on containers.
Persistent Volume (PV)	Kubernetes object used to map storage volumes on a cluster. External storage resources must be mapped to PVs before they can be used by applications.
Persistent Volume Claim (PVC)	Like a ticket/voucher that allows an app to use a Persistent Volume (PV). Without a valid PVC, an app cannot use a PV. Combined with StorageClasses for dynamic volume creation.
Pod	Smallest unit of scheduling on Kubernetes. Every container running on Kubernetes must run inside a Pod. The Pod provides a shared execution environment – IP address, volumes, shared memory etc.

Term	Definition (according to Nigel)
RBAC	Role-based access control. Authorization module that determines whether authenticated users can perform actions against cluster resources.
Reconciliation loop	A controller process watching the state of the cluster, via the API Server, ensuring observed state matches desired state. Moist controllers, such as the Deployment controller, run as a reconciliation loop.
ReplicaSet	Runs as a controller and performs self-healing and scaling. Used by Deployments.
REST	REpresentational State Trasfer. The most common architecture for creating web-based APIs. Uses the common HTTP methods (GET, POST, PUT, PATCH, DELETE) to manipulate and store objects.
Secret	Like a ConfigMap for sensitive configuration data. A way to store sensitive data outside of a container image, and have it inserted into a container at runtime.
Service	Capital "S". Kubernetes object for providing network access to apps running in Pods. By placing a Service in front of a set of Pods, the Pods can fail, scale up and down, and be replaced without the network endpoint for accessing them changing. Can integrate with cloud platforms and provision internet-facing load-balancers.
Service mesh	Infrastructure software that enables features such as encryption of Pod-to-Pod traffic, enhanced network telemetry, and advanced routing. Common service meshes used with Kubernetes include Consul, Istio, Linkerd, and Open Service Mesh. Others also exist.
Sidecar	A special container that runs alongside, and augments, a main app container. Service meshes are often implemented as sidecar containers that are injected into Pods and add network functionality.
StatefulSet	Controller that deploys and manages stateful Pods. Similar to a Deployment, but for stateful applications.
Storage Class (SC)	Way to create different storage tiers/classes on a cluster. You may have an SC called "fast" that creates NVMe-based storage, and another SC called "medium-three-site" that creates slower storage replicated across three sites.

Term	Definition (according to Nigel)
Volume	Generic term for persistent storage.
Worker node	A cluster node for running user applications. Sometimes called a "Node" or "worker".
YAML	Yet Another Markup Language. The configuration language you normally write Kubernetes configuration files in. It's a superset of JSON.

Outro

Thanks for reading my book. You're now ready to switch from impulse drives to warp speed as you explore the cloud native galaxy.

About the book's cover

The cover of this Starfleet collector's edition is similar in style to the LCARS (Library Computer Access/Retrieval System) operating system screens often seen in The Next Generation. The words *Aᐧ Astra Per Aspera* are the Starfleet motto and translate to *To the Stars Through Ships*. Below that, the words *Aᐧ Kubernetes Per Libros* translates to *To Kubernetes Through Books*. The image in the targeting brackets is a fusion of the Kubernetes logo and a Constitution Heavy Cruiser class of starship -- two of the spokes from the Kubernetes wheel merge into the struts for the starship's warp nacelles. The Big Dipper/Plough constellation is also on the front cover.

A word on the book's diagrams

There's a great set of Kubernetes community icons available in the following GitHub repo.

```
https://github.com/kubernetes/community/tree/master/icons
```

I like them, and I use them a lot in blogs and video courses. However, they didn't look good in printed copies of the book. As a result, I created my own similar set for use in the book. It took a very long time to create them, so I hope you like them.

In no way am I trying to replace the community icons or say they aren't good. They just didn't look good in printed editions of the book.

Connect with me

I'd love to connect with you and talk about Kubernetes and other cool tech.

You can reach me at all of the following:

- Twitter: twitter.com/nigelpoulton
- LinkedIn: linkedin.com/in/nigelpoulton
- Mastodon: @nigelpoulton@hachyderm.io
- Web: nigelpoulton.com
- YouTube: youtube.com/nigelpoulton

Feedback and reviews

Books live and die by Amazon reviews and stars.

I've spent well-over a year of my life writing this book and keeping it up-to-date. Soooo… I'd love it if you left a review on Amazon.

Ping me at tkb@nigelpoulton.com if you want to suggest content or fixes for future editions.

Index

The ~~end~~ beginning...

... of an exciting chapter of your career!

Show the book some love

Smash the KCNA cert

Made in the USA
Monee, IL
09 September 2023